# INHALE

## Reflections from a Beginner on the Path to Mastery

Philosophy, Writing, and Photography
by Michael Foley, MD

Book Design & Production by
Groom Creative

Published April 27, 2019. Copyright, Michael R. Foley, M.D., All rights Reserved.
Cover Image: Ketchikan, AK; ISO 100 f/11 1/250 sec

## Note to Readers:

All of the enclosed writings are original. The thoughts that generated these reflections, however, are a product of 50-plus years of martial arts training, 30-plus years of medical training and practice, and a host of influential teachers. These include Dan O'Keeffe, Idahlynn Karre, Fred Corbus, Gabriel Vargas, Carl Clarizio, Jr., Terrence Webster-Doyle, Toby Hecht, teachers and students at The Center for Humane Living, and most of all, my wife, Lisa Dado, and my children, Bonnie, Molly and Michael.

**Don't believe anything you read in this book.**

**Investigate everything for yourself.**

**Discover your own PERSONAL truth.**

Paradise Valley, AZ
ISO 100 f/16 1/6 sec

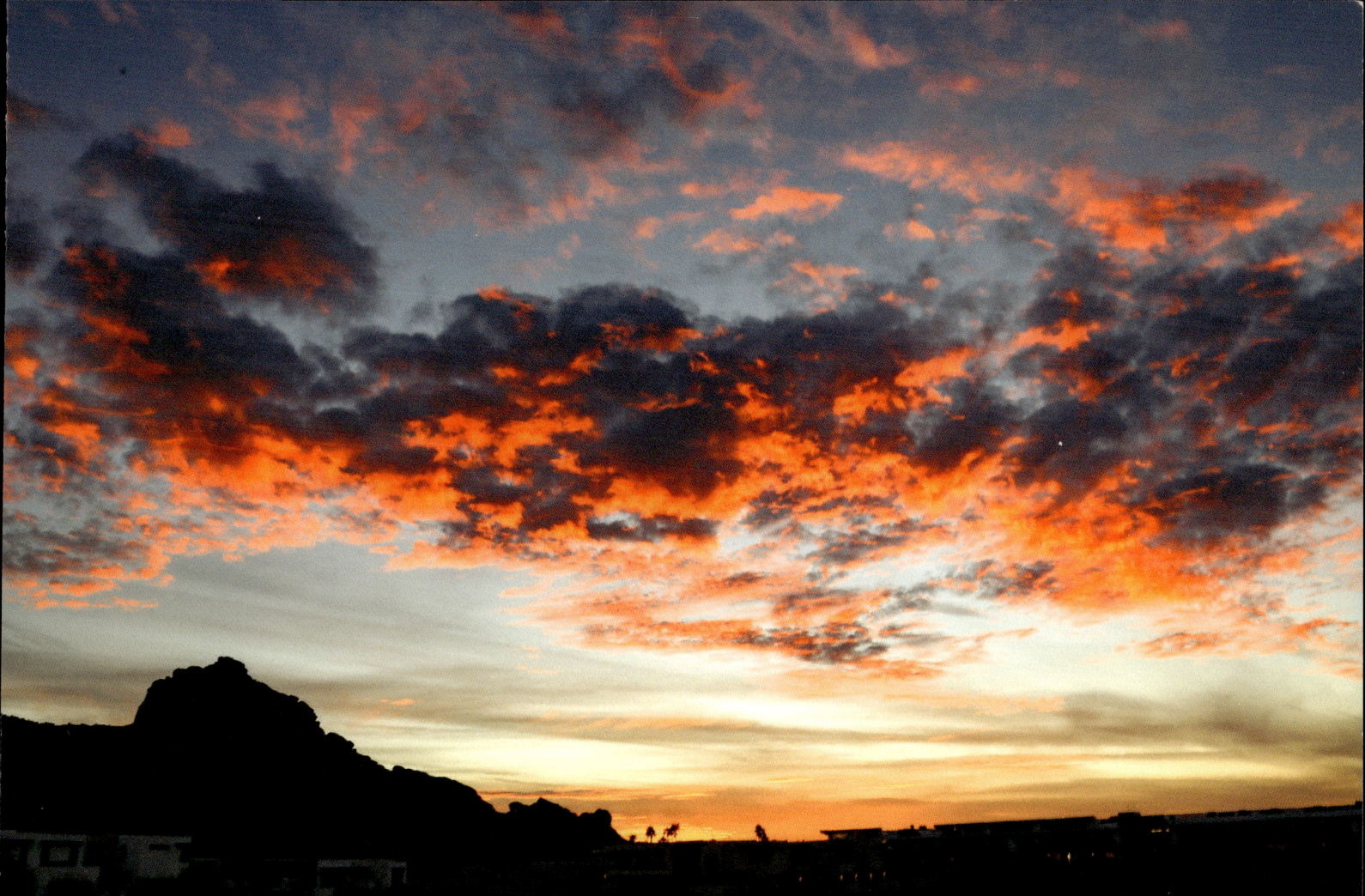

To **"master"** something means you have acquired complete knowledge and skill in a given domain. Paradoxically, embracing a **"beginners mind"** to pursue lifelong learning is the goal of the Master.

*Is it possible to actually be open for new learning if complete knowledge and skill have already been obtained?*

**Perhaps a real Master is a "beginner on the path to mastery?"**

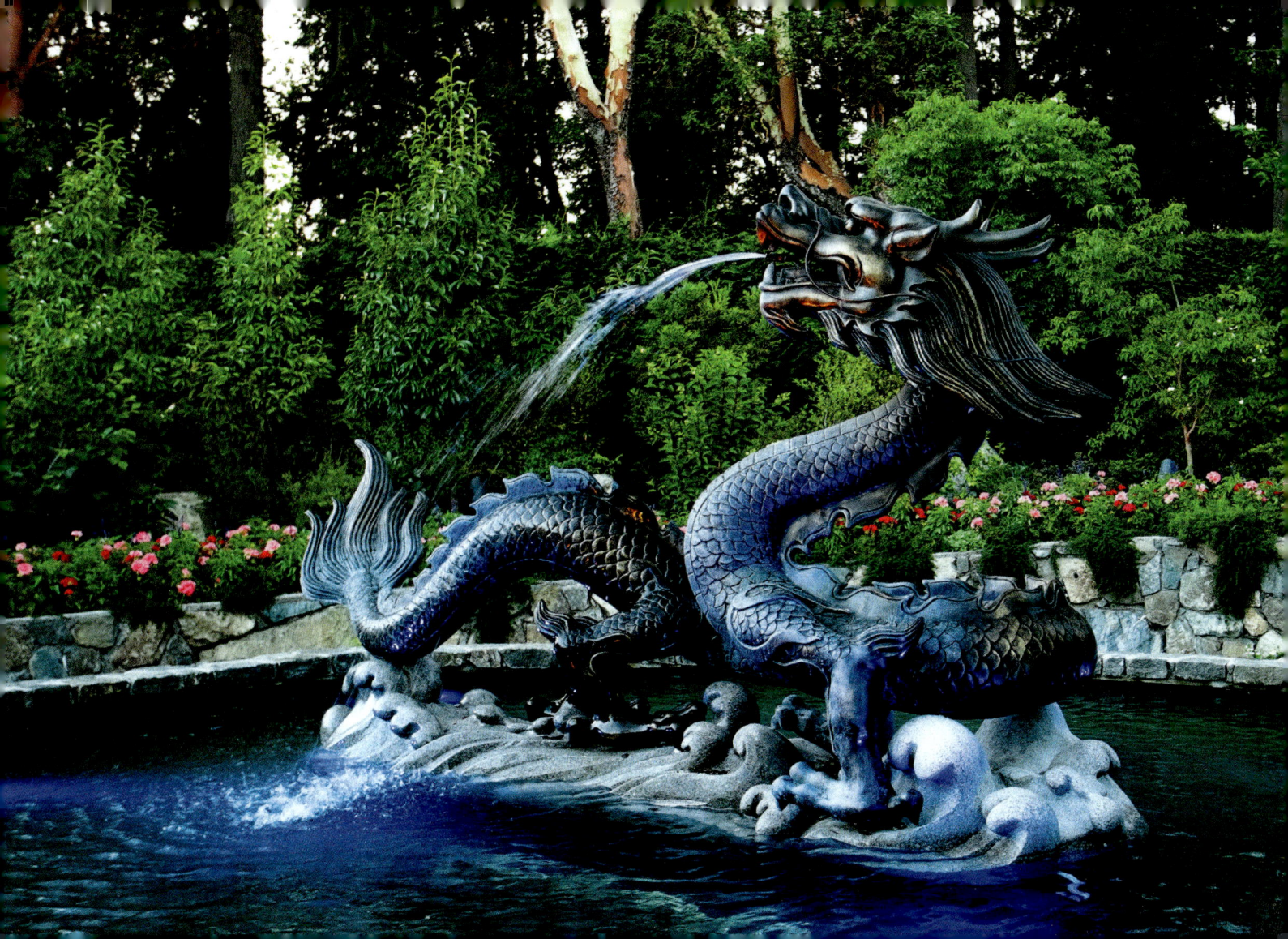

By **breathing out**, we care for others.

By **breathing in**, we care for our self.

We cannot survive unless we breathe both in *and* out.

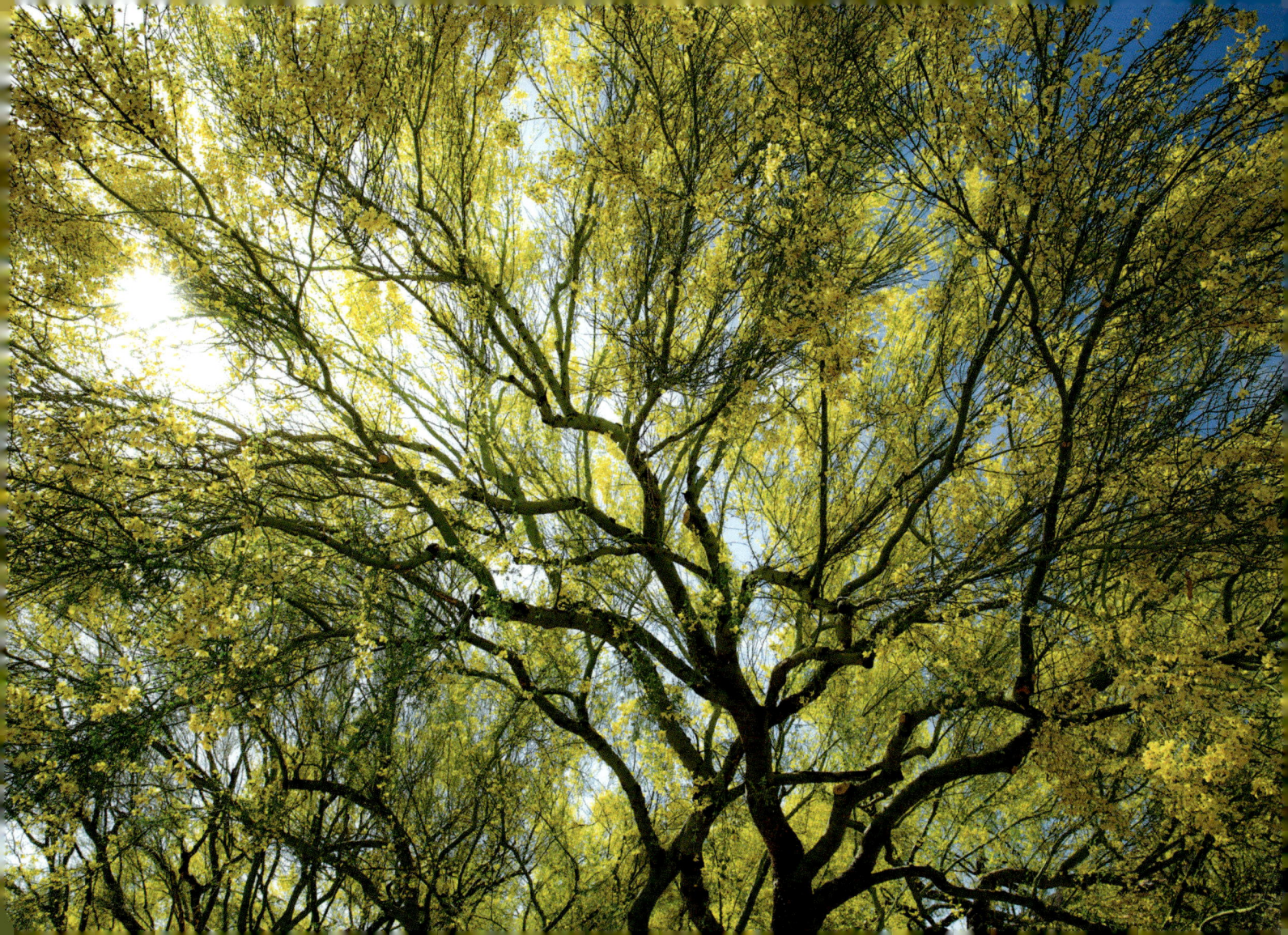

The unique way we think and act is a product of our psychosocial conditioning influenced by our culture, faith, family, environment and life experiences.

*This is how we see the world and how the world sees us.*

Conflict emerges when we fail to embrace our underlying humanity while myopically focusing on our differences.

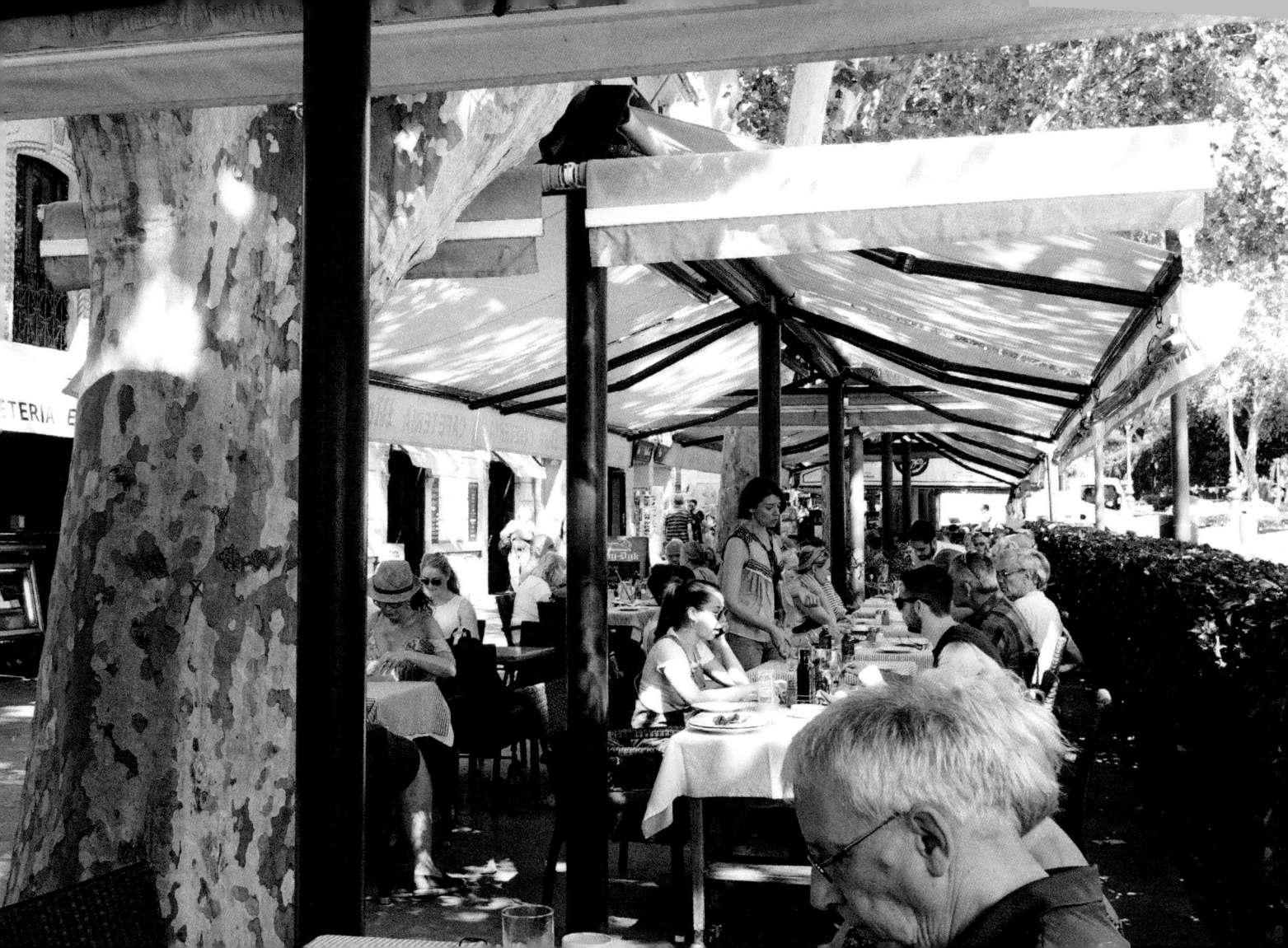

By establishing boundaries separating what is acceptable from what is not acceptable in any relationship, we expand our capacity to consistently express tolerance, empathy, compassion, and love.

**Secure your perimeter.**

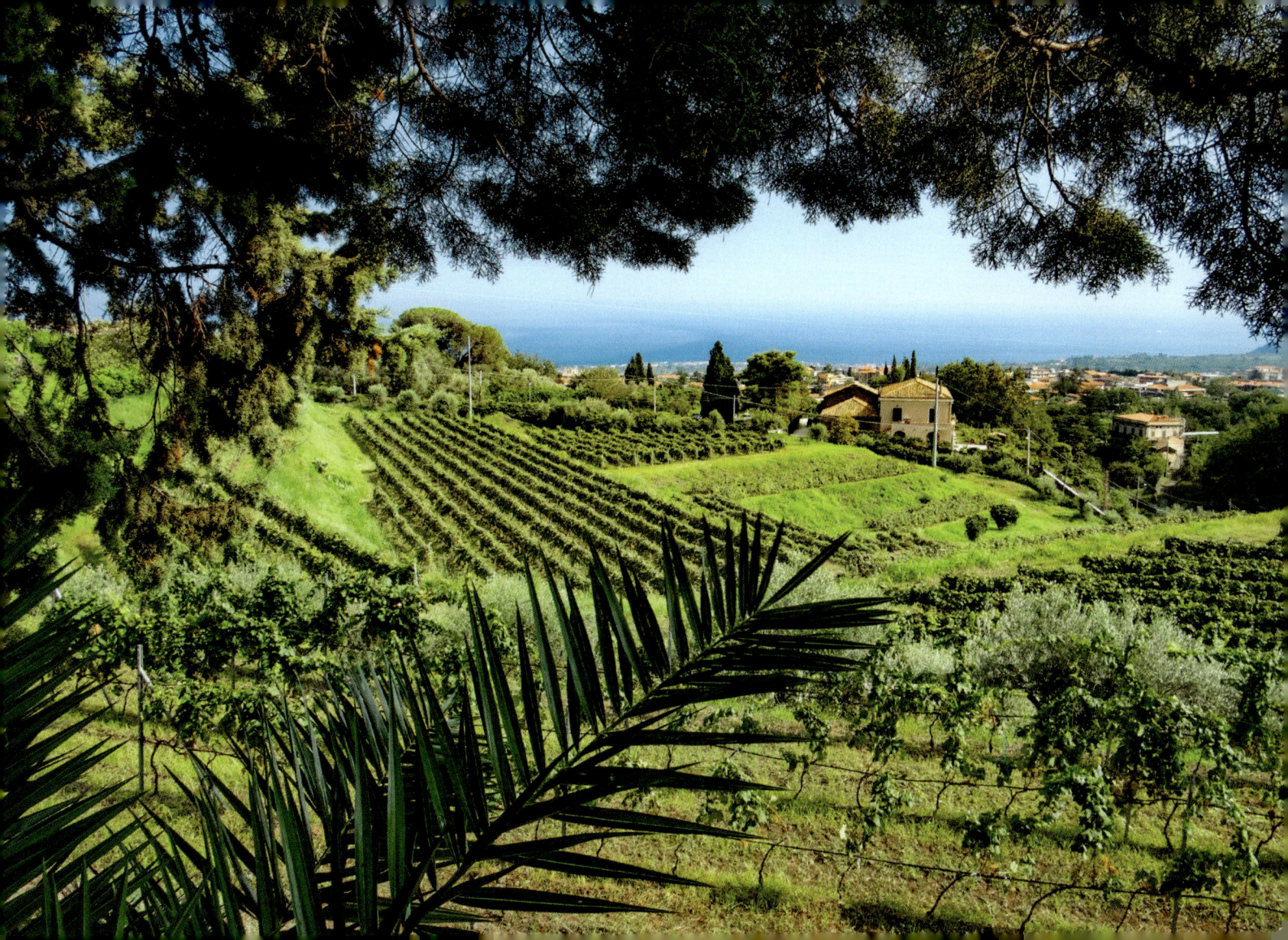

You **must** fully accept and love yourself before you can truly develop meaningful relationships with others.

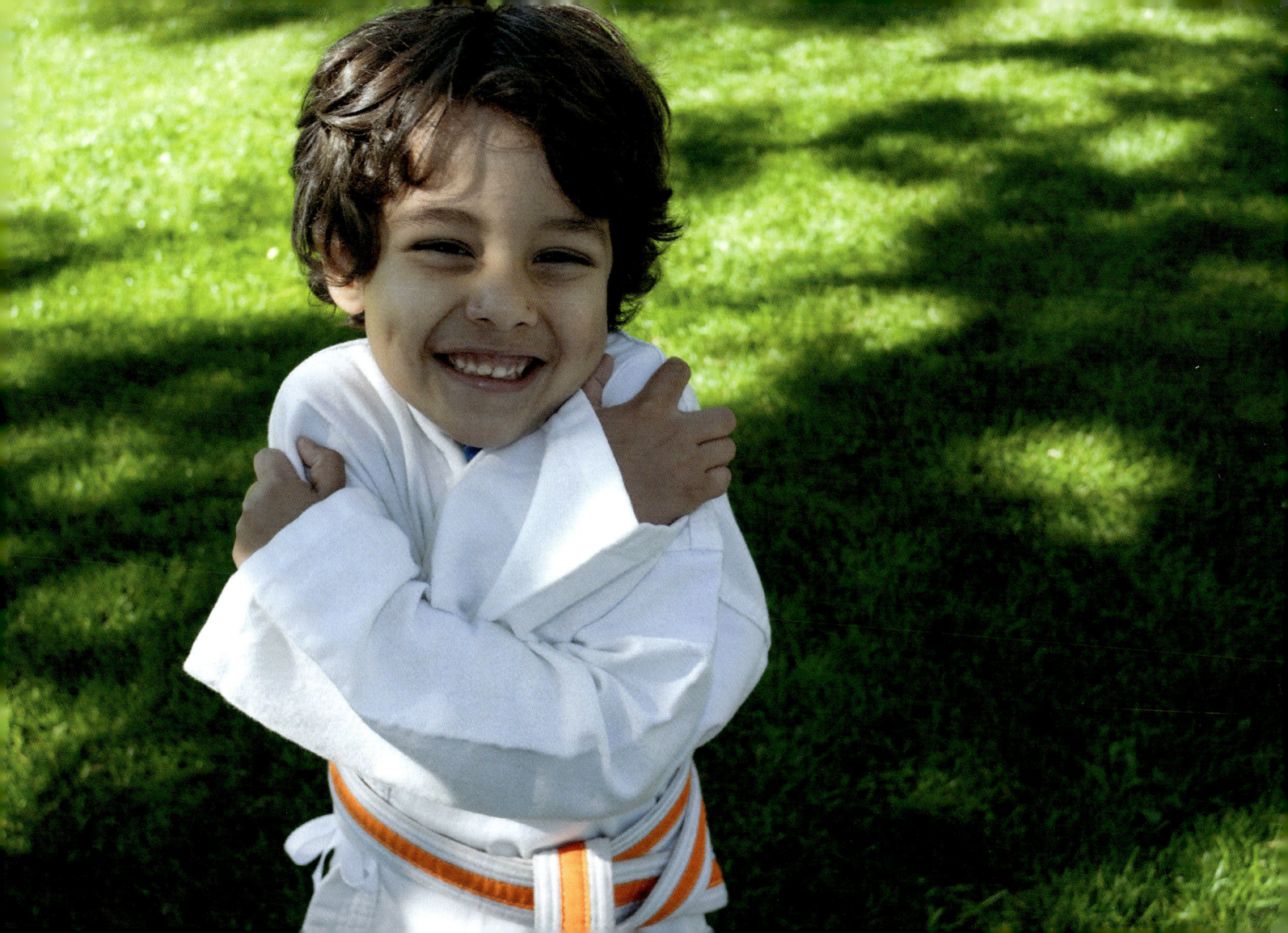

To live a happy life,

focus on harmonizing

the **relationships** you have with

*yourself*, *others* and *our environment*.

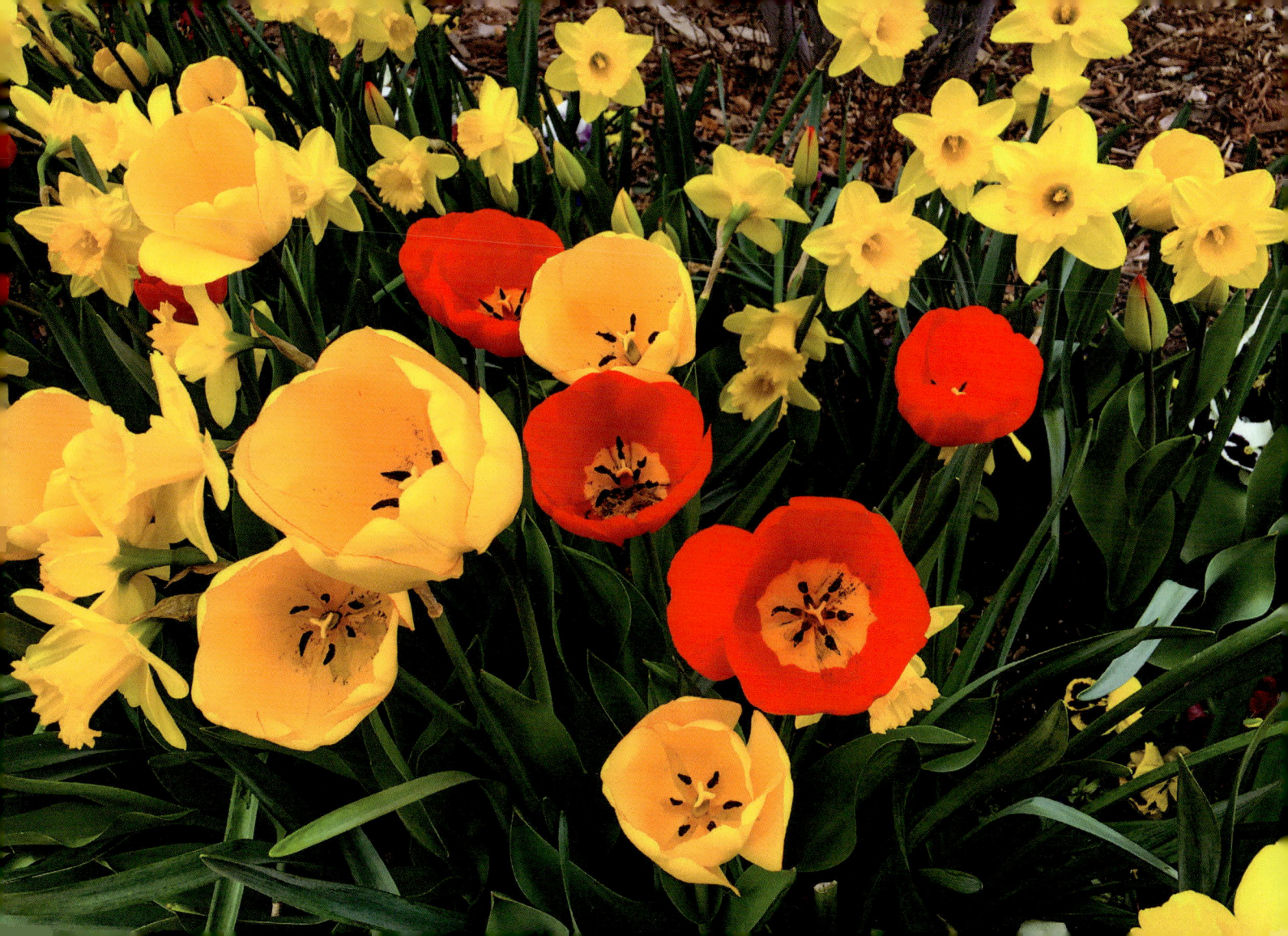

Change

**only**

occurs


when the pain of staying the same becomes *greater* than the pain of change itself!

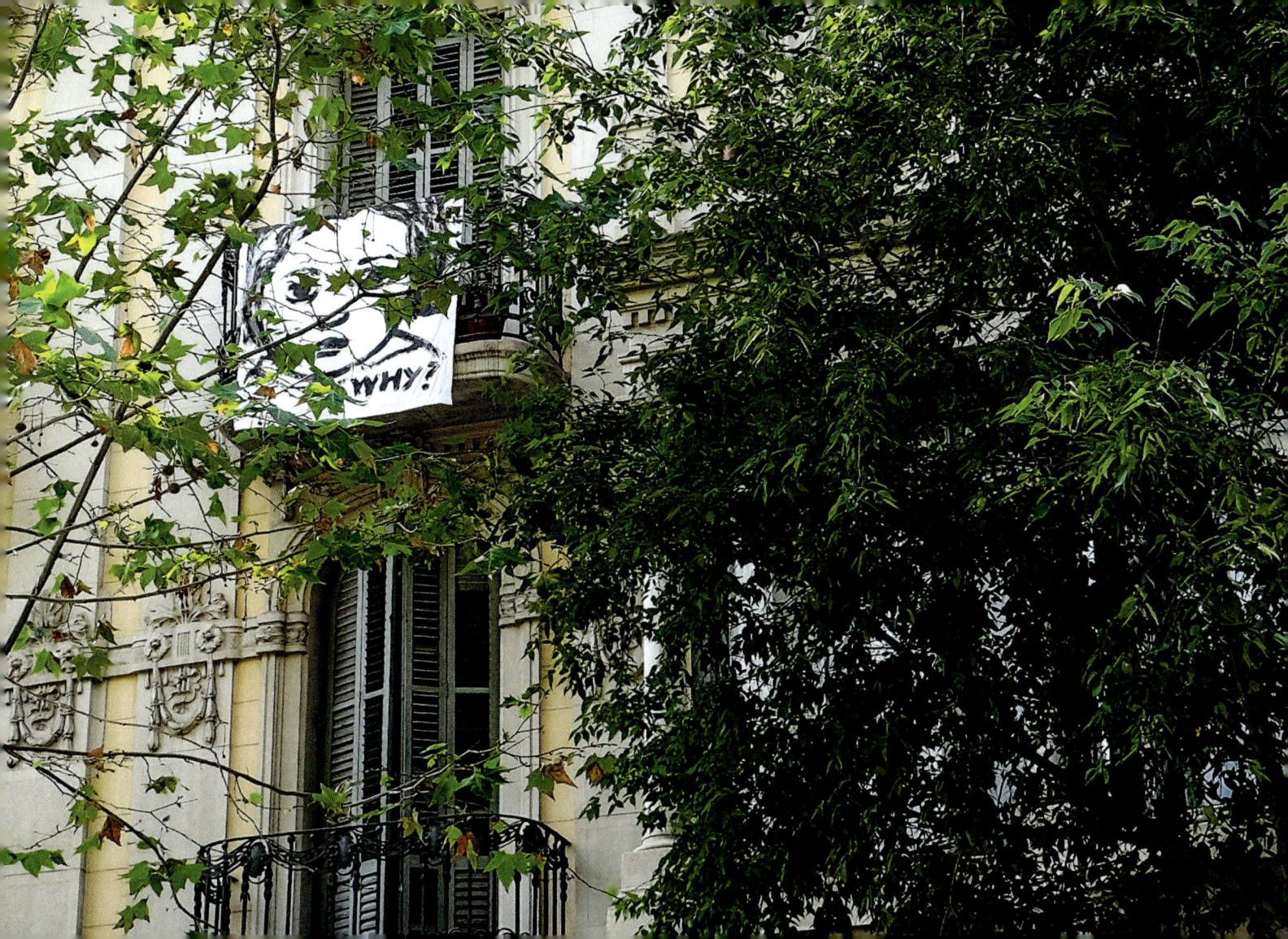

*"To be nobody to everybody you must first be somebody to yourself."*

You must develop a foundation of love and respect for yourself in order to be open and receptive (nobody) to those around you.

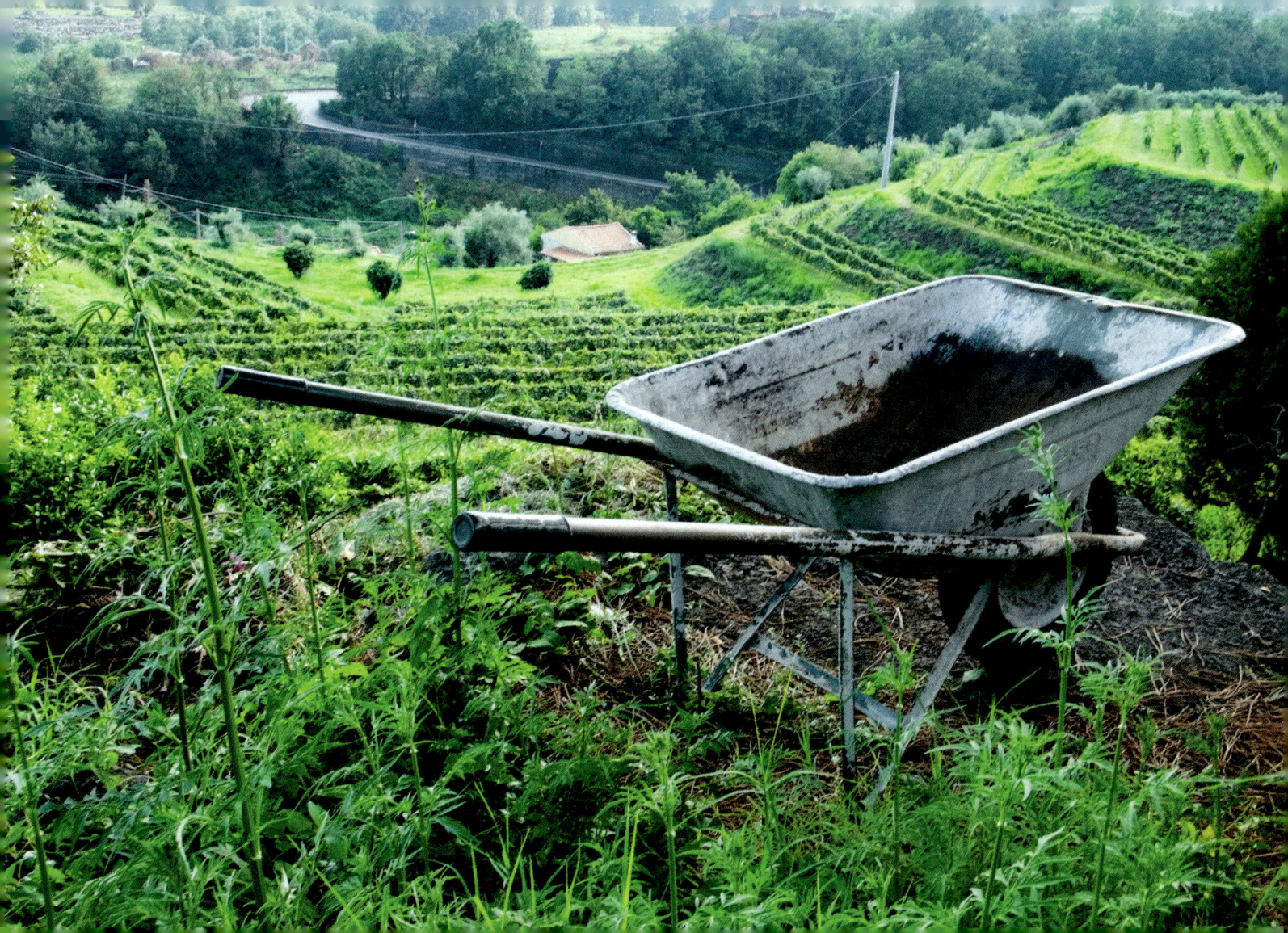

## Pain exists only from resistance.

When two forces meet in opposition, pain for the lesser is inevitable. Blending with the force without resisting allows for better control and acceptance without pain.

*Are you in a painful relationship?*

*If so, where are you resisting?*

*Where can you blend?*

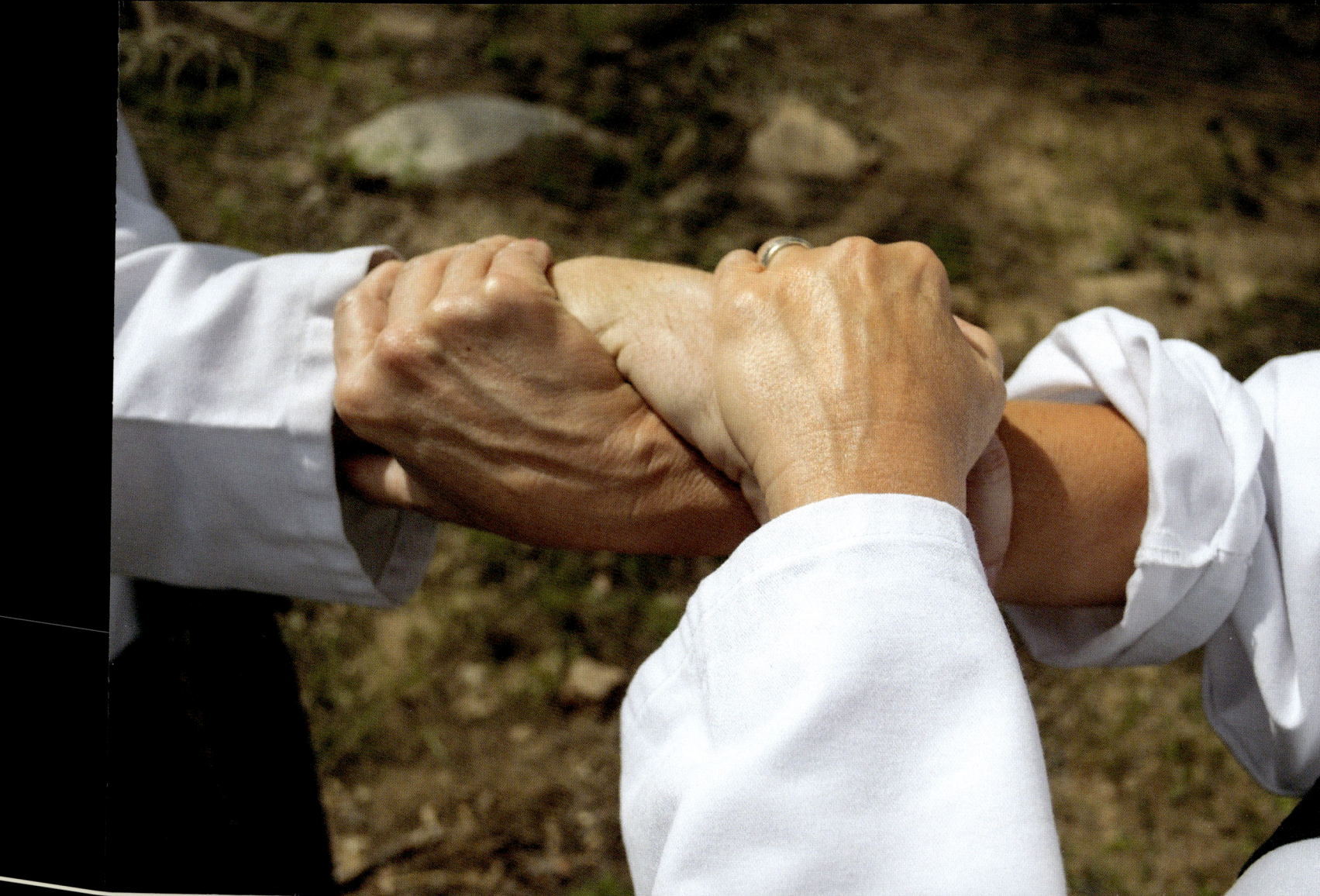

Demonstrating gratefulness and generosity provides a longer—lasting fulfillment to the *giver* than to the *recipient*.

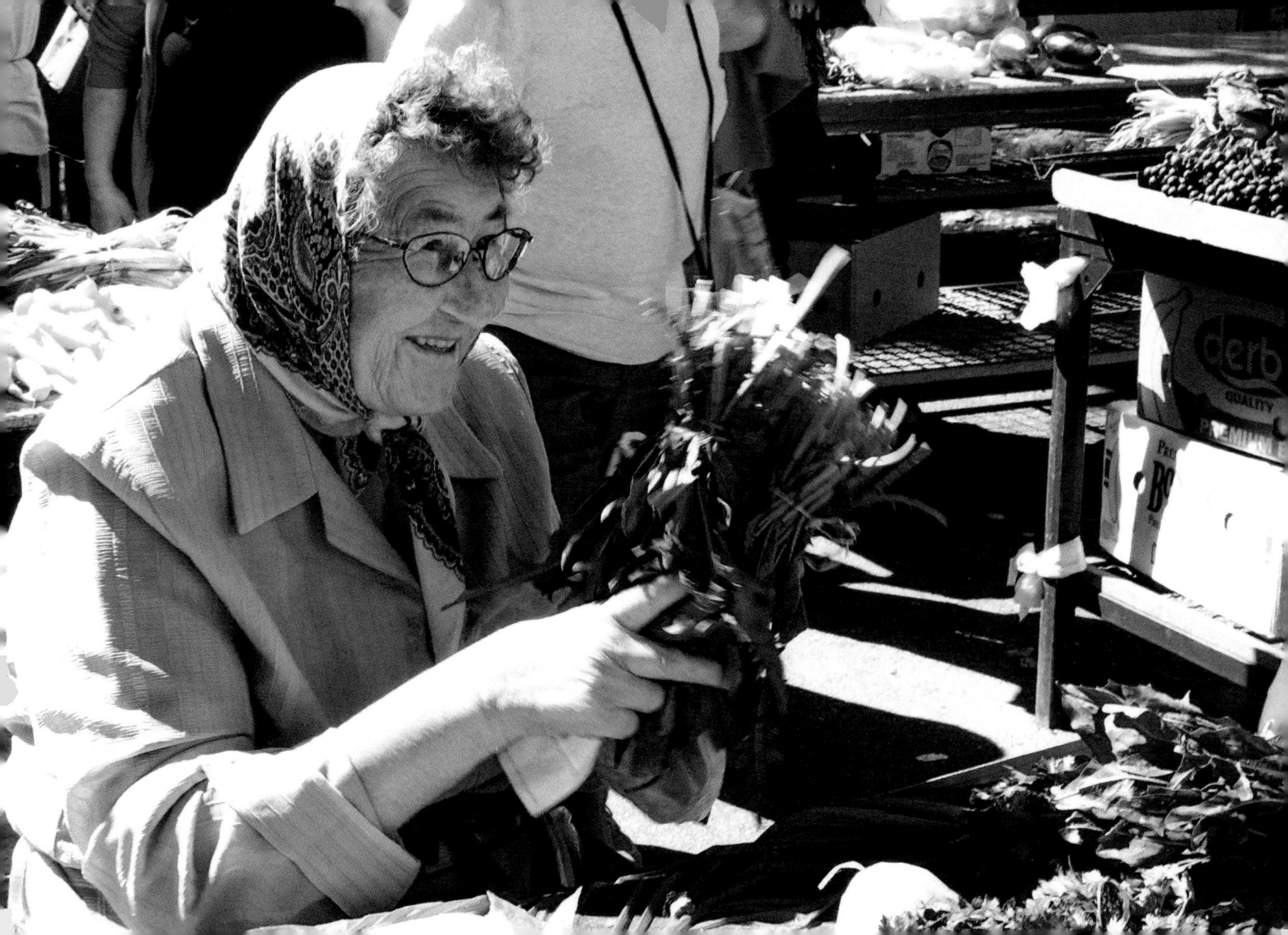

Learn first to be self-aware—

*then lovingly manage.*


Next-learn to be socially aware—

*then lovingly share.*


Peace emerges from this place.

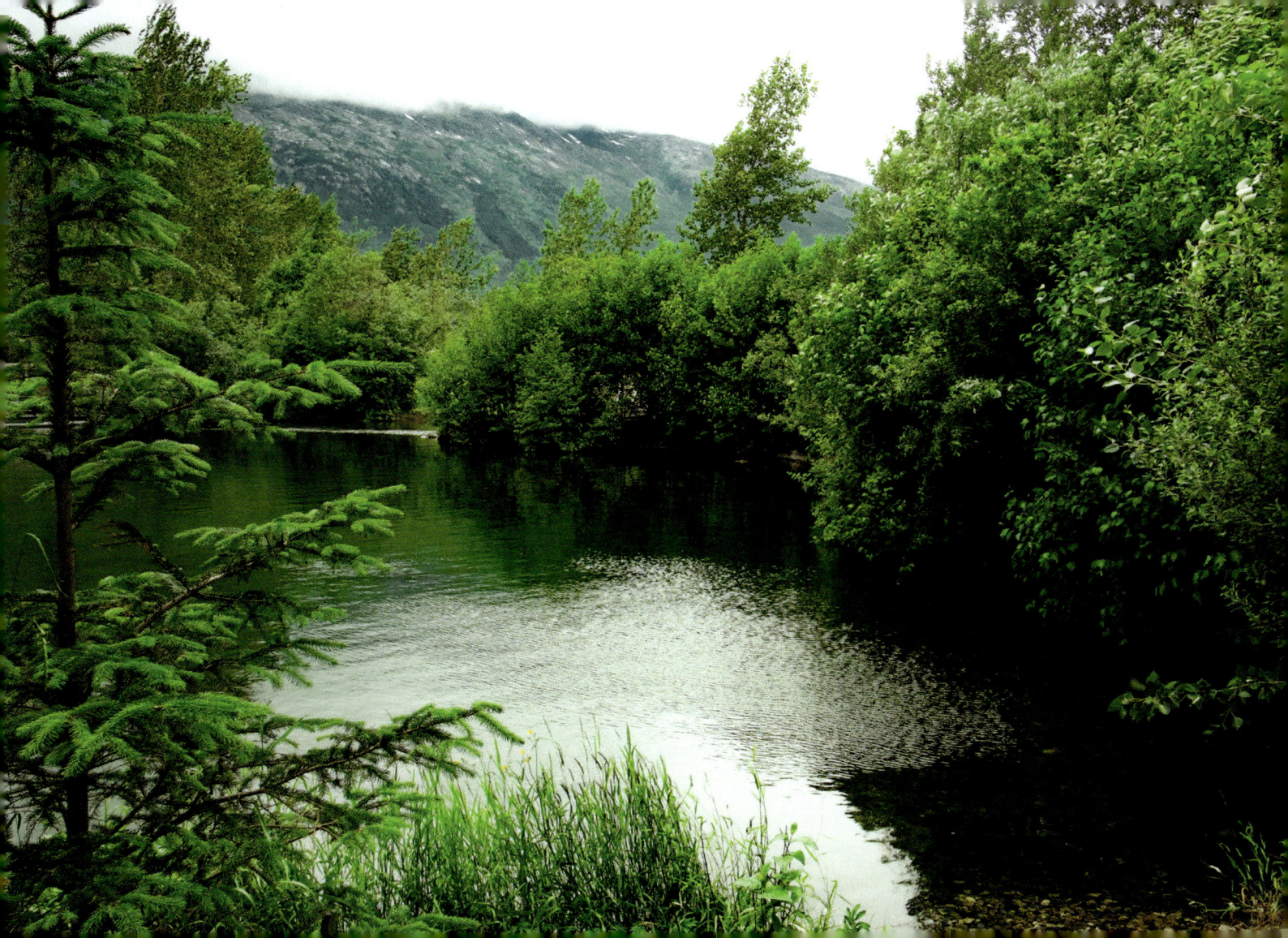

Be accountable to being a *"giver,"* not entitled to being a *"taker."*

**Life fulfillment depends on it.**

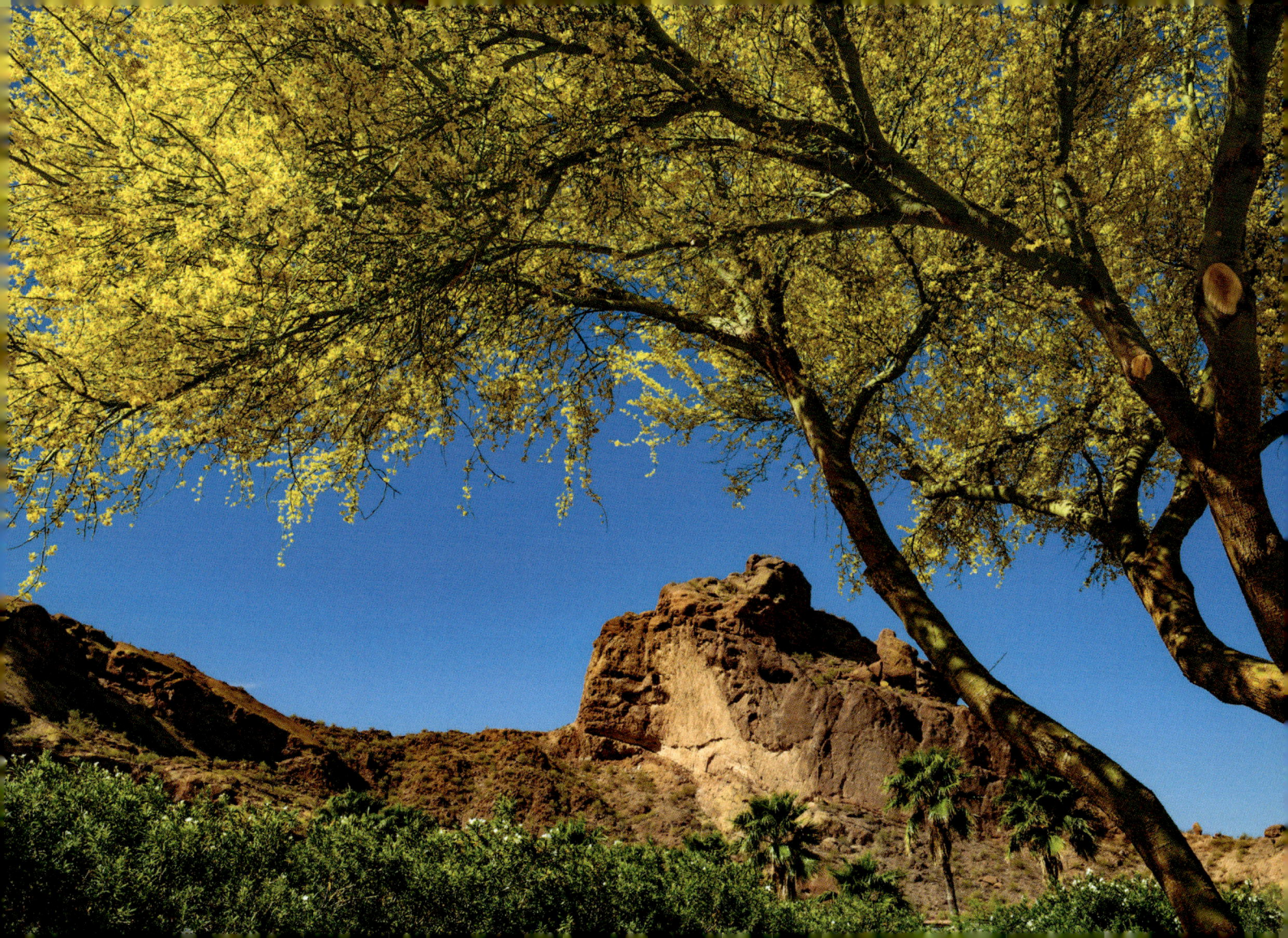

**Happiness only comes from within.**

It is rooted in the soil of a positive mindset and blossoms radiantly as life success.

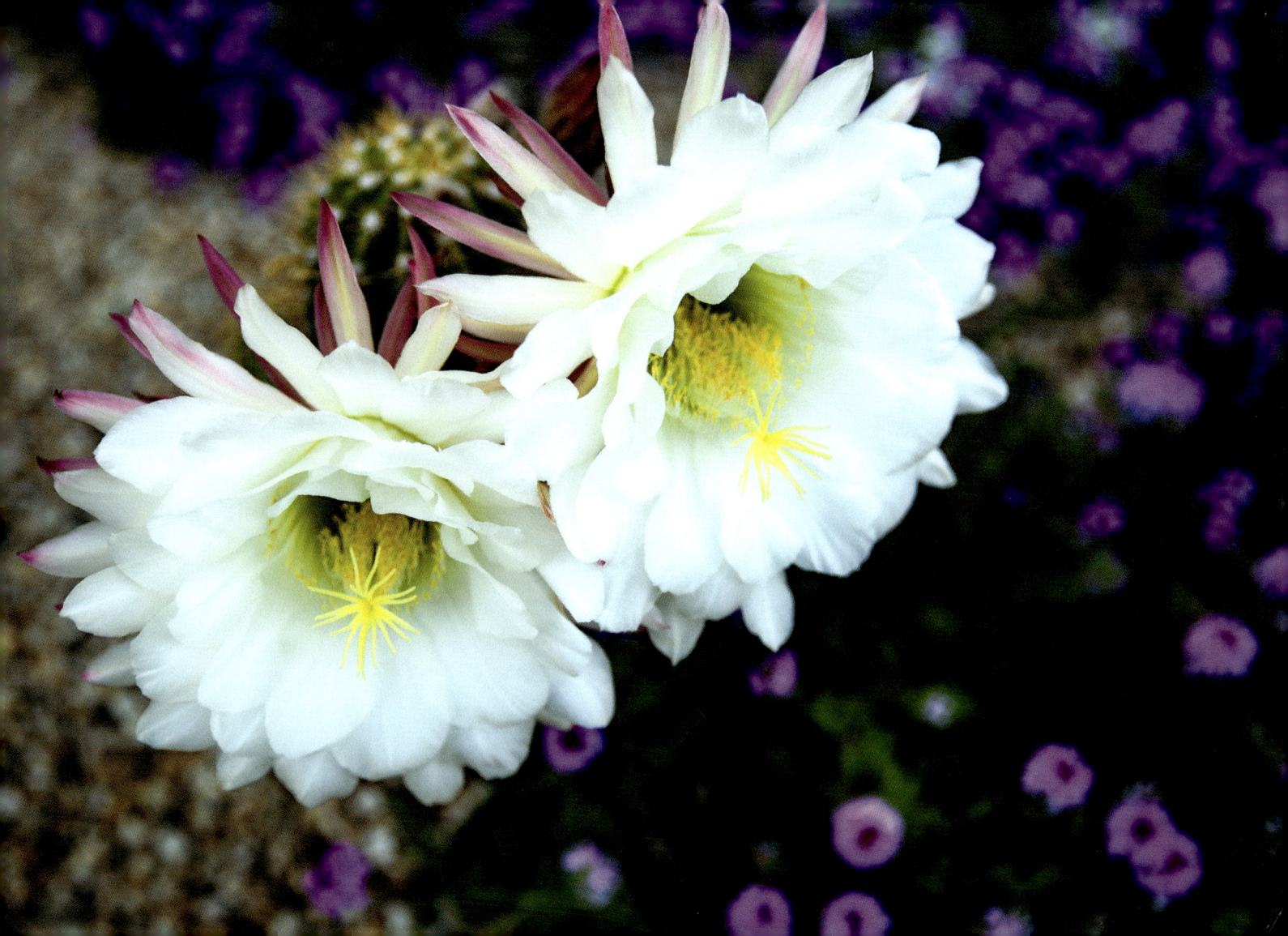

**Truth** lies with the **non-abiding mind** that *sees* all perspectives and is *not limited* by the myopic perspectives of others.

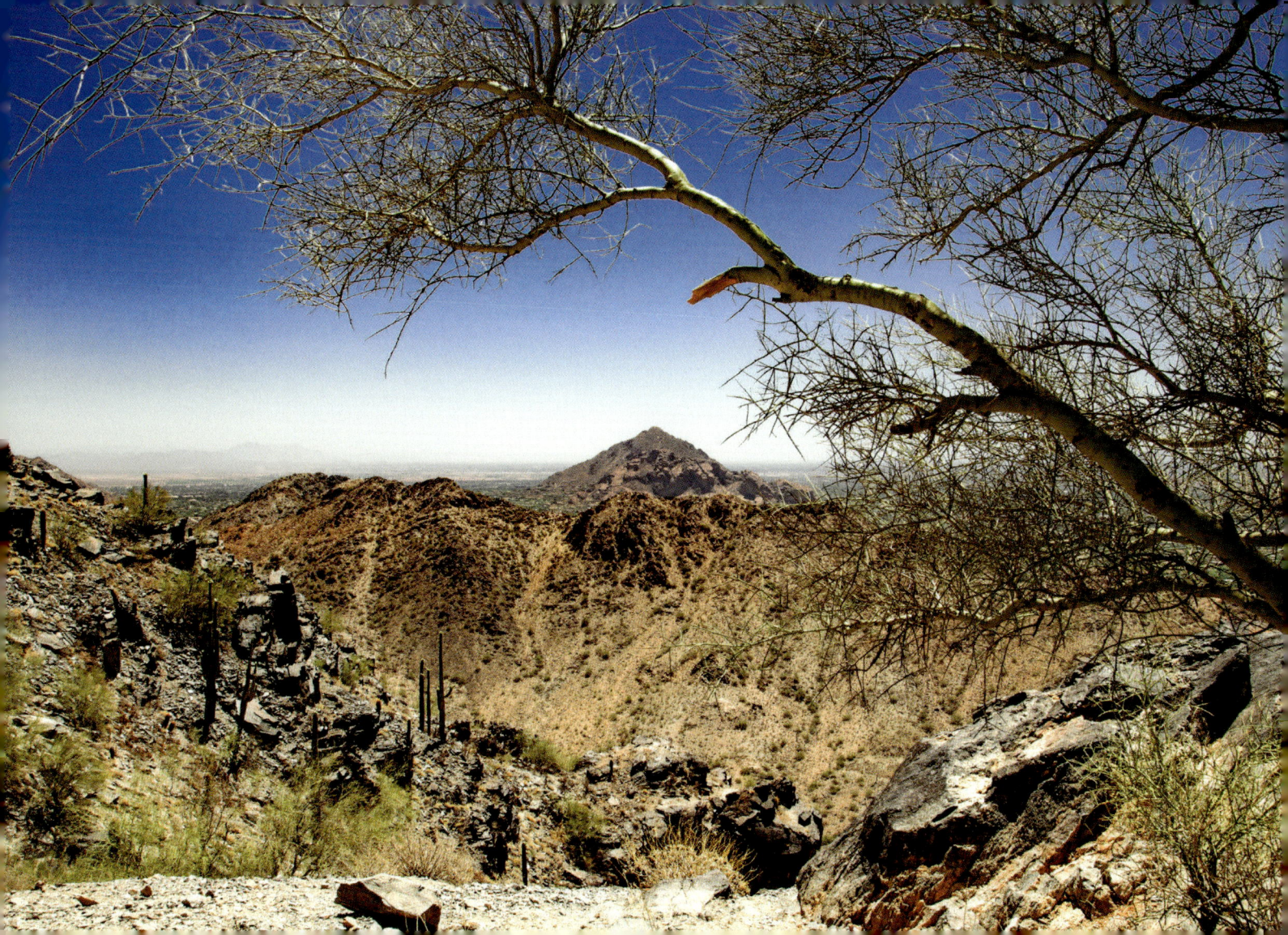

When having conversations that really matter,
work on preparing your self first.

# Humanize others.

Avoid the self-perpetuated narratives of villain, victim and helplessness to focus on the safety of mutual respect and common purpose.

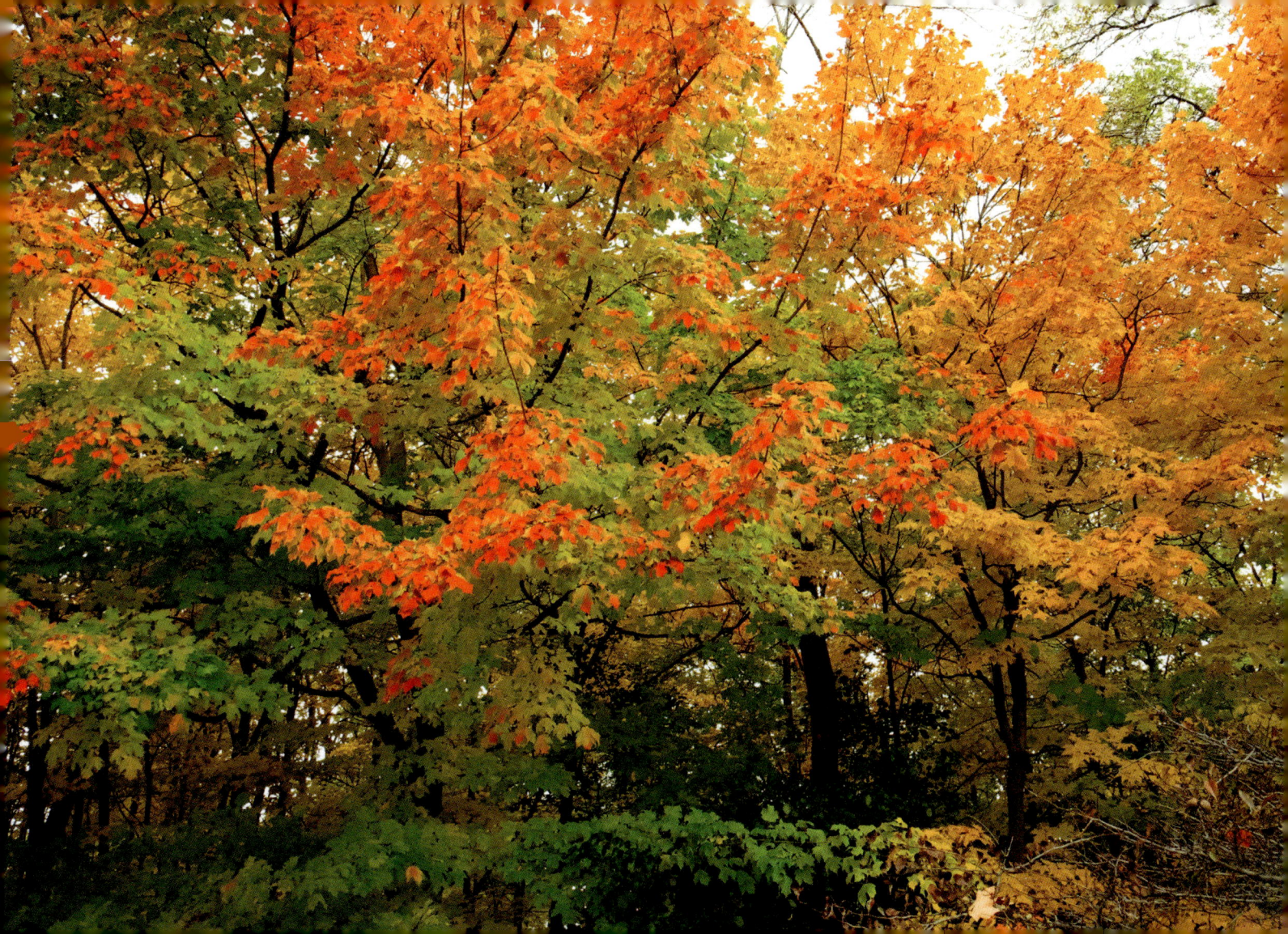

All learning opportunities must be approached with

**a clear and receptive nature.**

The mind is like a teacup and new knowledge is like tea...
when the teacup is full, *no new tea can be added.*

When you think you have all the answers, there is no room for new learning.

To truly embrace life, we need to empty our cups frequently to make room for lifelong learning.

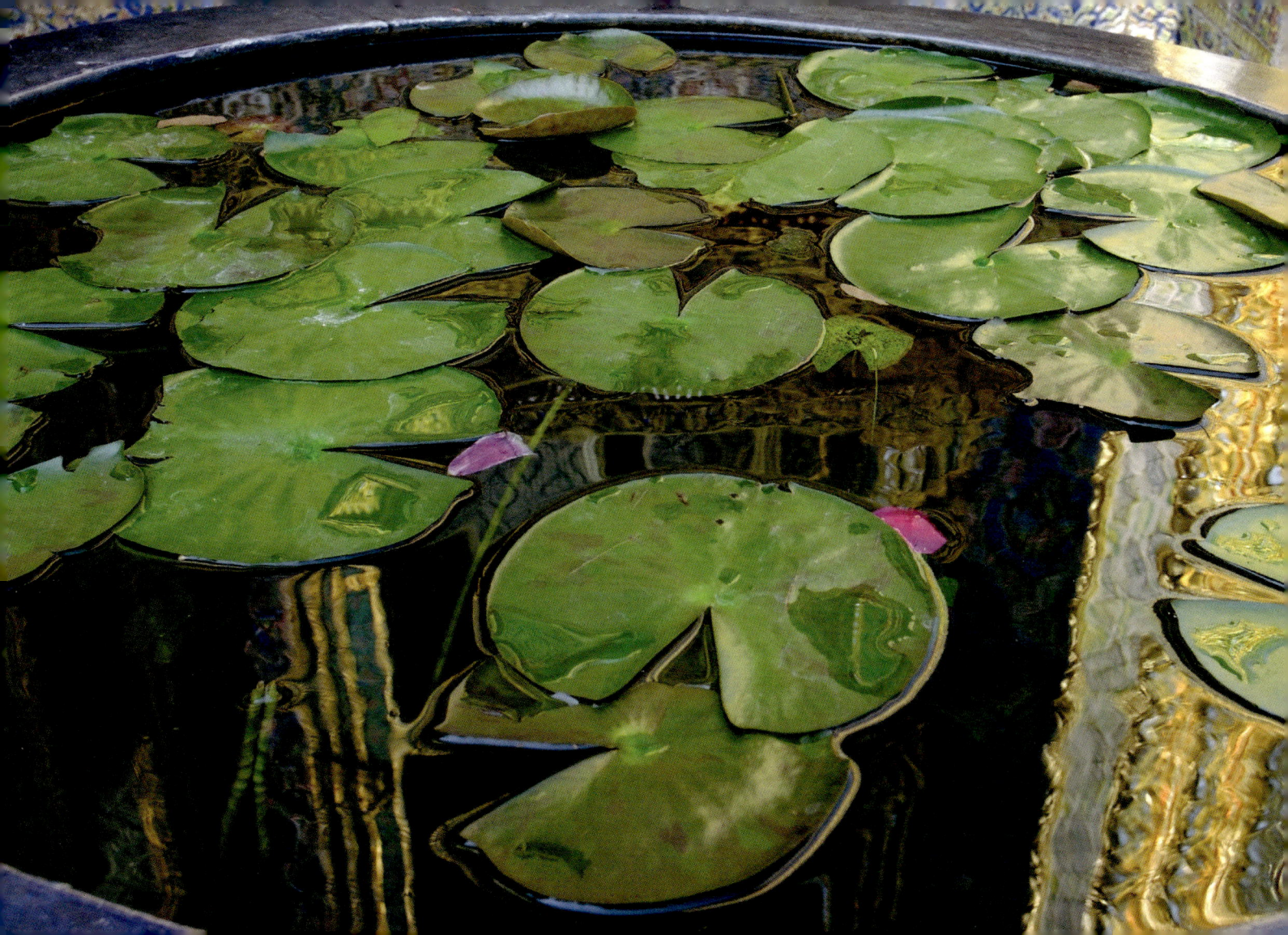

Sorrow, anger, ambivalence and inappropriate humor represent the many "faces" of human fear.

Treat them *all* with compassion.

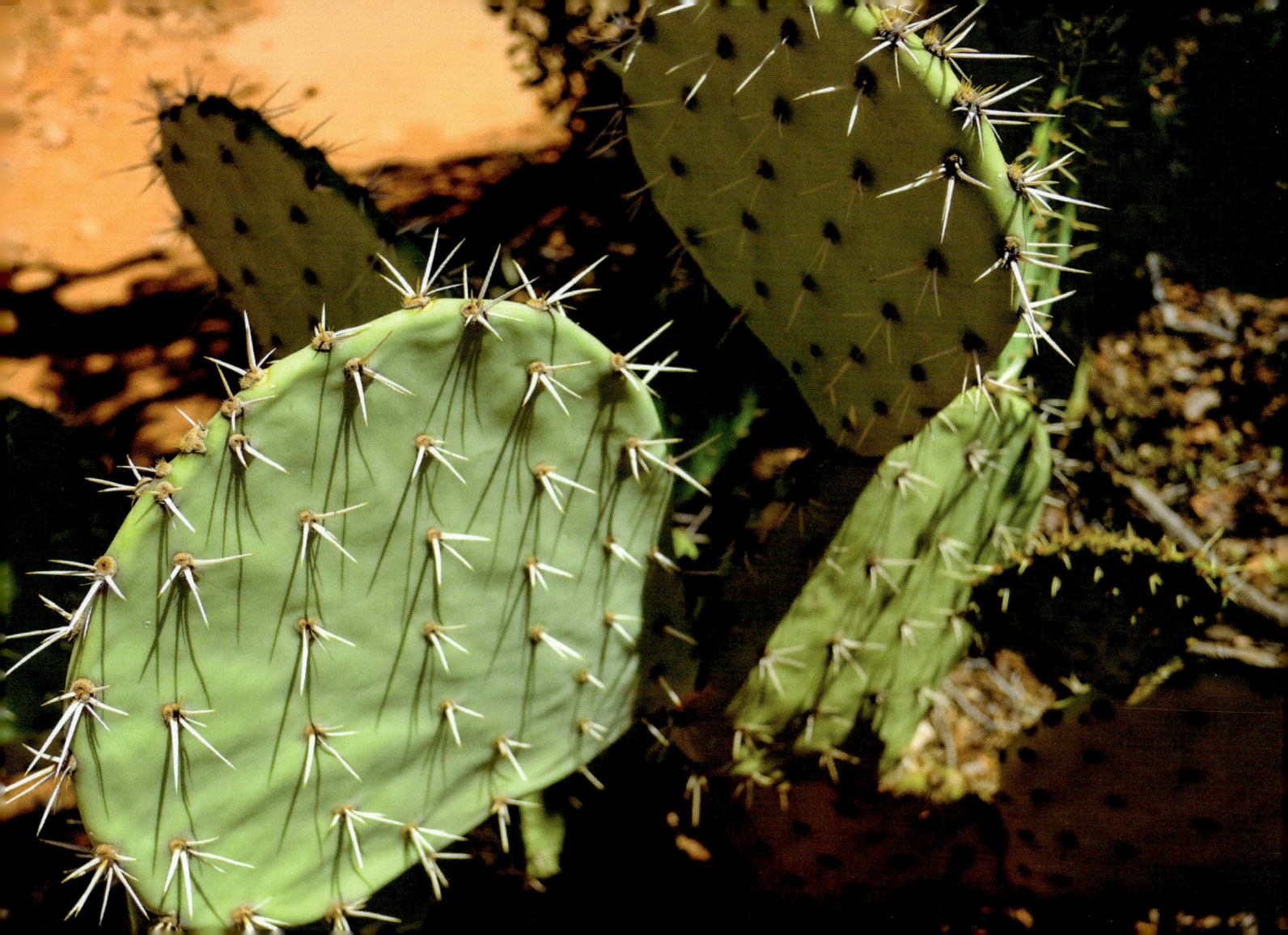

Trust is a metaphorical three-legged stool.

Each leg provides foundational stability.

To be trustworthy, you must demonstrate **sincerity, competence** and **reliability**.

Without the support of each of these legs, trust erodes and topples over.

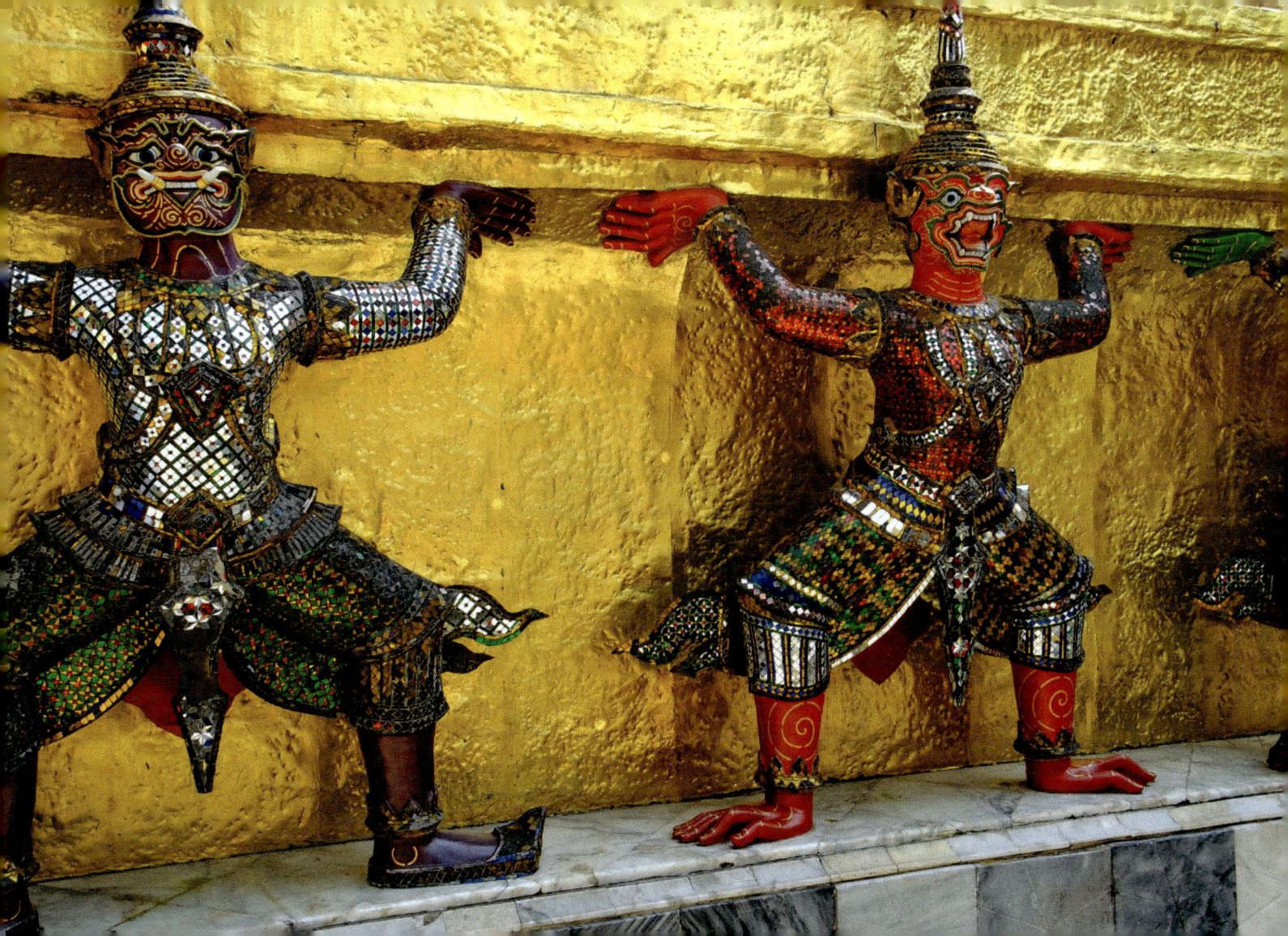

Treat all perceived disrespect as if it comes from ignorance, illiteracy or immaturity.

**Teach** and **educate** instead of belittle or punish.

Set clear expectations and rigorous boundaries to enforce future accountability.

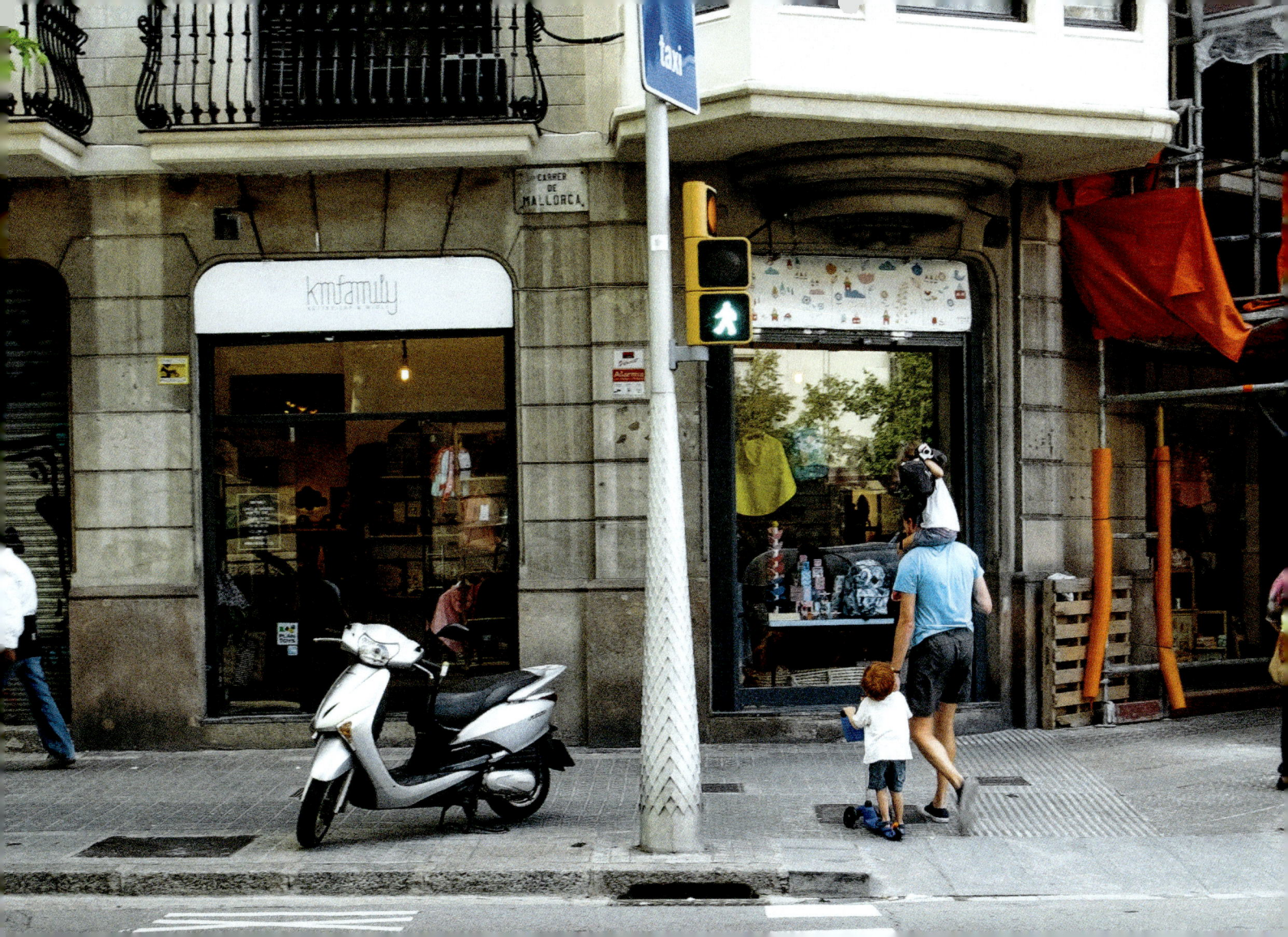

Hedonic happiness is an attempt to find life fulfillment by acquiring material possessions.

*Fulfillment is ultimately elusive.*

True happiness is eudaimonic and comes from enriching the lives of others by sharing our strengths and talents.

*Fulfillment becomes the inevitable result.*

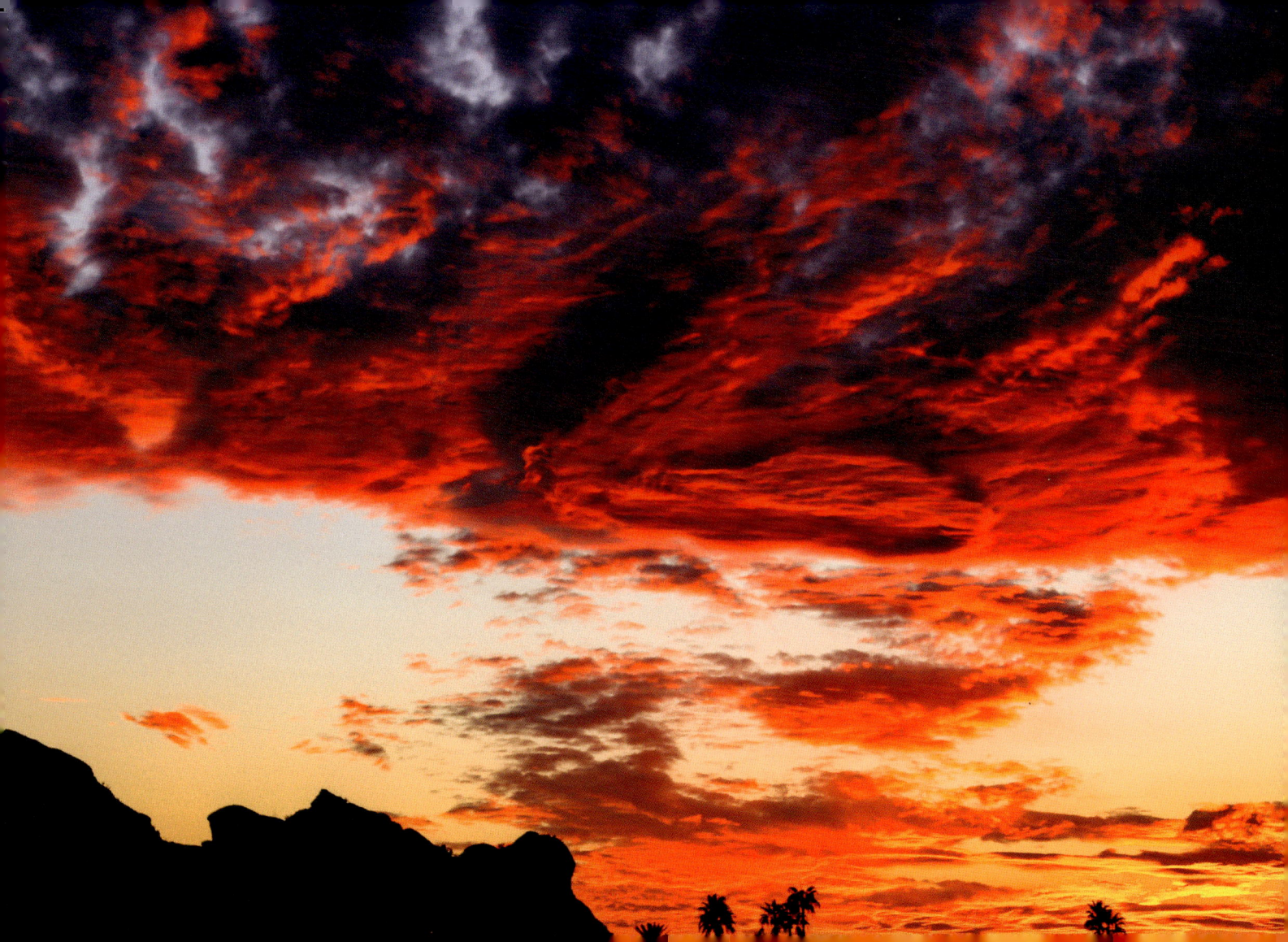

**Being truly grounded and centered means we move through life with the intent to do good things.**

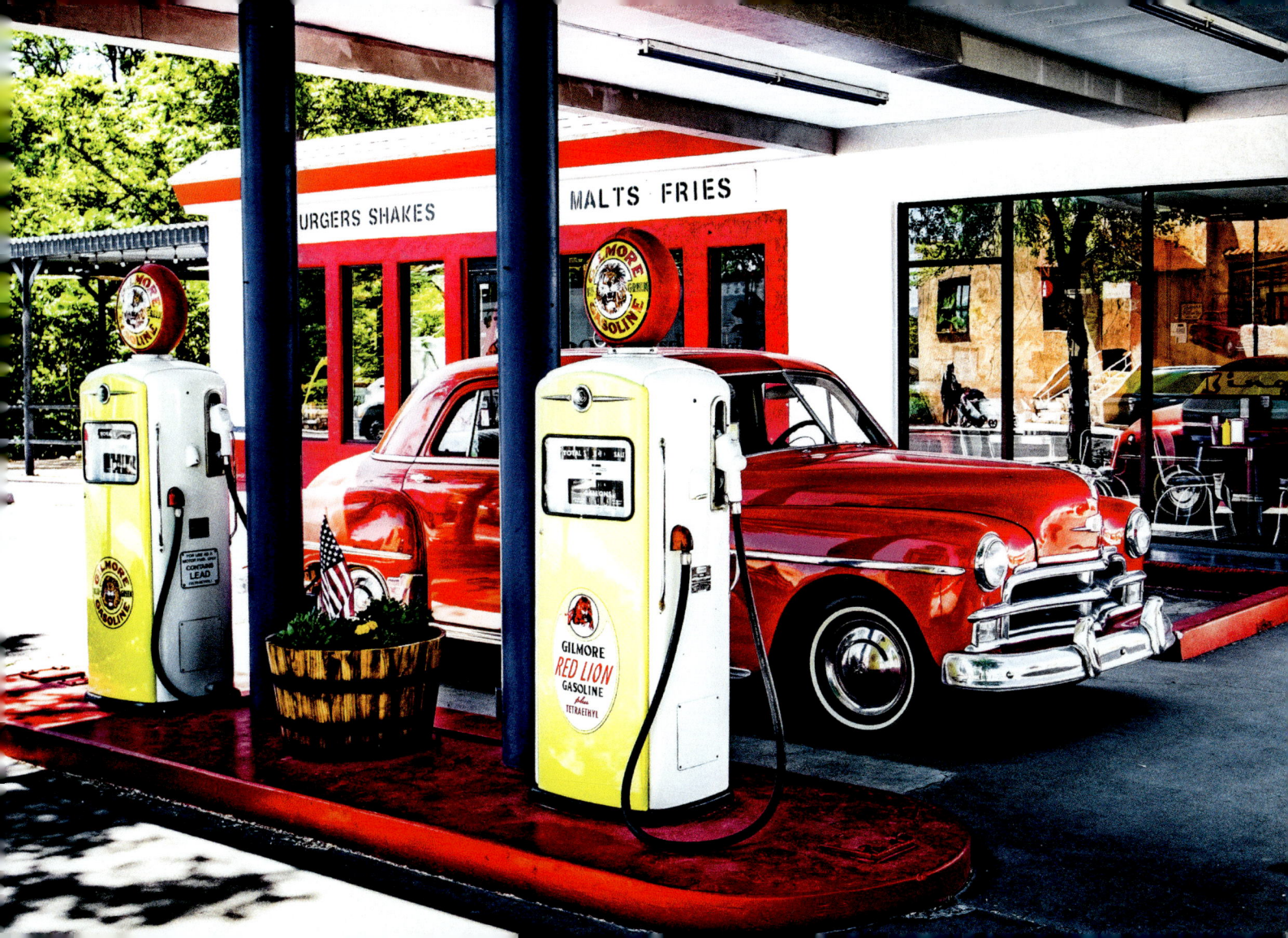

Only through the expression of **reciprocal vulnerability** can we push relationships beyond the superficial to allow the emergence of deeper, trusting friendships.

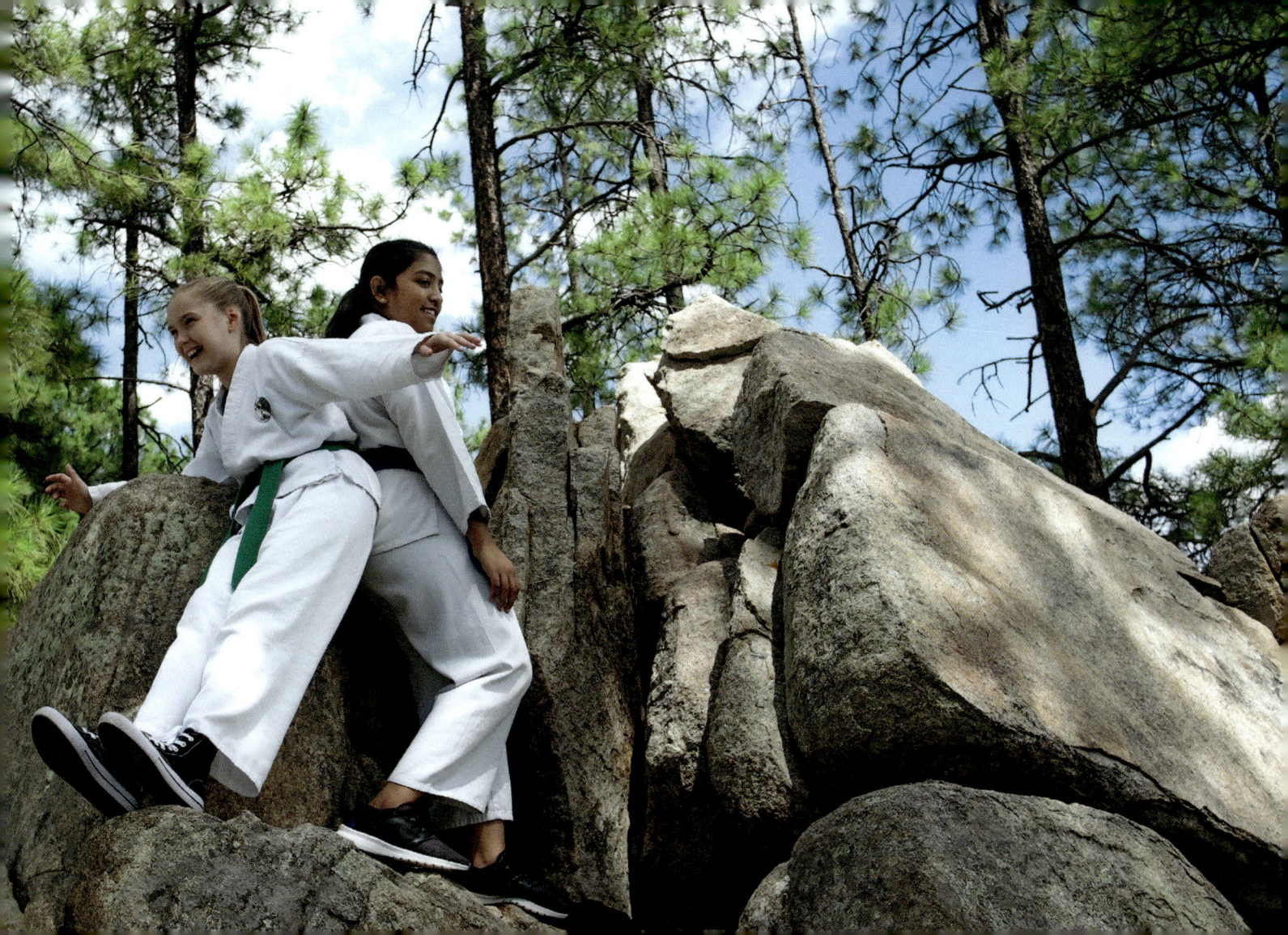

To break free from negative assumptions and self-doubt about what we can accomplish in life, we need courage, skill and follow-through.

**Courage** is needed to step into the unknown.

**Skill** is required to survive the uncertainty.

**Follow-through** provides the opportunity for success.

Glacier Bay, AK
ISO 500 f/3.6 1/1000 sec

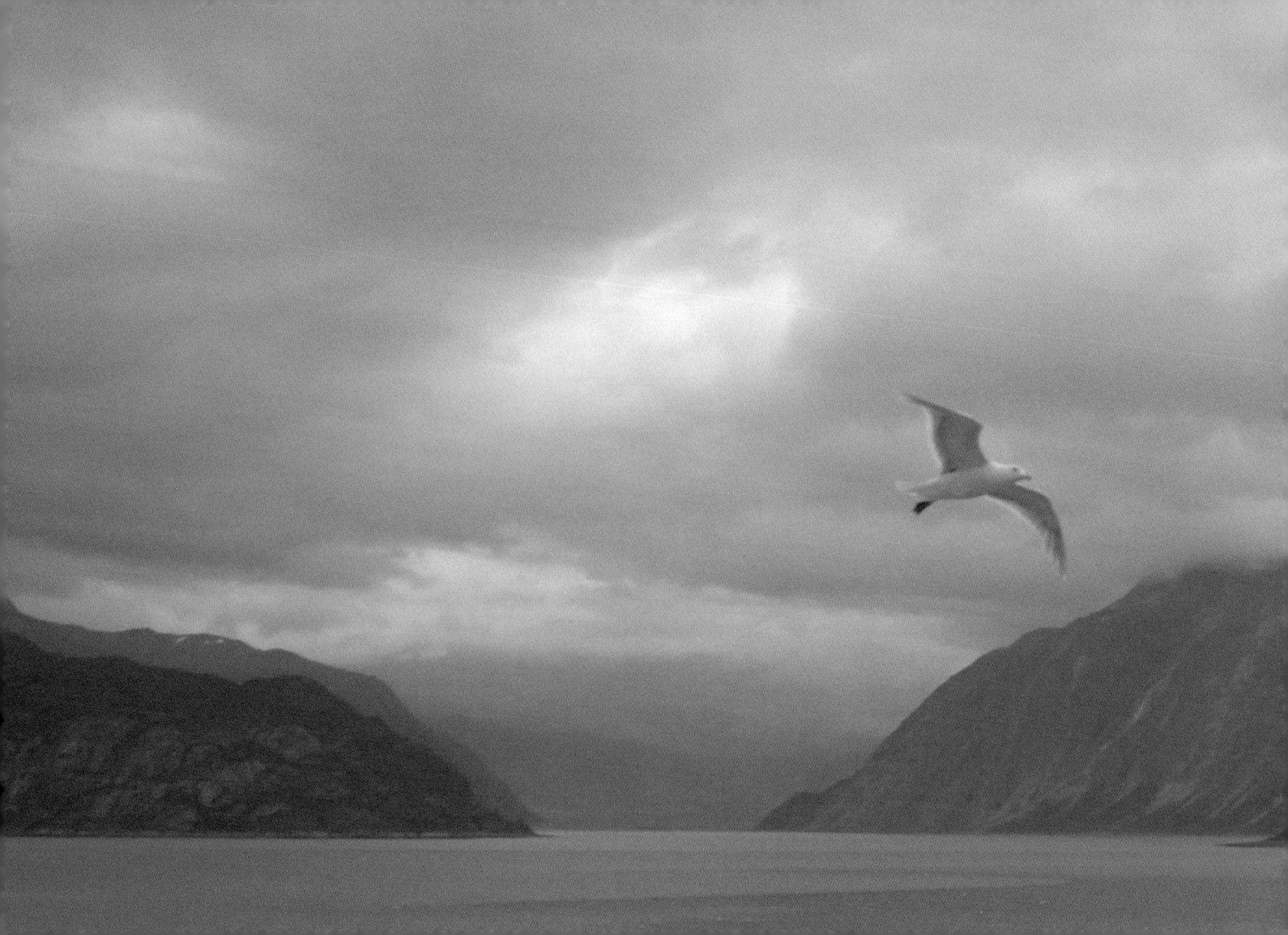

Escape the shackles of tradition to explore the rewards of innovative action.

**_Shu – Ha – Ri_**

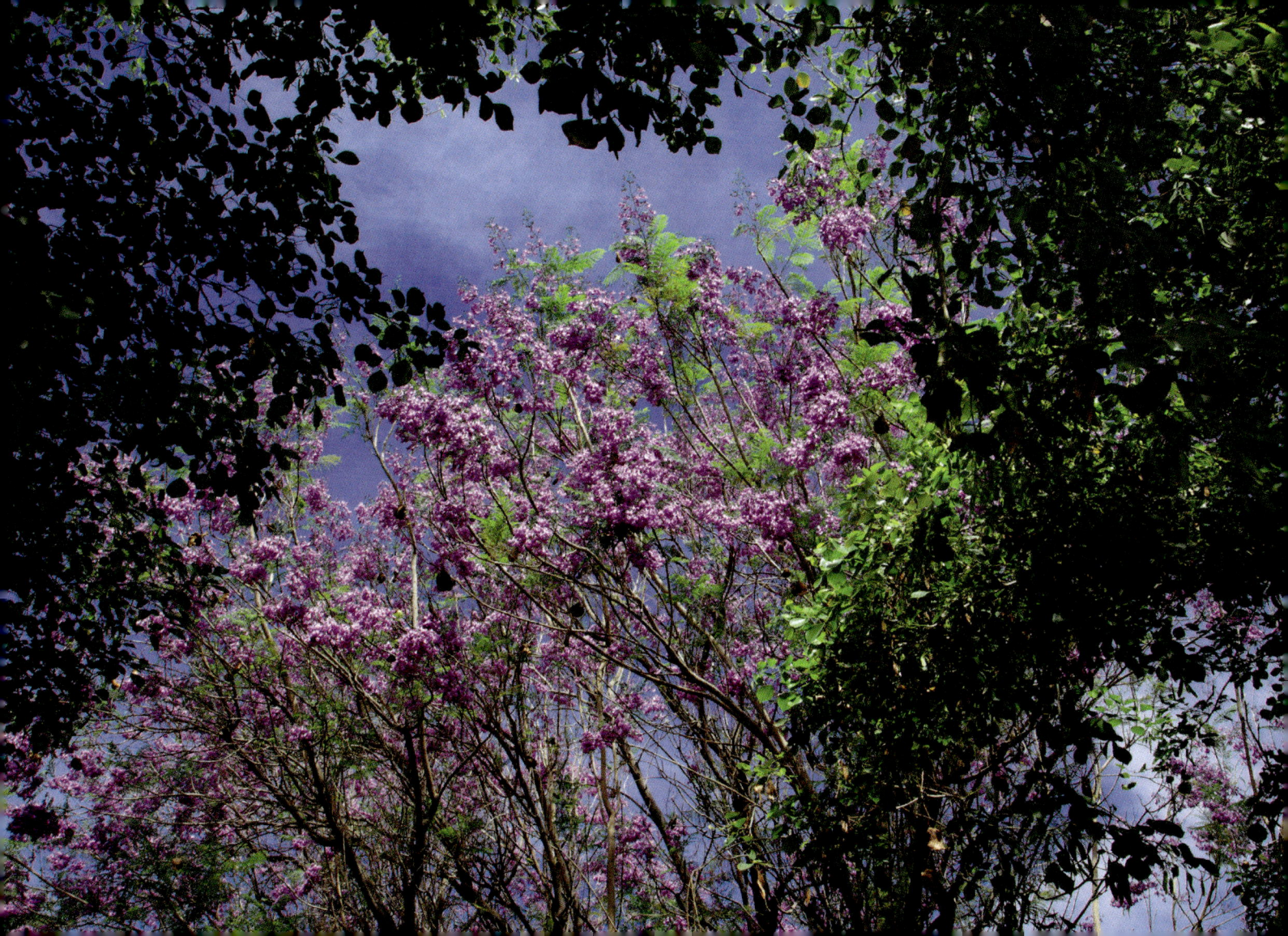

When we bow to someone to show respect – we release excessive ego and silently say,

*"You are more important than I am."*

This metaphorical practice provides insight for conflict transformation.

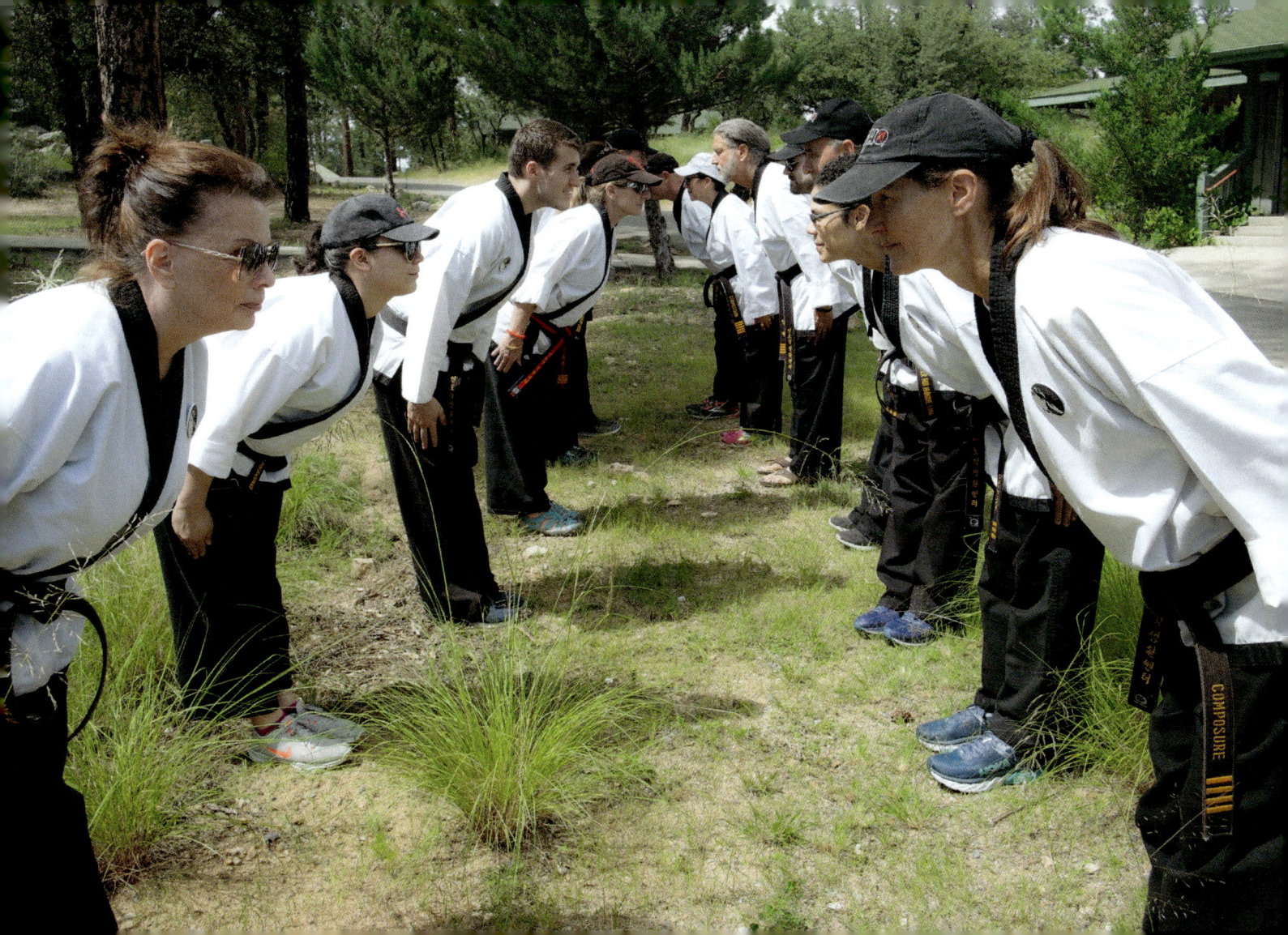

When we take the time to discover what color eyes the other person has during a dialogue,

**we engage**,

demonstrate sincerity and begin earning their trust.

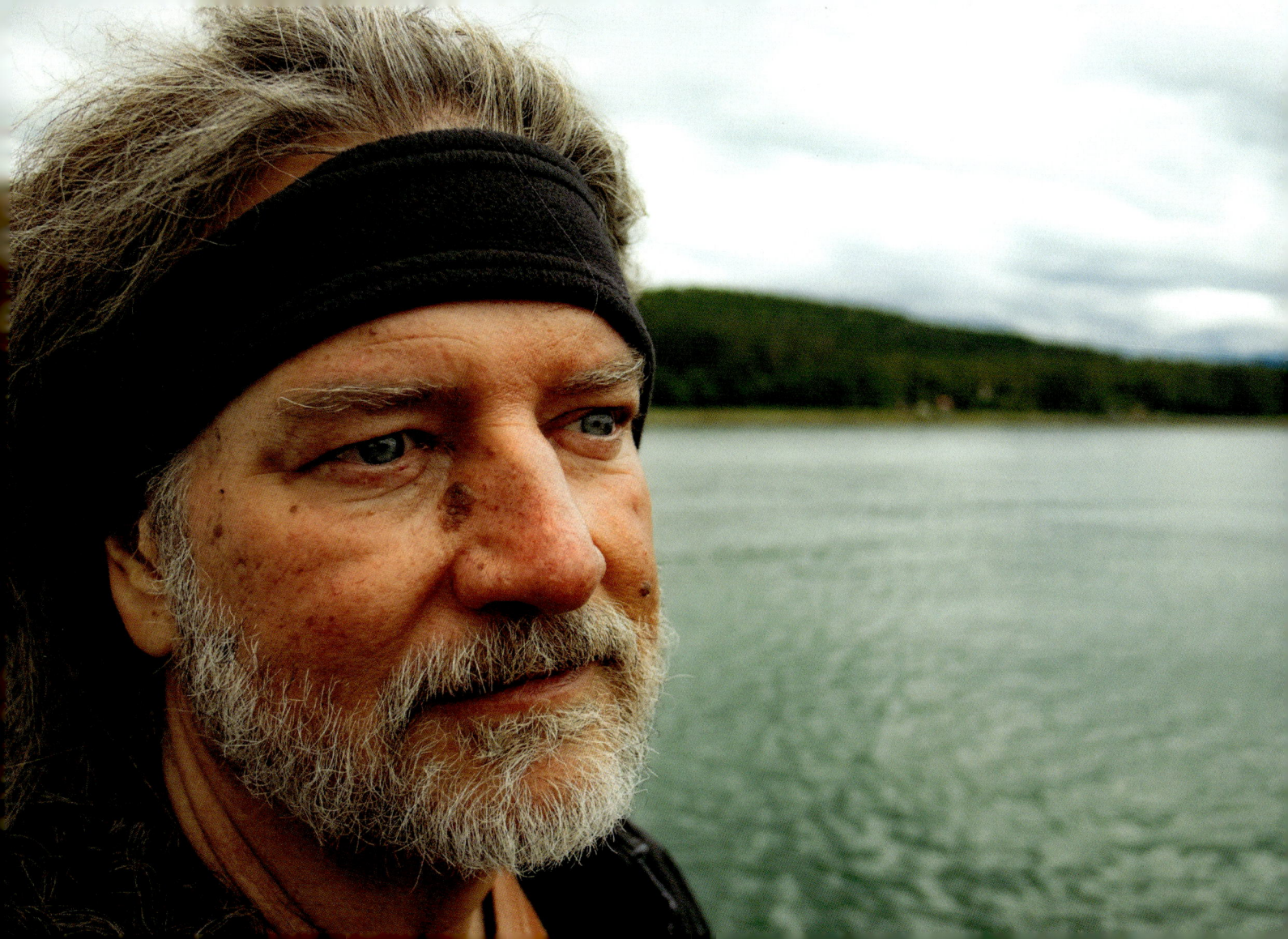

The power of *process* and *discovery* ultimately reveals more fulfillment and reward than the endpoint or product.

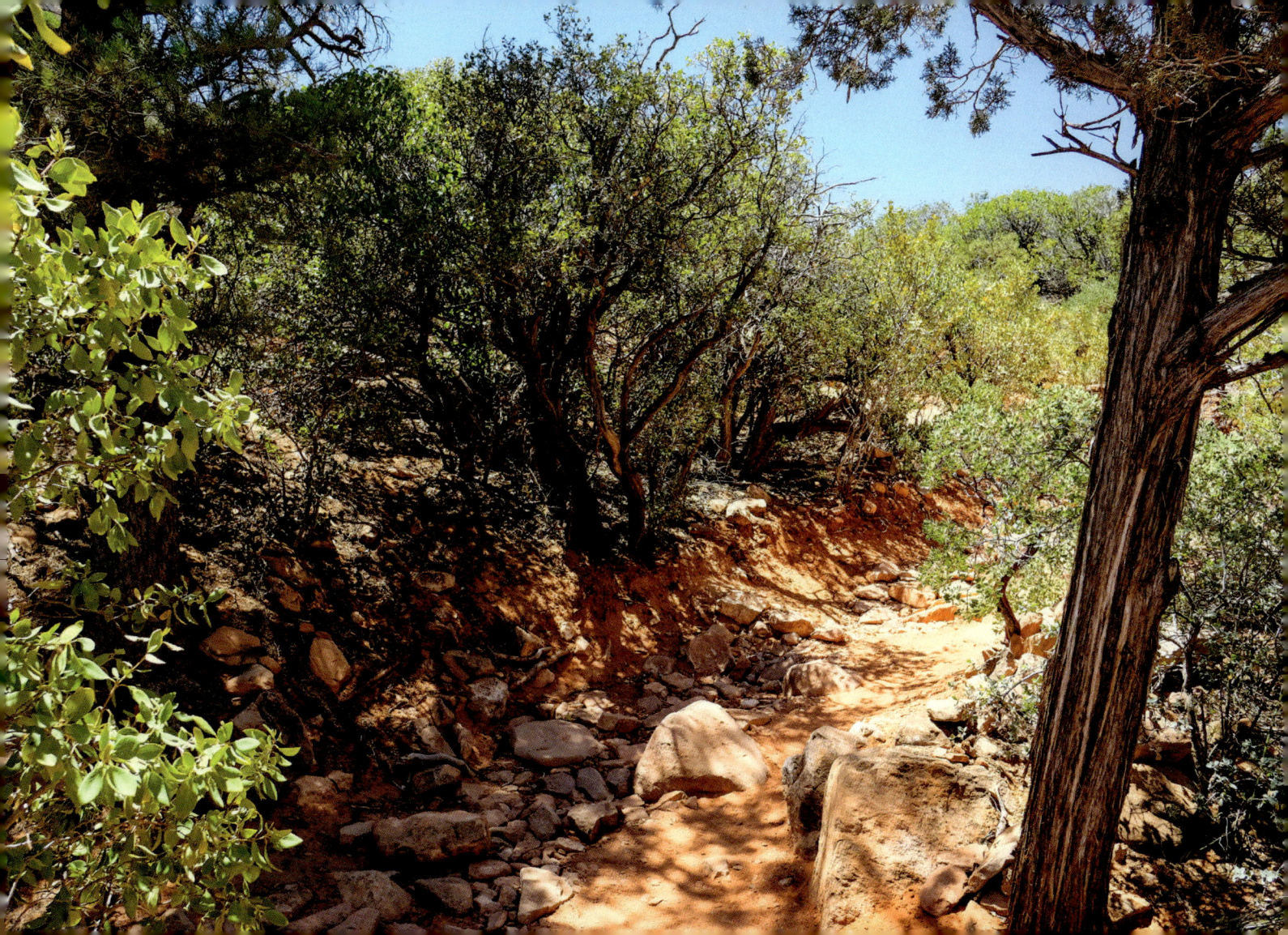

People don't really care what we know

*Until...*

They really know that we care.

**Relationships always come first.**

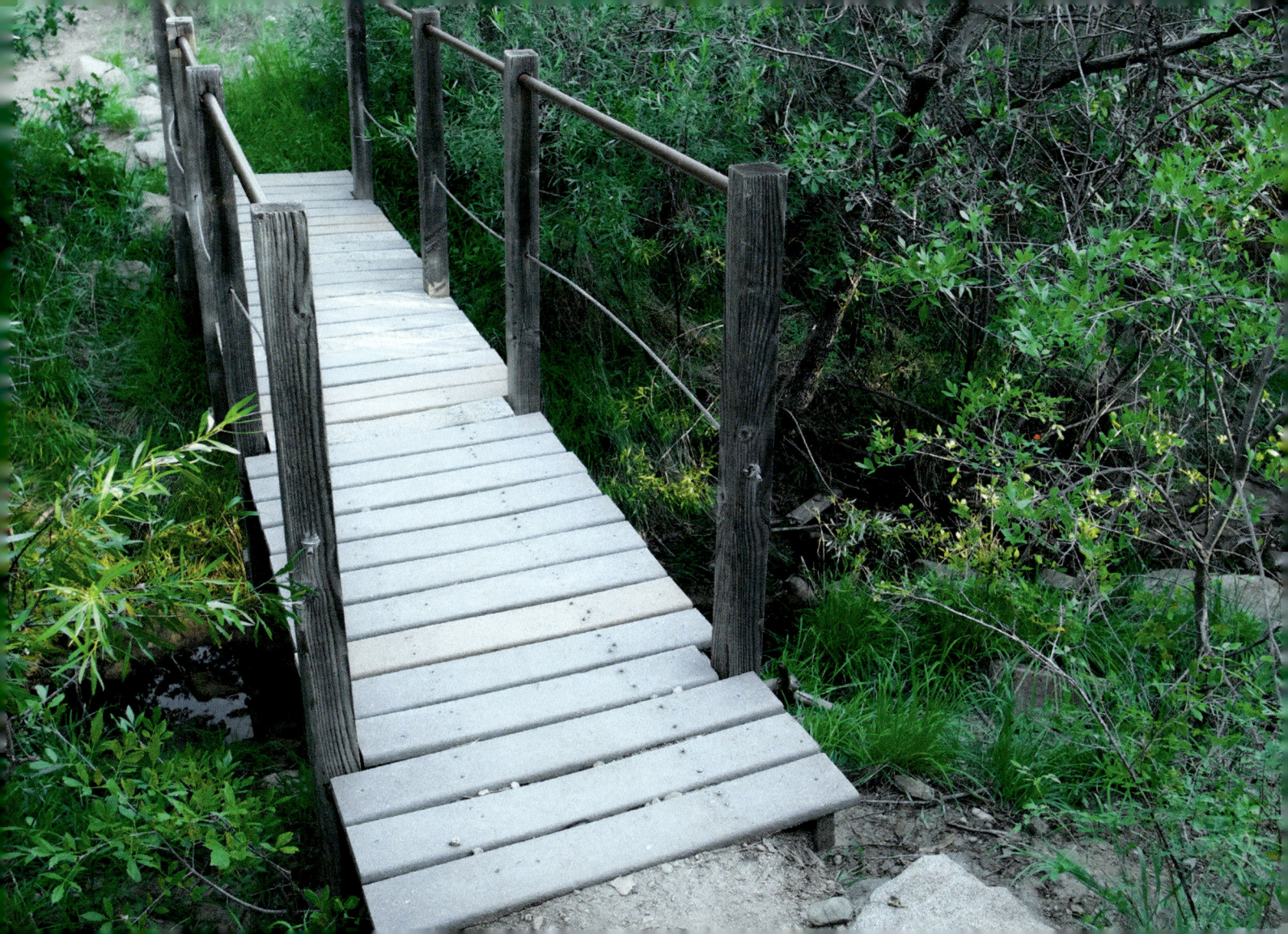

Spreading negative rumors is like emptying a bag of feathers into the wind.

Once released, *retrieving them*

*is nearly*

*impossible.*

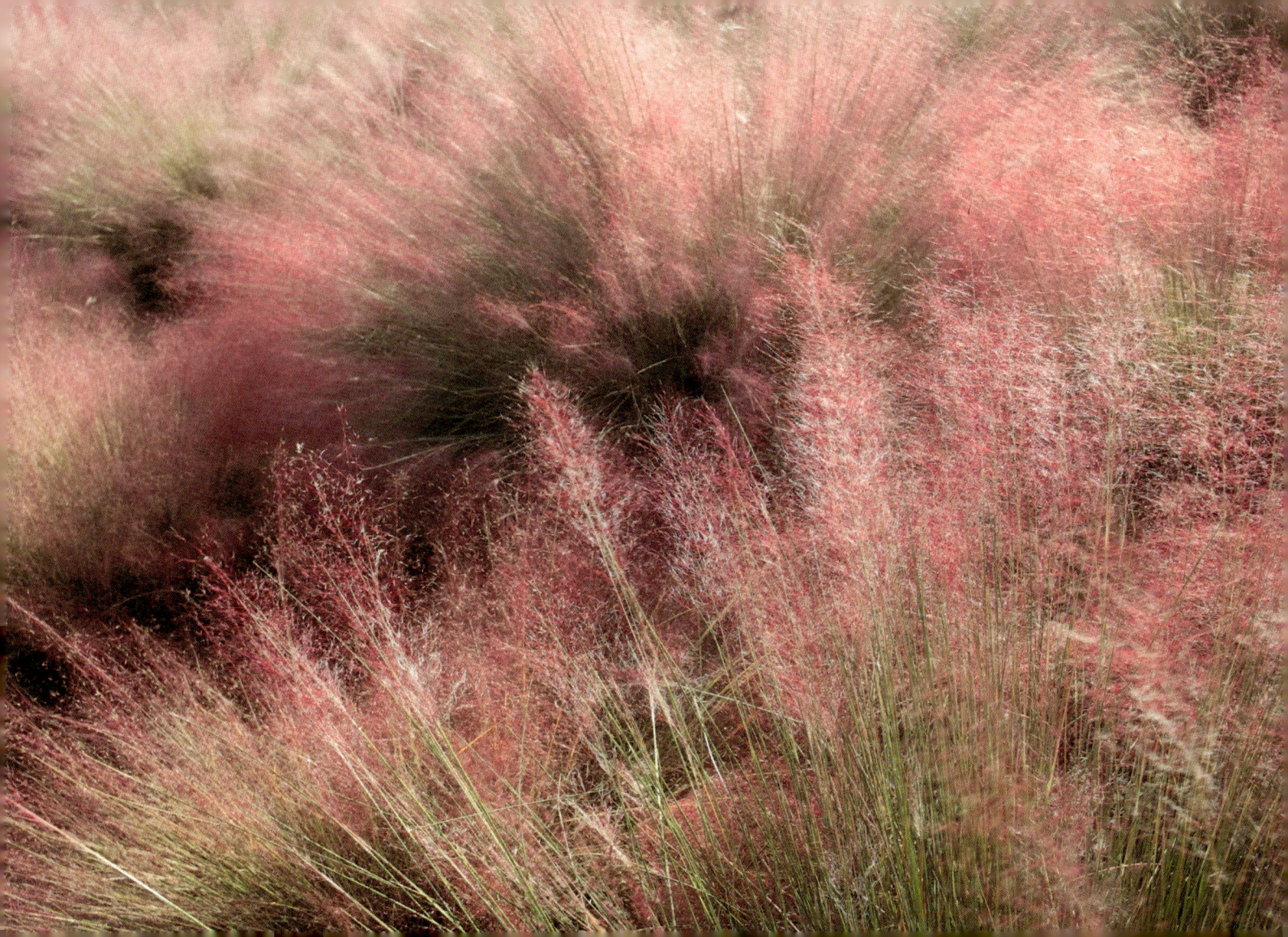

A fundamental component of living a happy life is to learn to *desire all that we have* instead of having all that we desire.

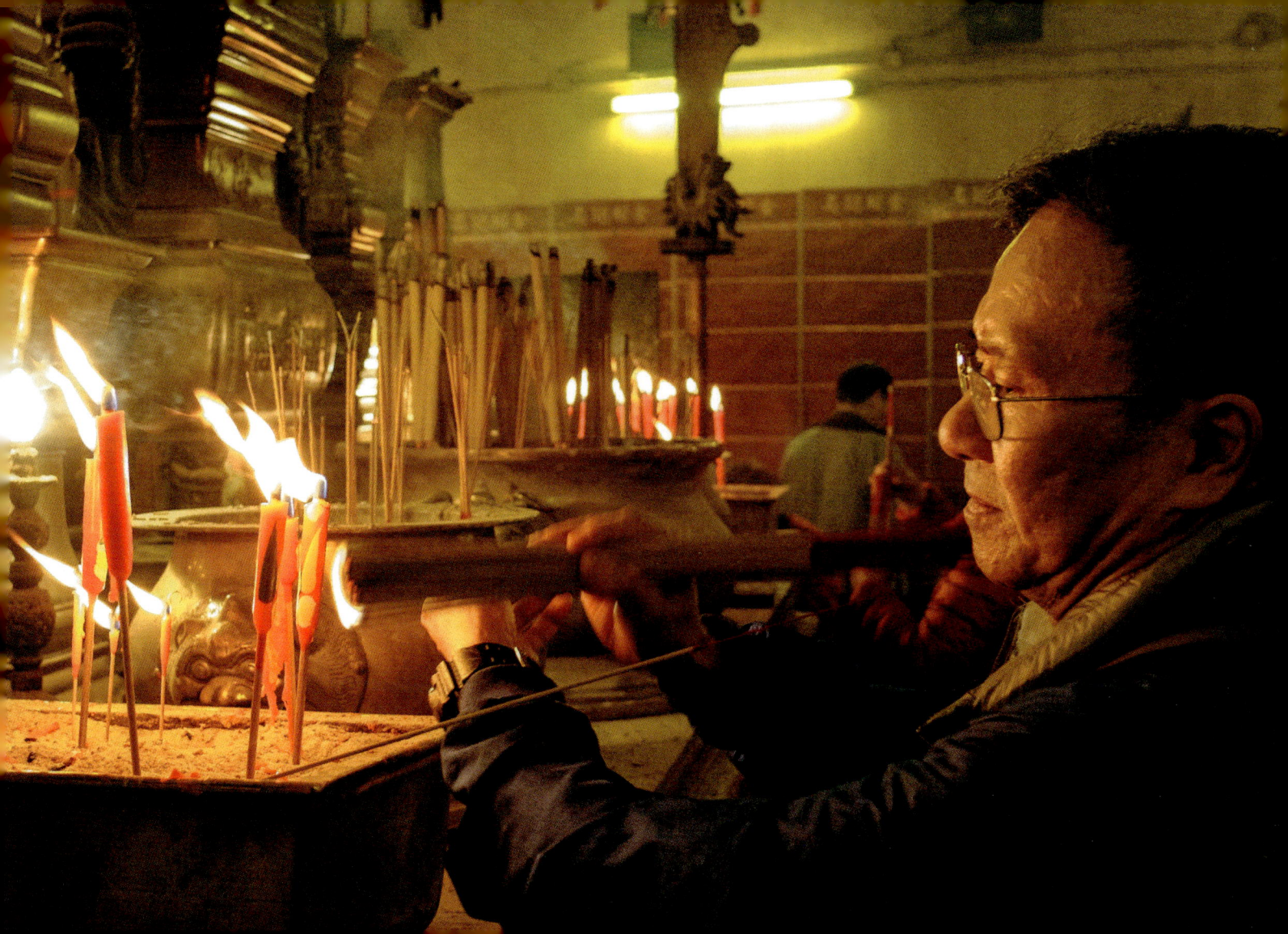

To consistently "act with confidence" instead of "reacting from fear," we must be **acutely aware** and **meticulously prepared**.

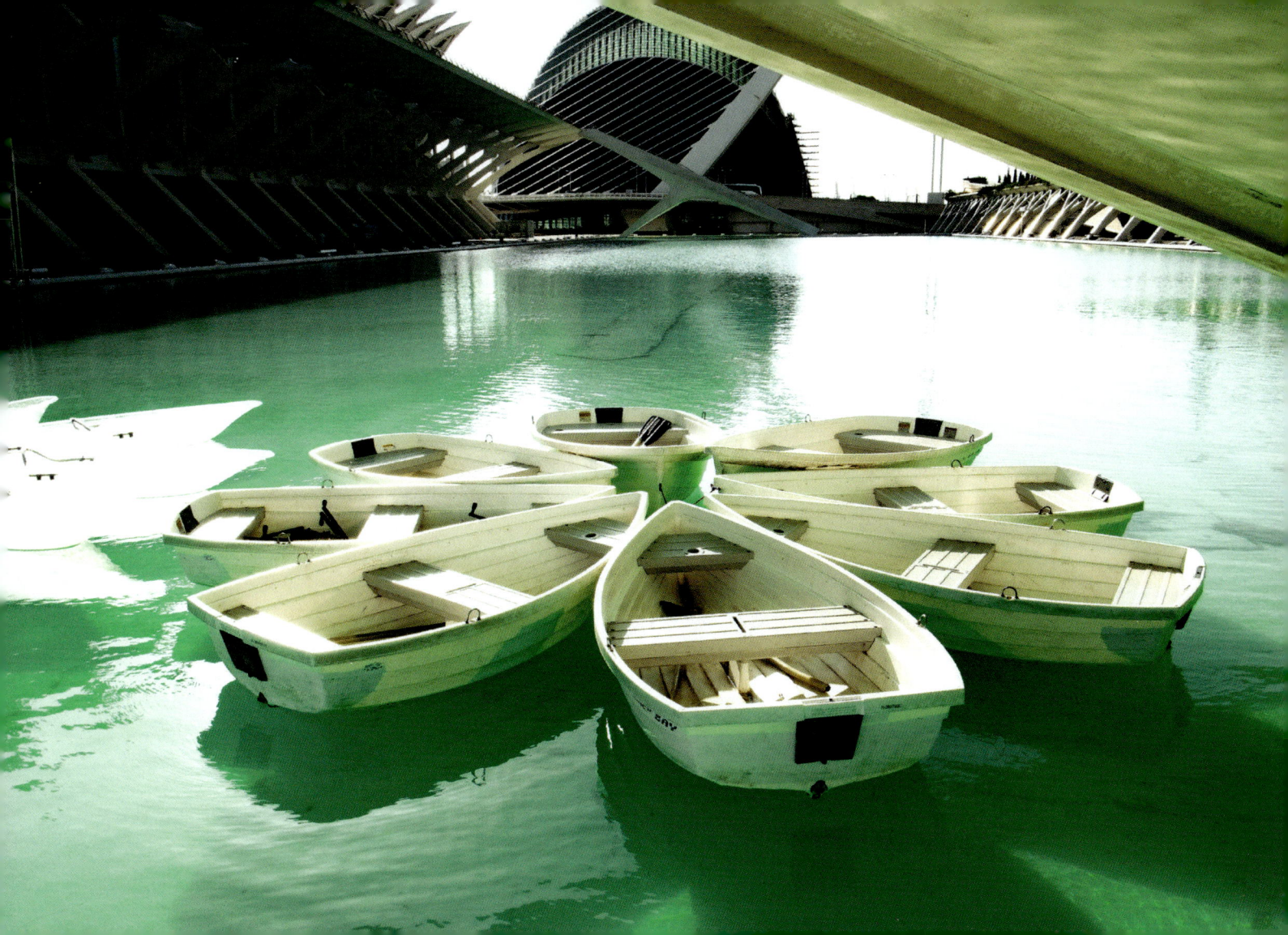

Sometimes we need to stop "beating ourselves up" over difficult situations.

*Innovative solutions often arrive only when we stop trying so hard to make them happen.*

Keep in mind those whispered words of wisdom,

**"Let it be."**

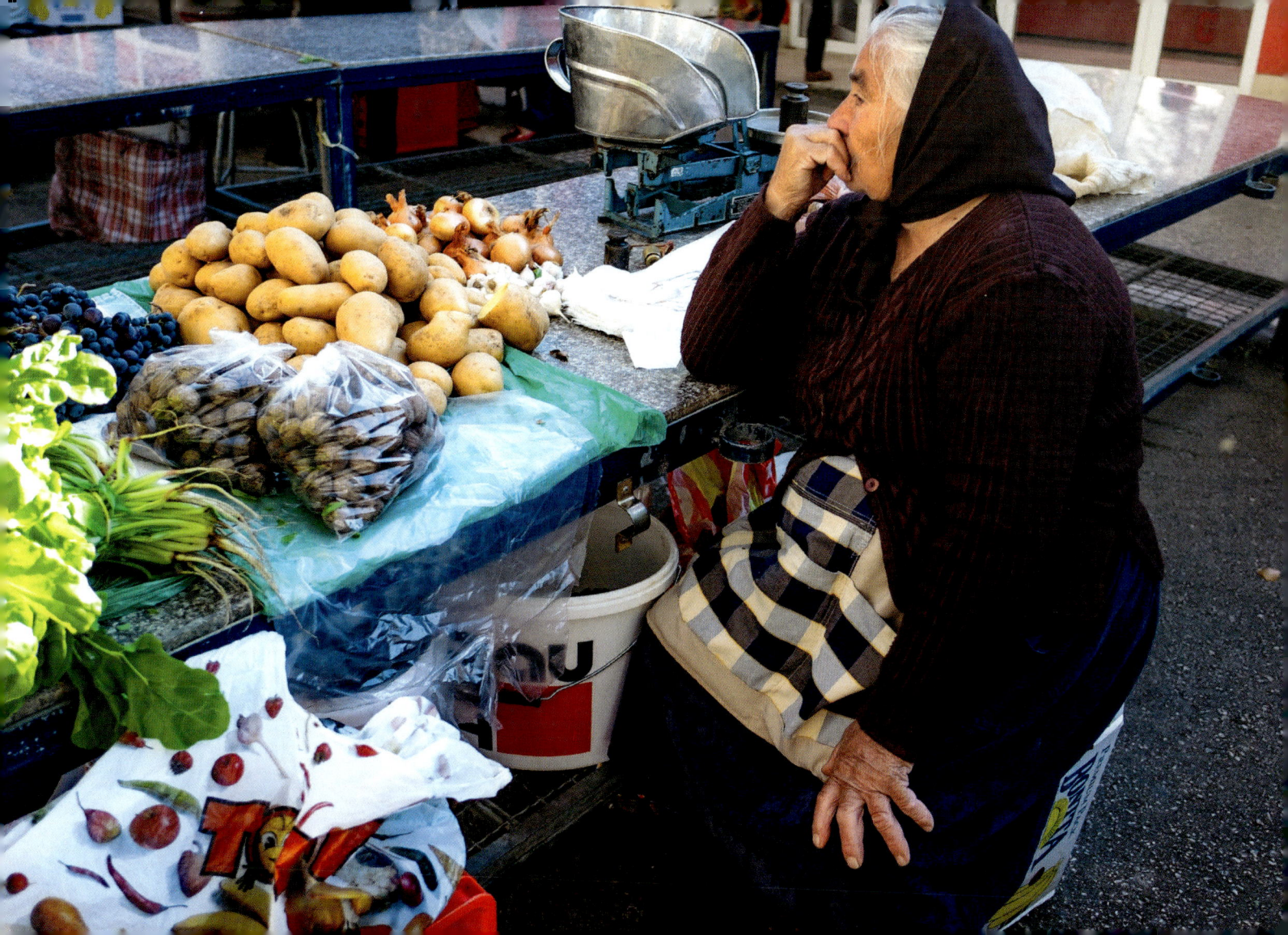

To avoid pain and gain control in a conflict situation, we must focus less on resisting and more on *blending*.

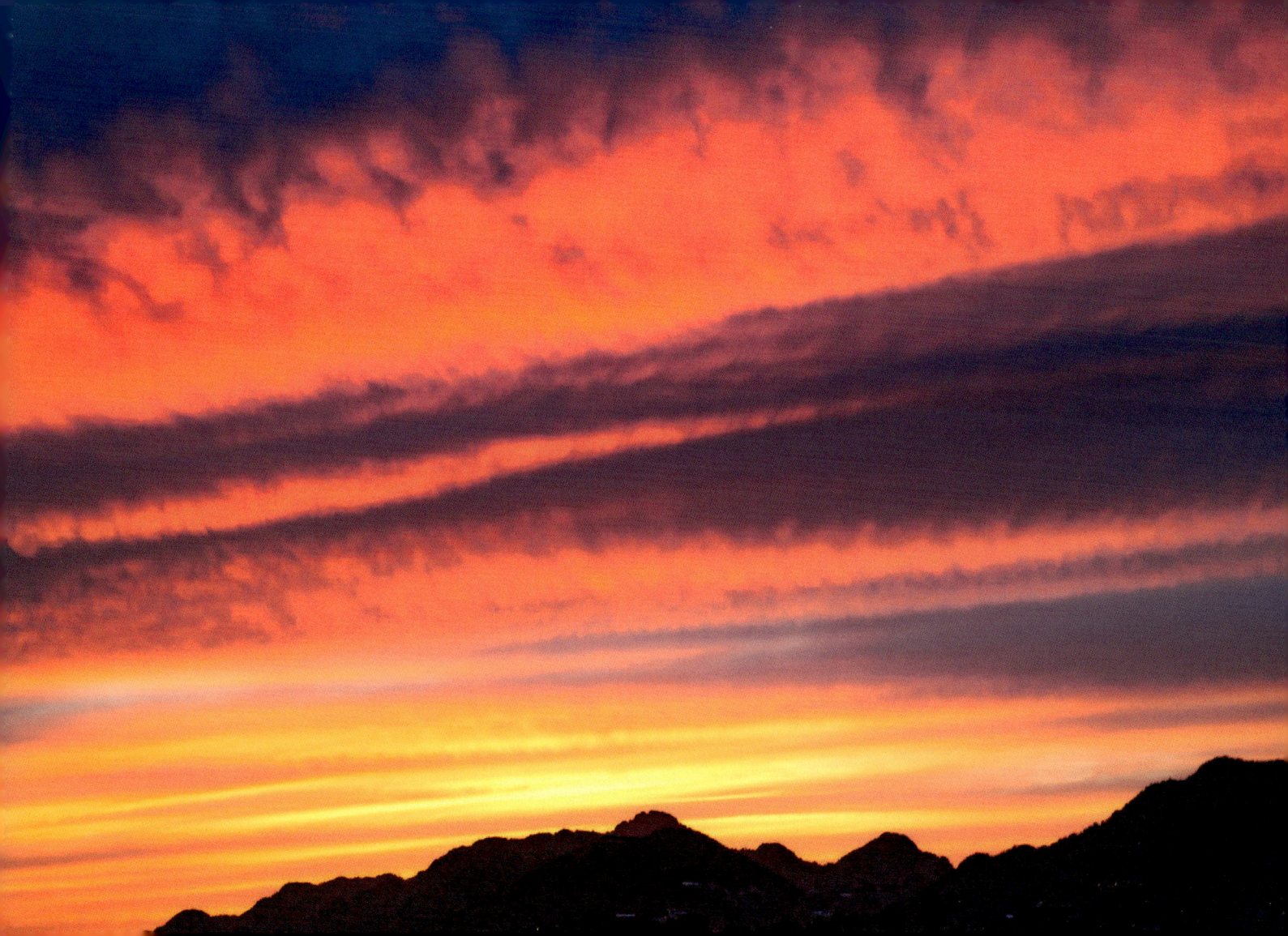

*Be like bamboo —*

Be durable, yet flexible, to endure change.

Have the capacity to be humble and forgiving.

Be able to bend instead of break

when conditions become harsh.

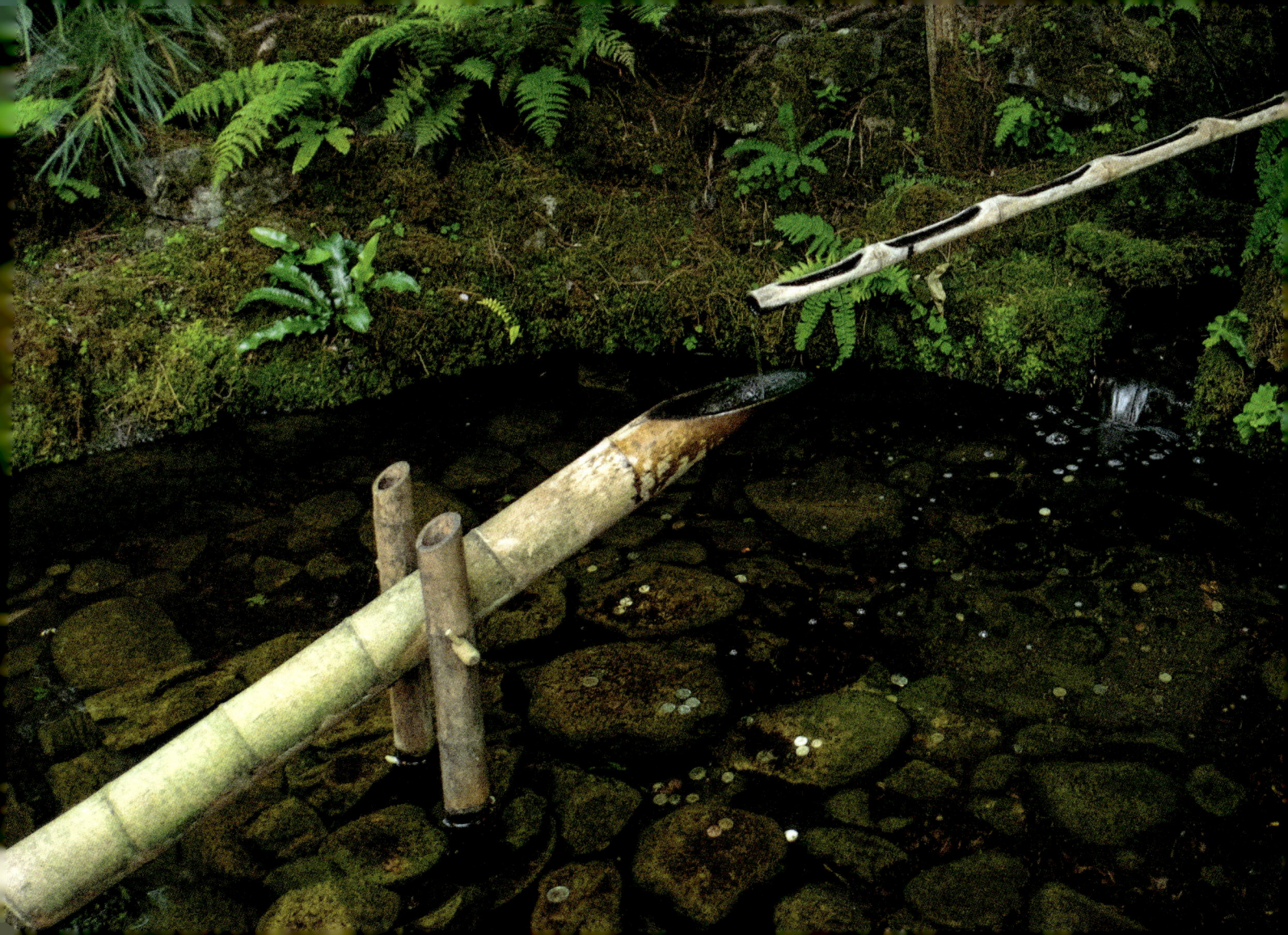

While standing at the beach attempting to maintain balance as the waves crash precariously at our knees and the sand retreats beneath our feet, we must purposefully adjust our stances to find stability.

Our life is much like balancing in the surf where the waves of uncertainty and the retreating sands of broken promises are always attempting to

knock
us
down.

To sustain our balance, we must rely on the stability provided by our "life-stance" structured from our irrevocable personal truths and unwavering life commitments.

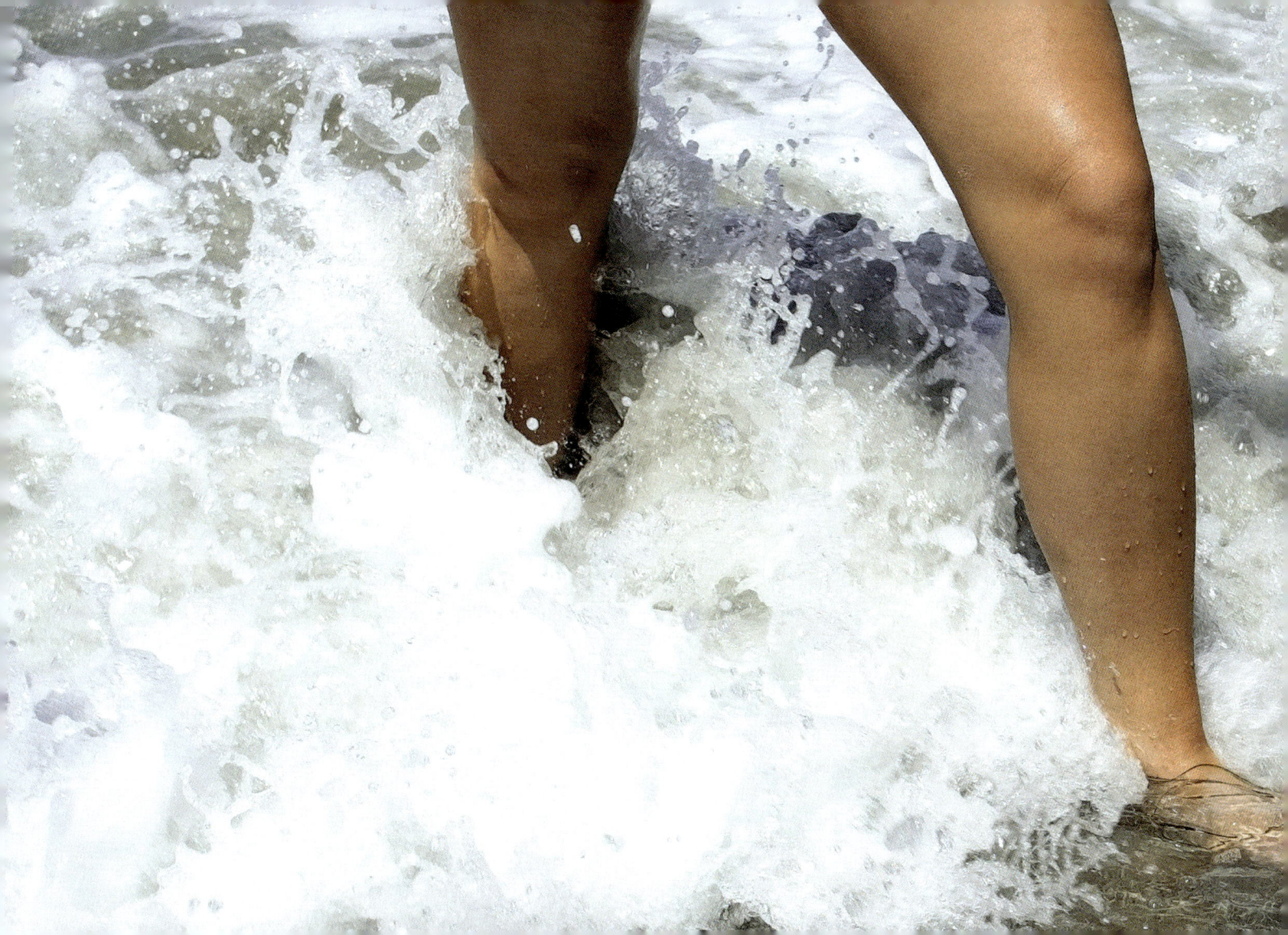

Meaningful motivation emerges from having a **clear purpose**, the **autonomy** to make it happen and the **opportunity** to continuously improve.

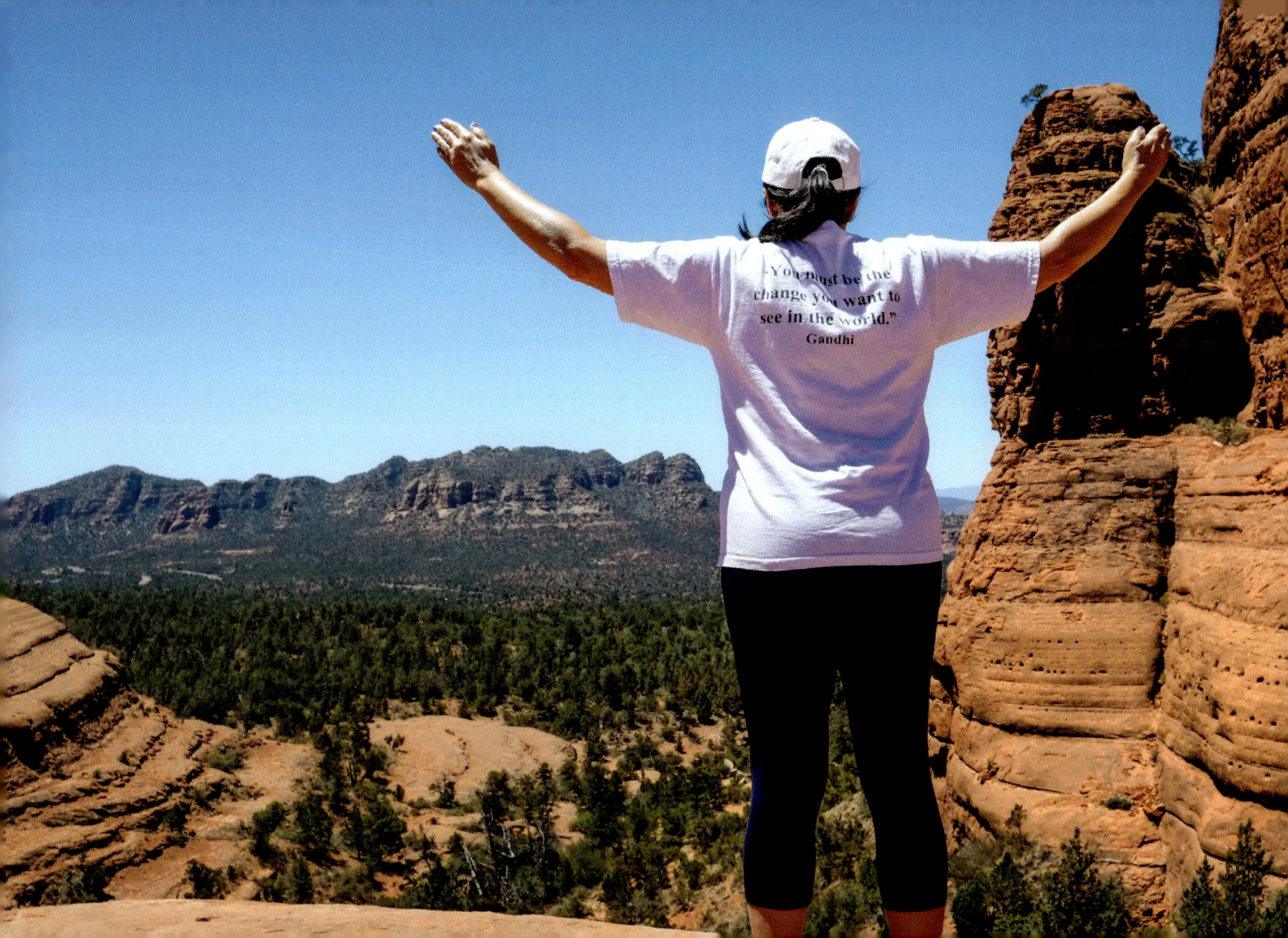

Stop trying to live a balanced life. It is exhausting and impossible to keep the "teeter-totter of life" always level in the air.

***Focus instead on living a life of harmony.***

Carefully tune each string of the metaphorical instrument of life by establishing meaningful goals in the domains of your career, family, personal life, community work, spirituality and finances.

Through this process, we establish control, reduce the fatigue of attempting to live in balance and ***become free to play a beautiful and harmonious "life" chord.***

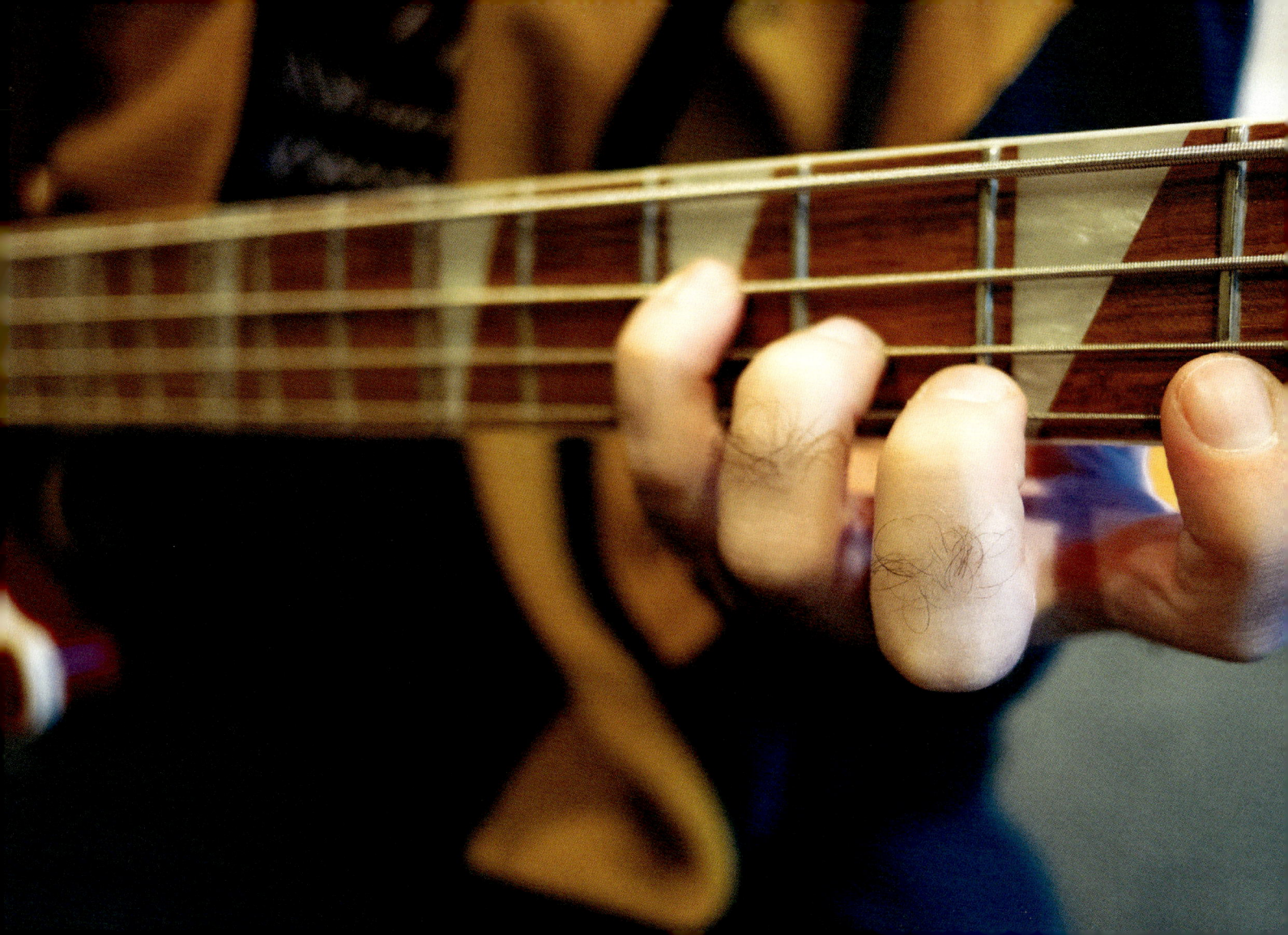

**Caring** leaders provide fair, inclusive and transparent leadership.

They **foster hope** by consistently articulating an inspiring future.

They **demonstrate compassion and empathy** for the plight of their followers.

They **enable trust** to be at the center of all relationships.

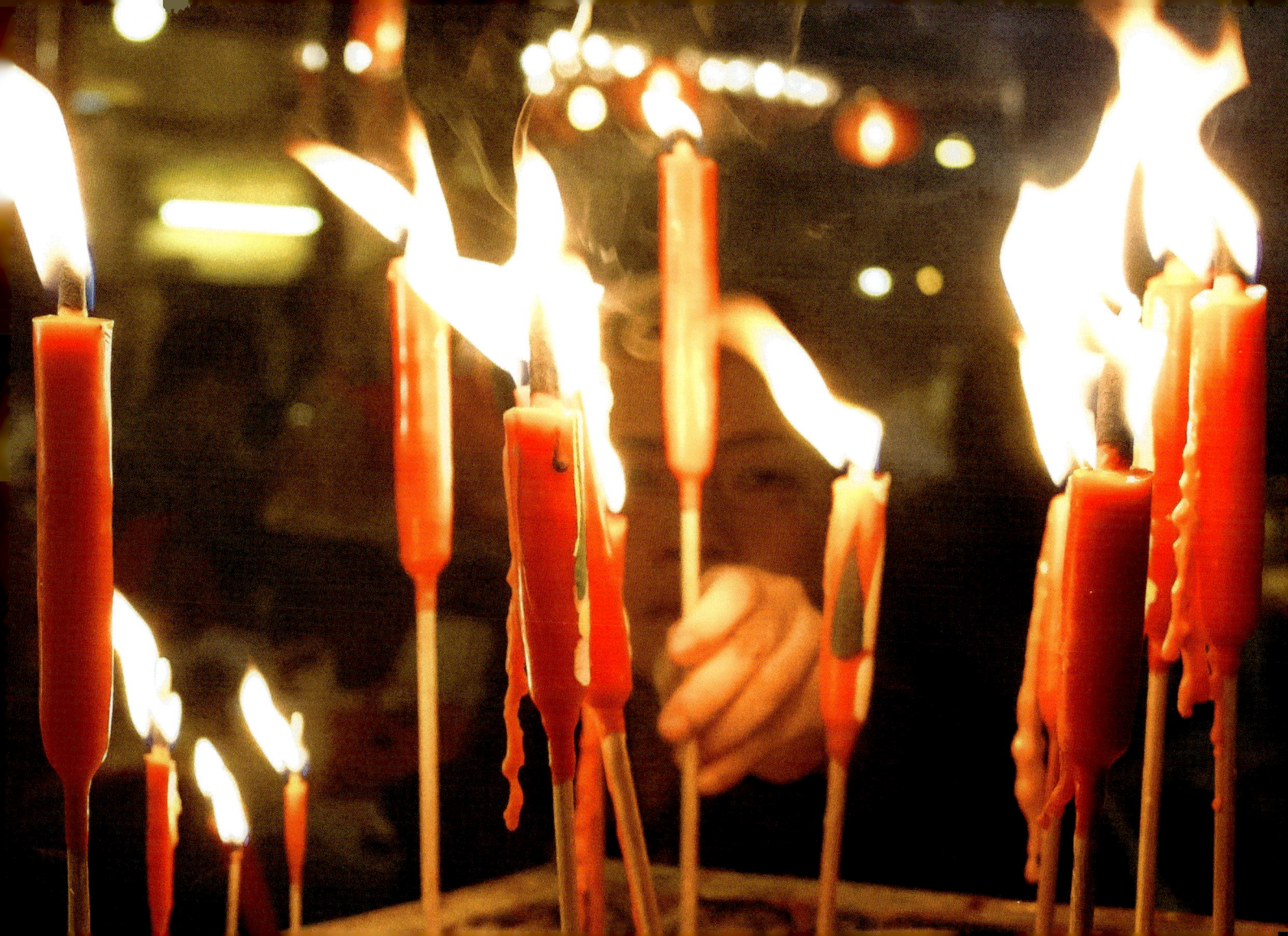

**Maintaining a positive mindset opens the door to happiness.**

**To walk through that door, we must commit to six-to-eight hours of sleep, a healthy diet, exercise and strong interpersonal relationships.**

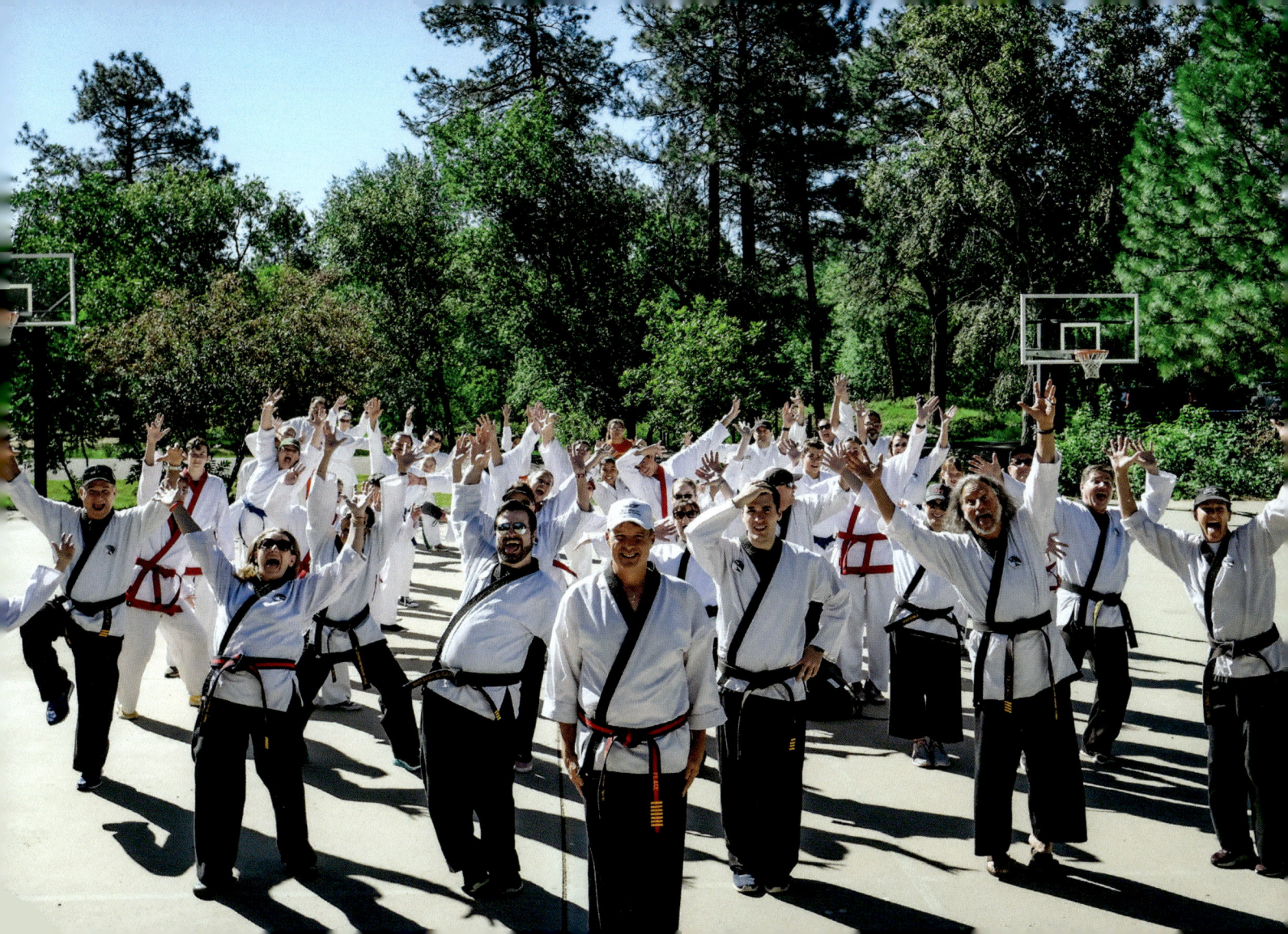

Email and texting lack the necessary context to communicate intent.

Gaps of uncertainty become filled by self-invented victim, villain and helpless narratives.

Meaningful conversations should occur only *face-to-face*

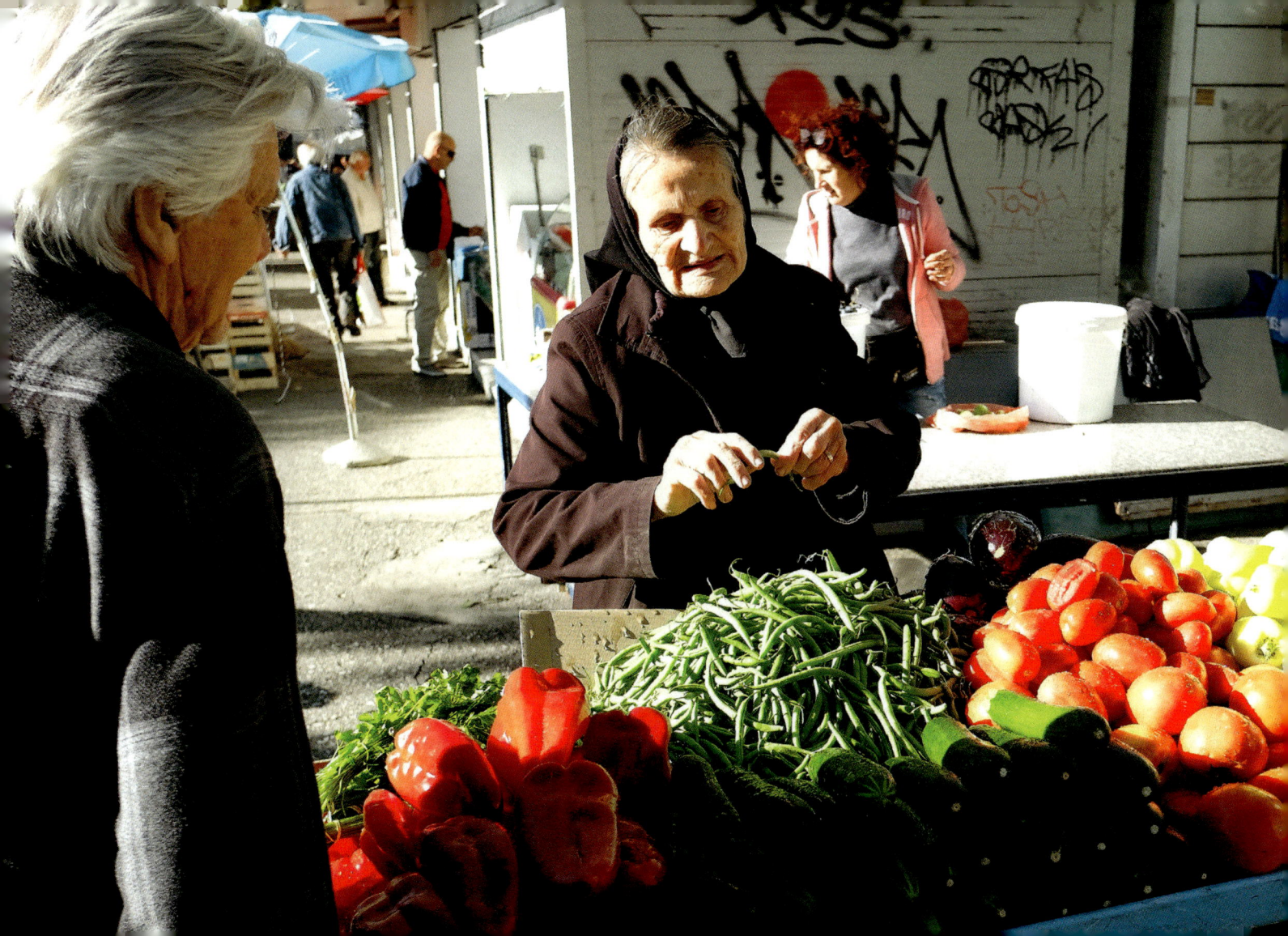

If we can give *purpose* to our *pain*

we can remarkably *alleviate* our suffering.

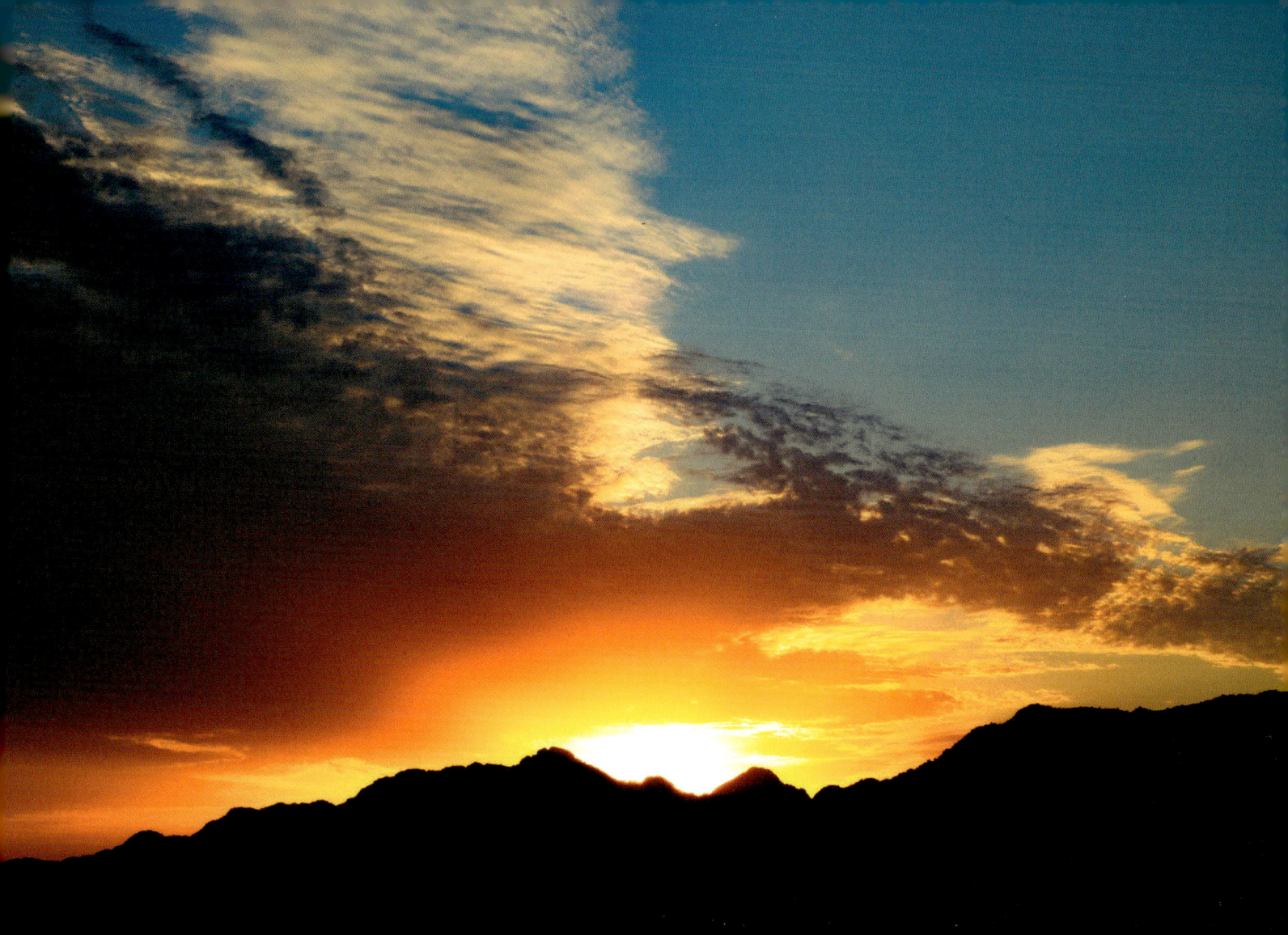

Bullies are *victims*.

They are fighting a personal battle that nobody knows anything about.

Their self-esteem "bucket" is empty and they need *us* to fill it.

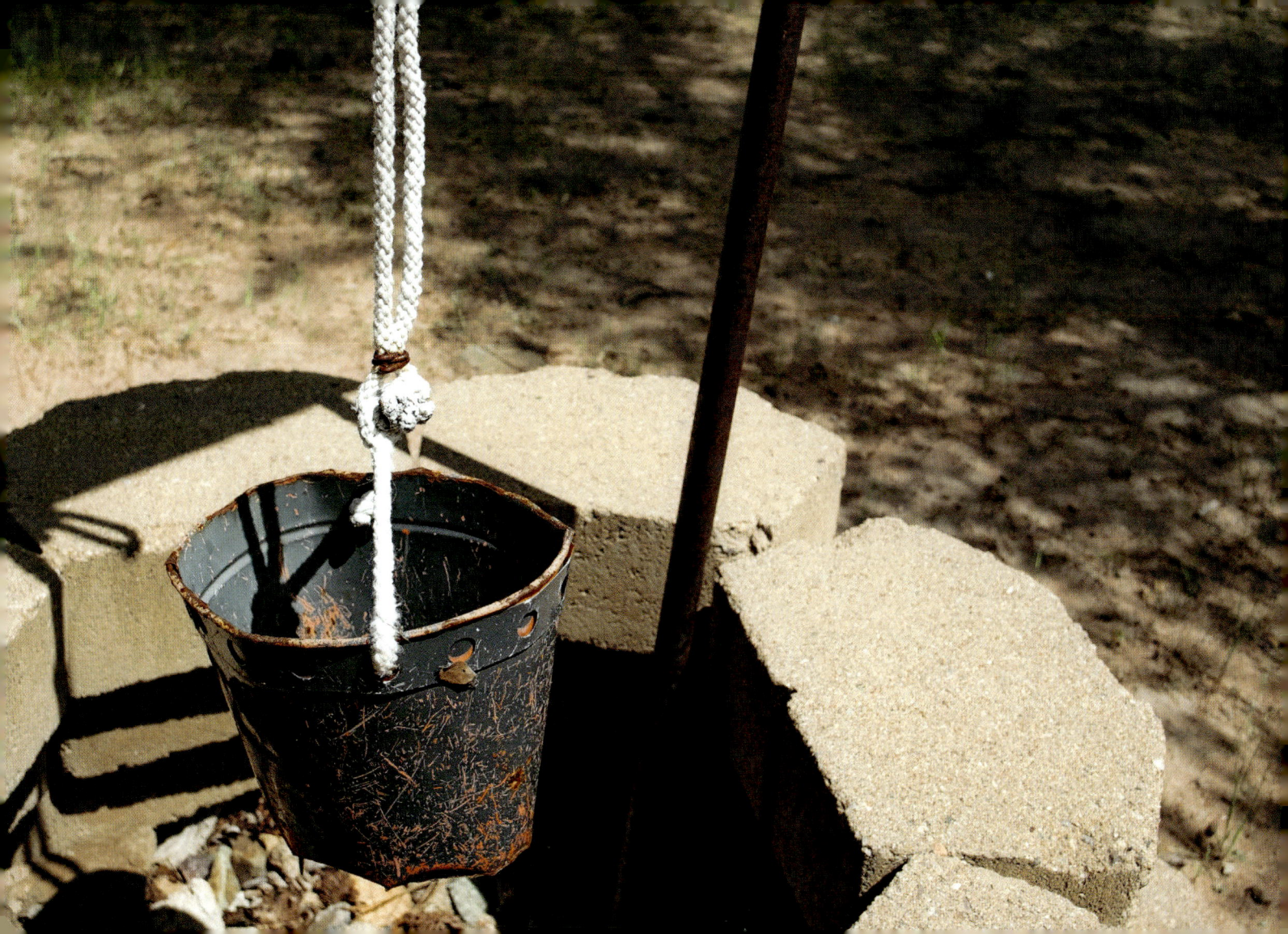

Our best teachers are always to our left, right, front and behind.

*Seldom are they at the podium.*

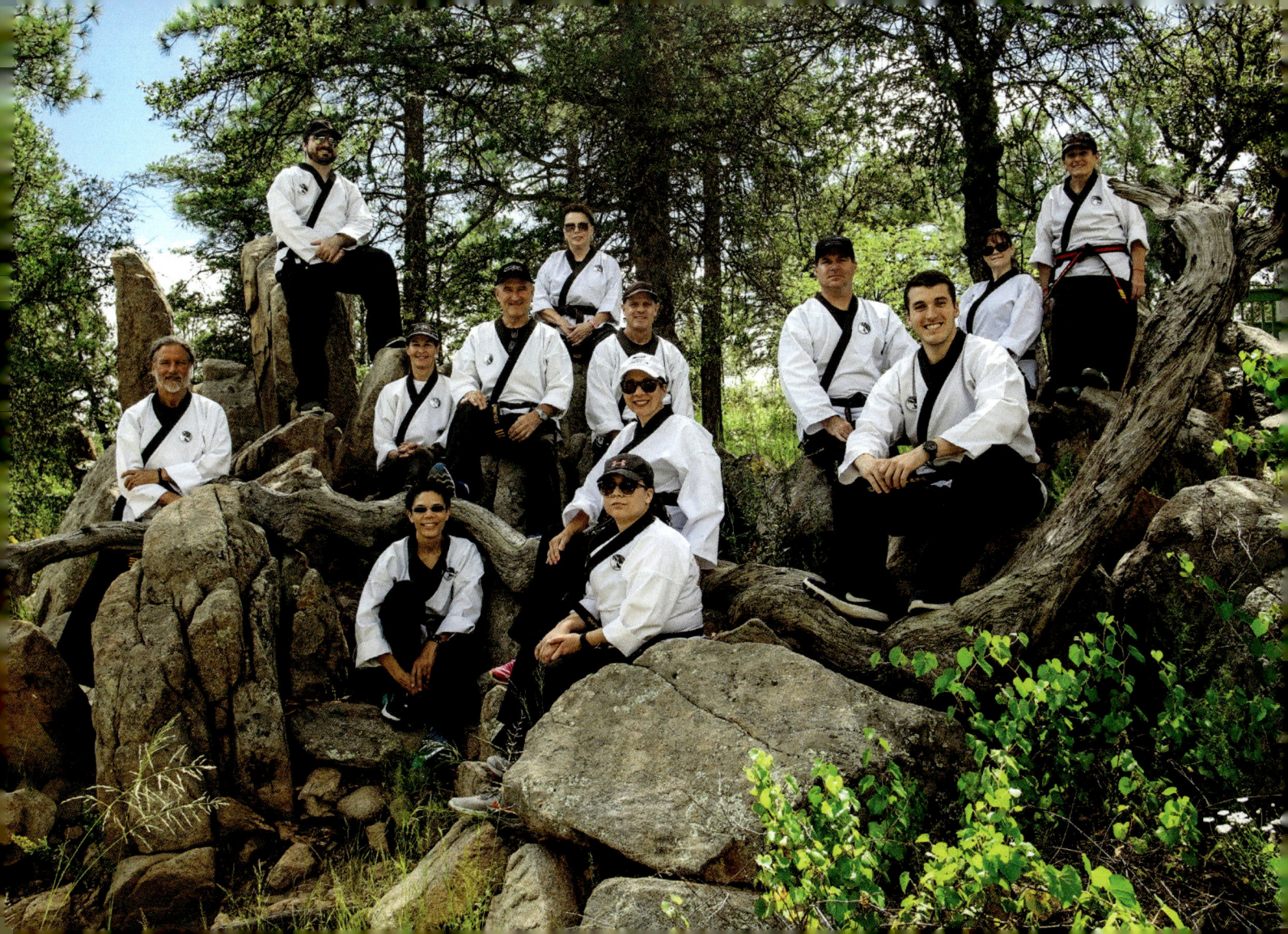

*"We don't get out of this world alive."*

**Be present and fully embrace life *actively* and *lovingly*.**

Photo taken by Dr. Lisa Dado

Venice, Italy
ISO 1000 f/4.0 1/60 sec

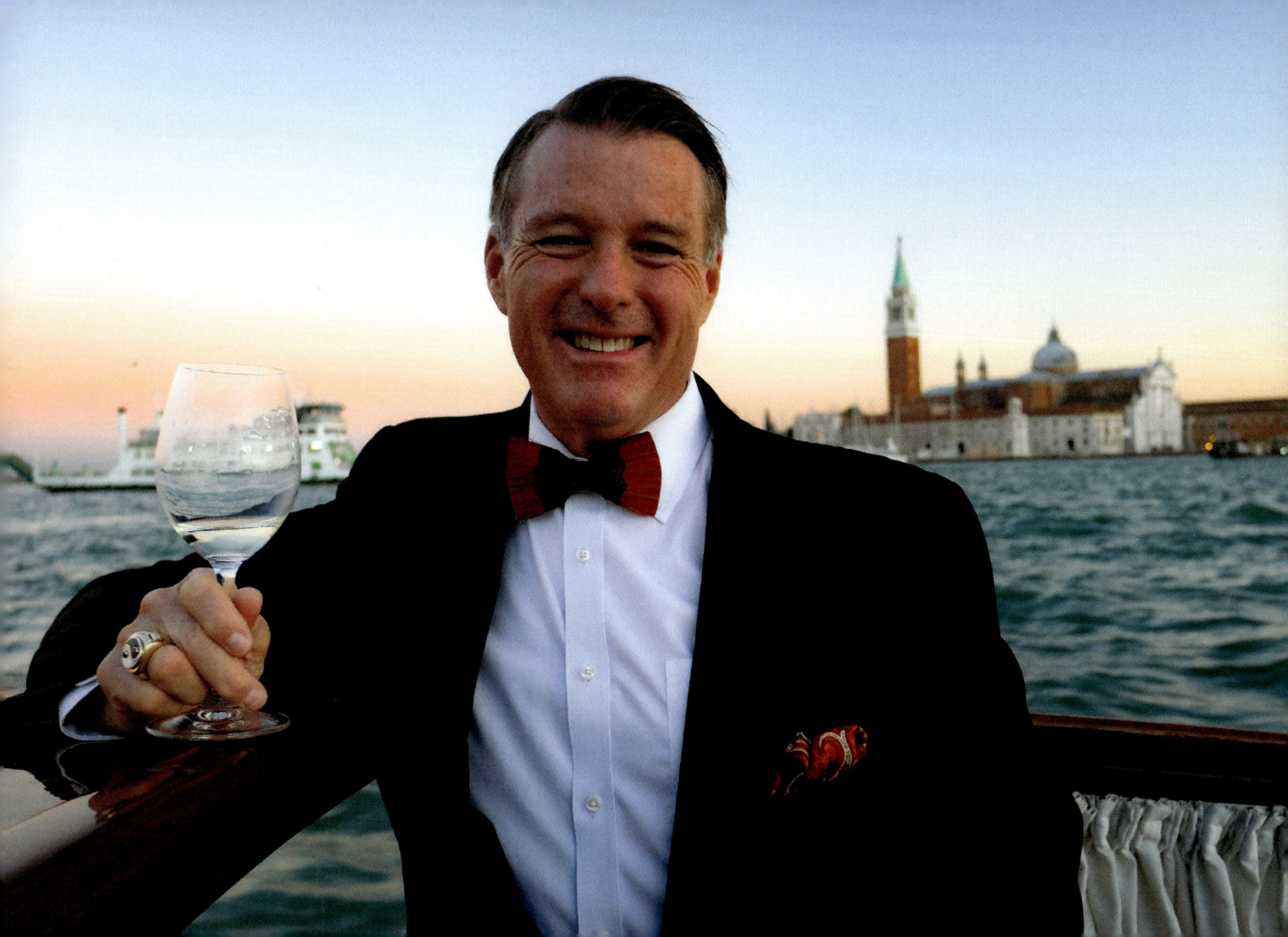

There are people around us who energize us, foster our happiness and help us express feelings of confidence and satisfaction.

Others, however, deplete our energy and sense of well-being.

Surround yourself with those who energize.
*Establish clear boundaries for those who don't.*

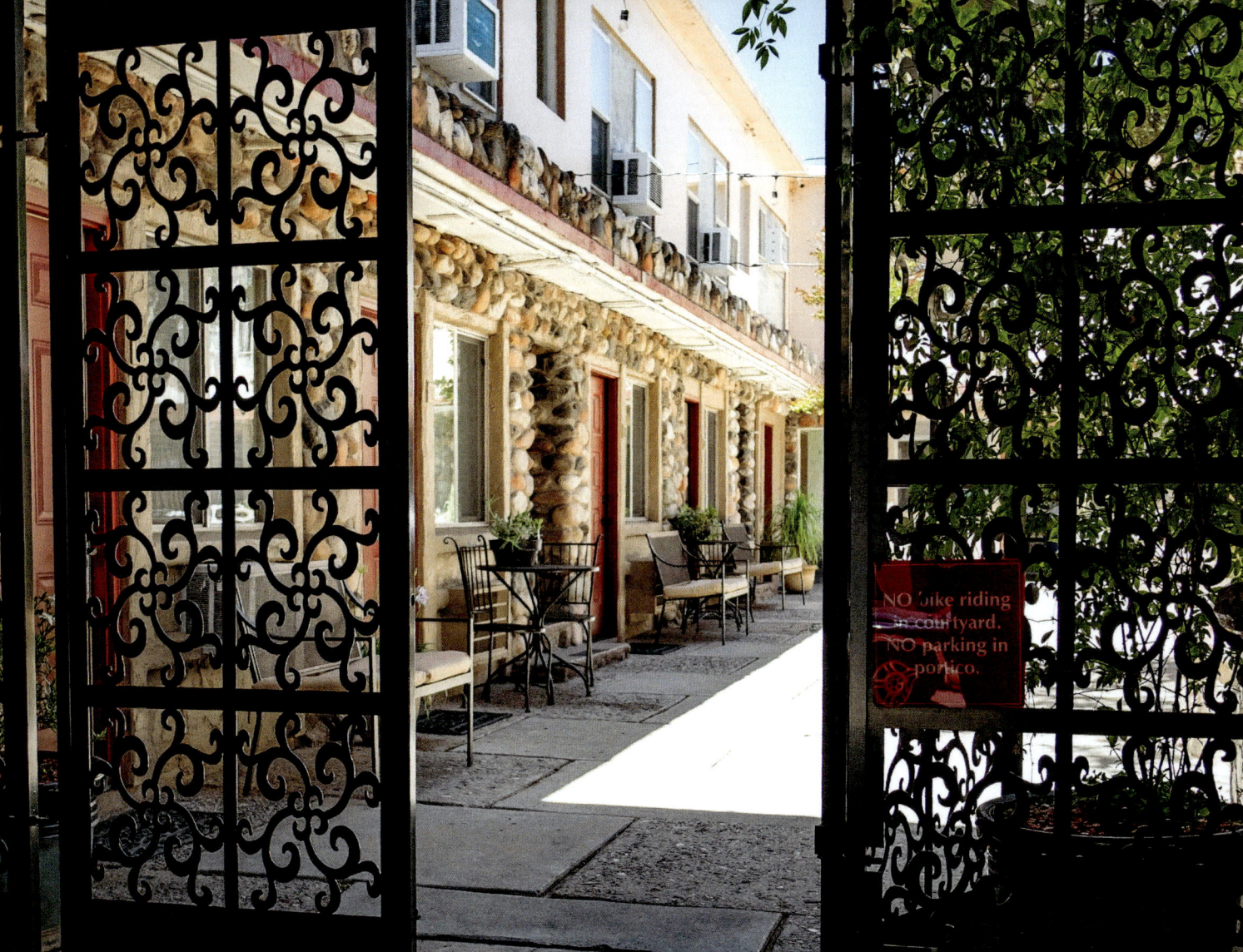

write and display positive affirmations for a desired future.

Perseverate powerfully.

Fully embrace the Law of Attraction.

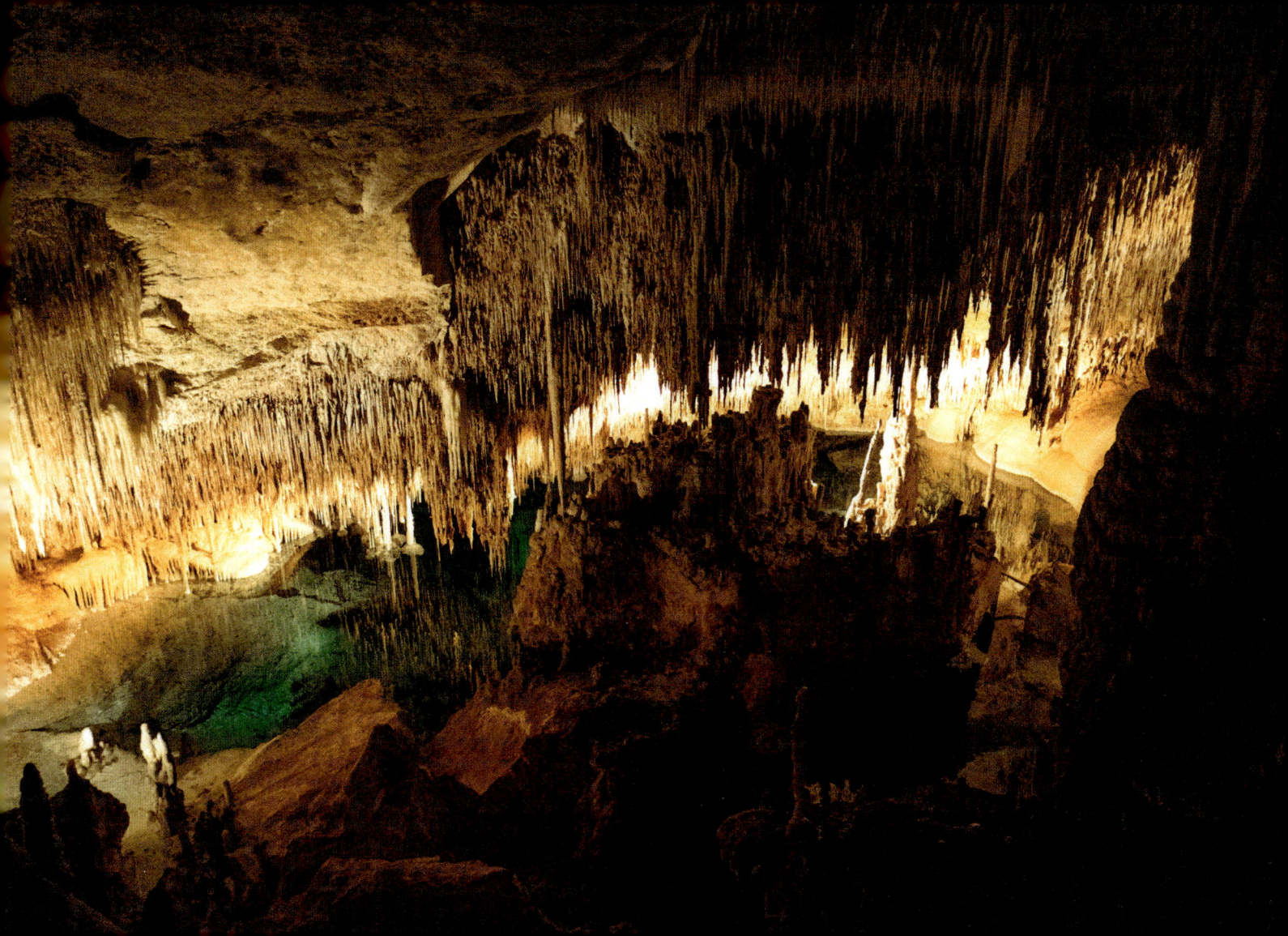

**Mushin** or **"no mind"** is a state of absolute awareness and clarity.

It is a mindset of *knowing* and *being*, not one of thinking and doing.

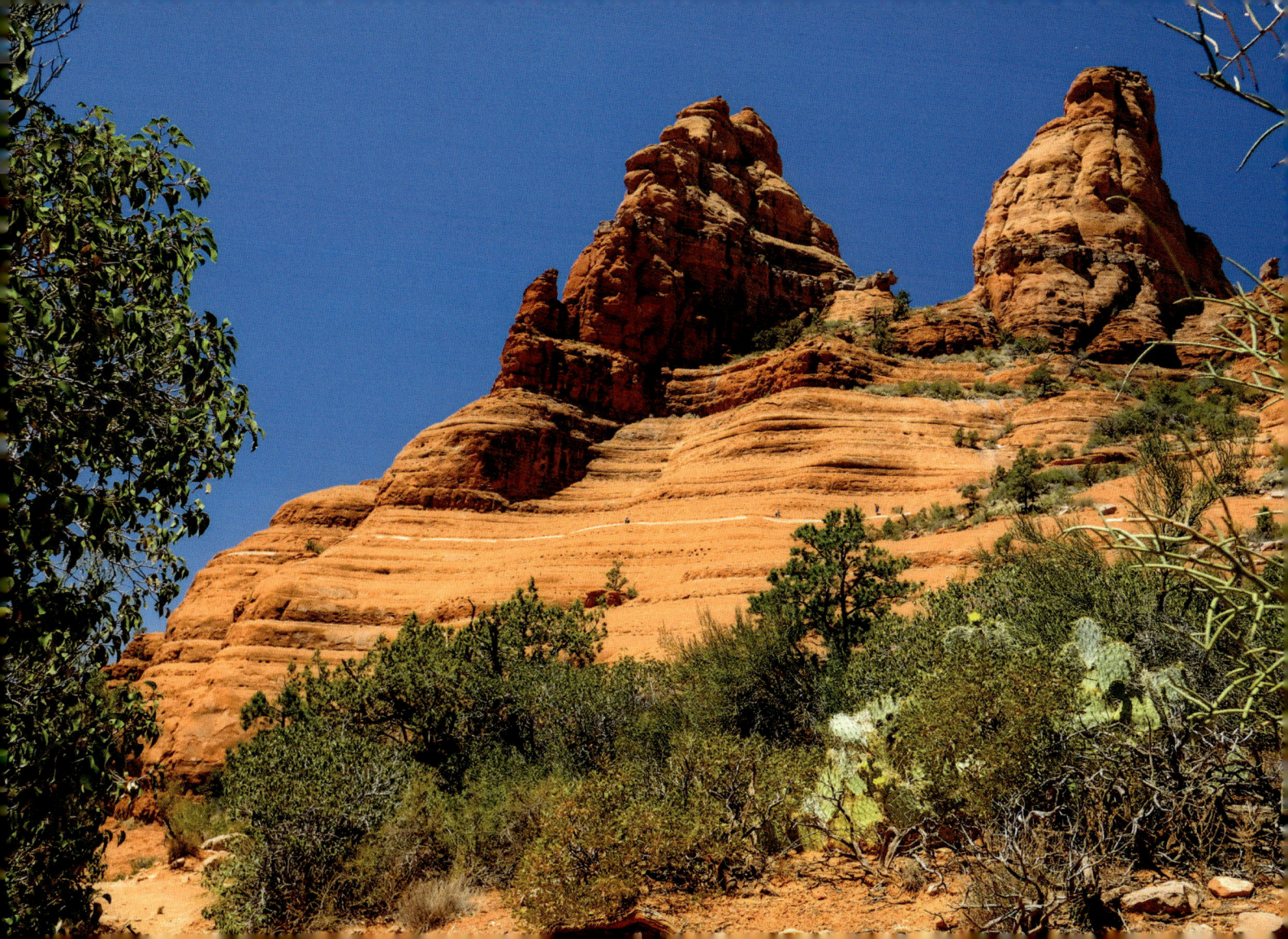

**By expressing our talents and strengths passionately in our careers, family and play, we will never work a day in our lives.**

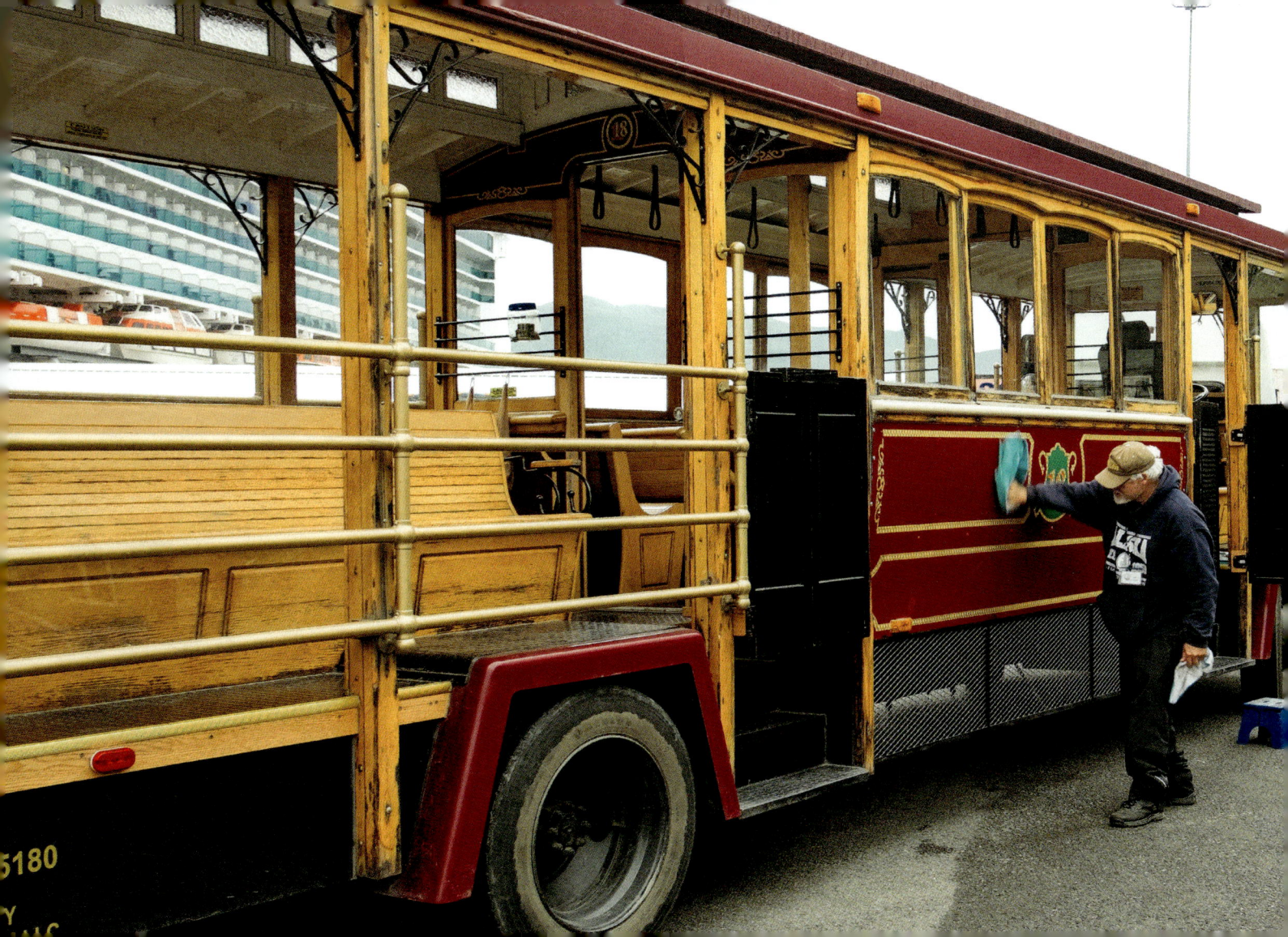

The expression of gratefulness and gratitude
is a road to *continued generosity and future giving*.

The path of expectation and entitlement...

is a *dead-end*.

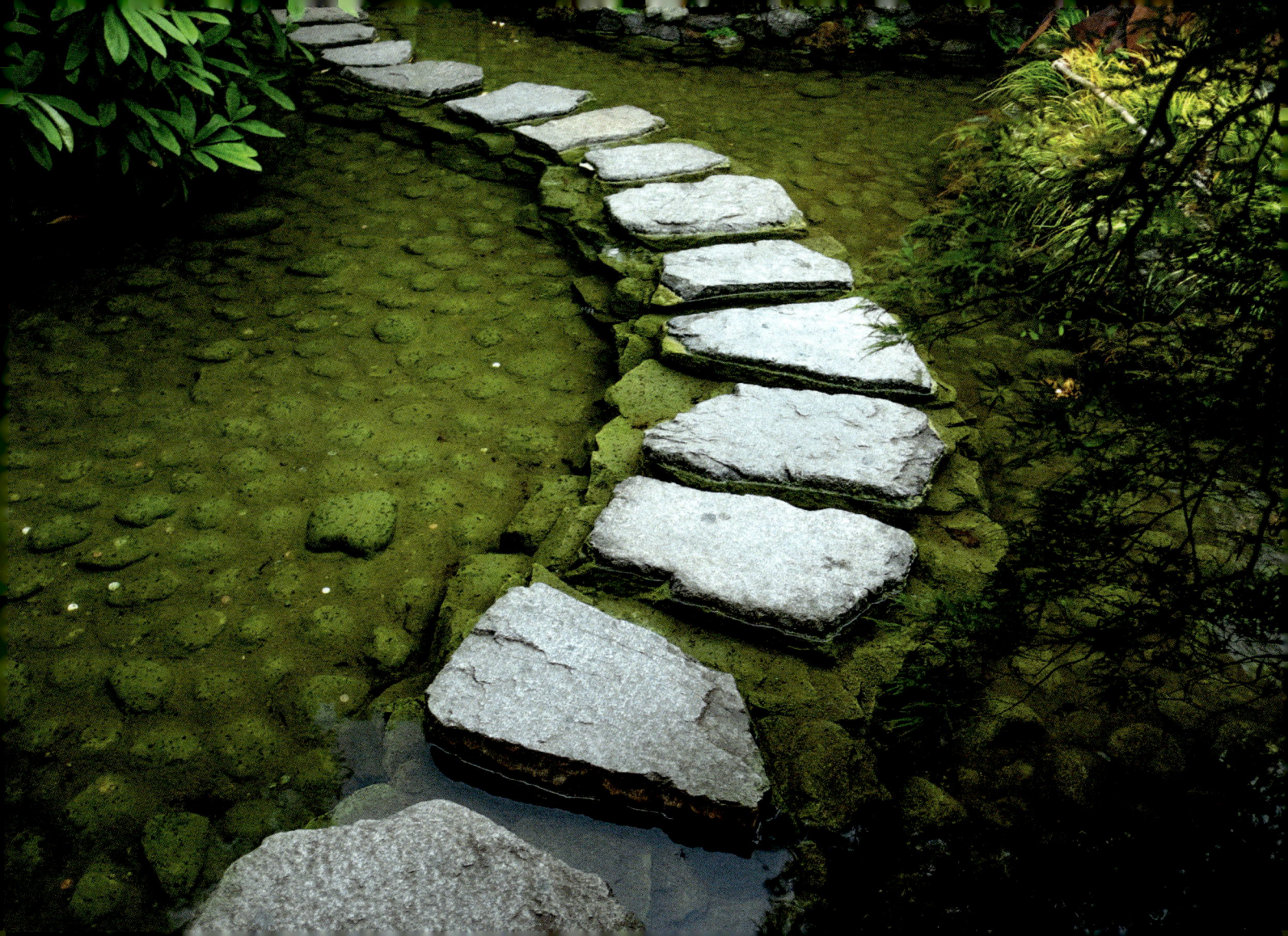

**Don't let fear paralyze you.**

**Harness the "fight or flight" power within to create a "superhero" advantage.**

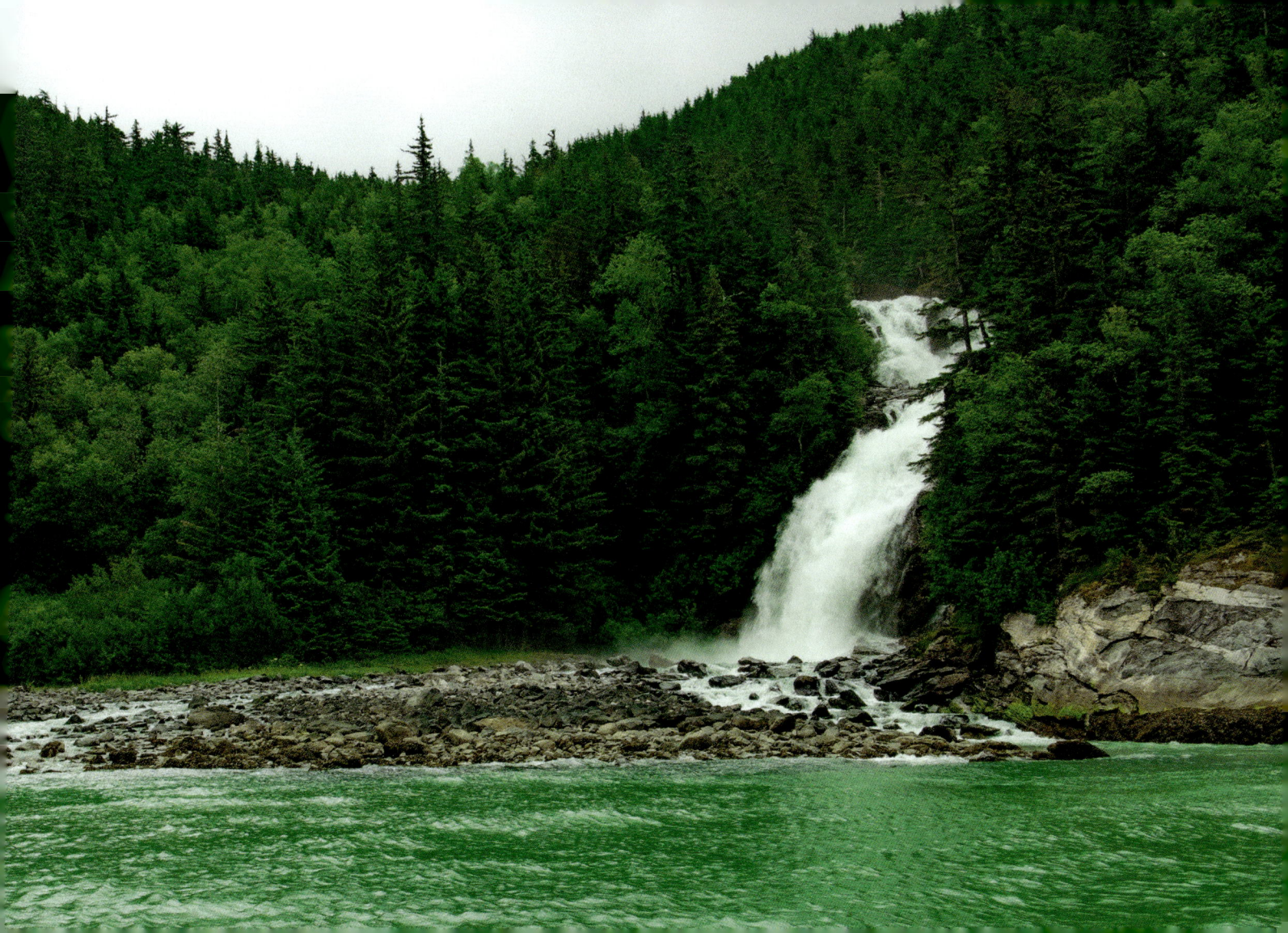

Great leaders find their success in making those they lead **more successful.**

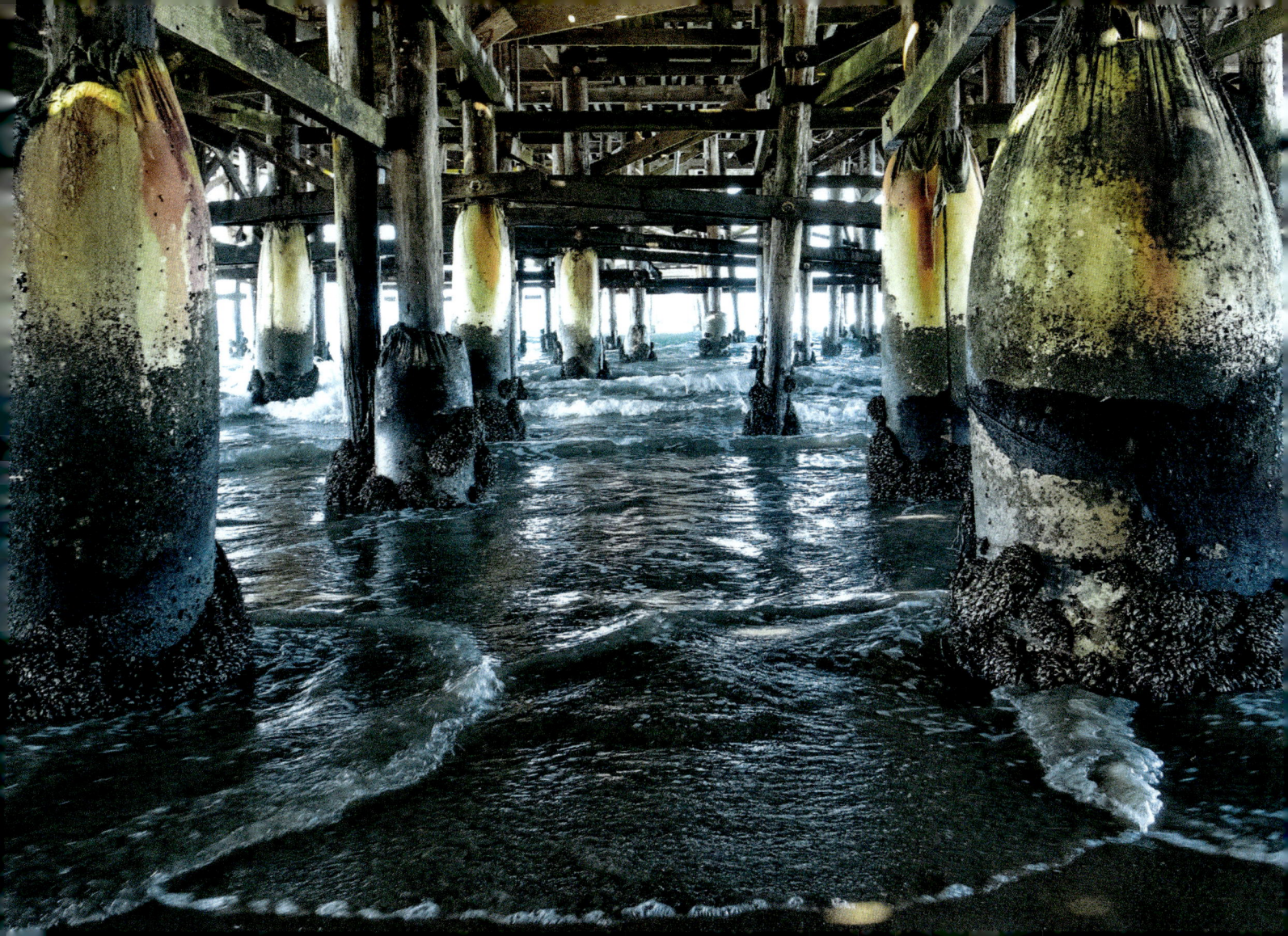

The only difference between a Master martial artist and a beginner is the Master has failed many more times than the beginner.

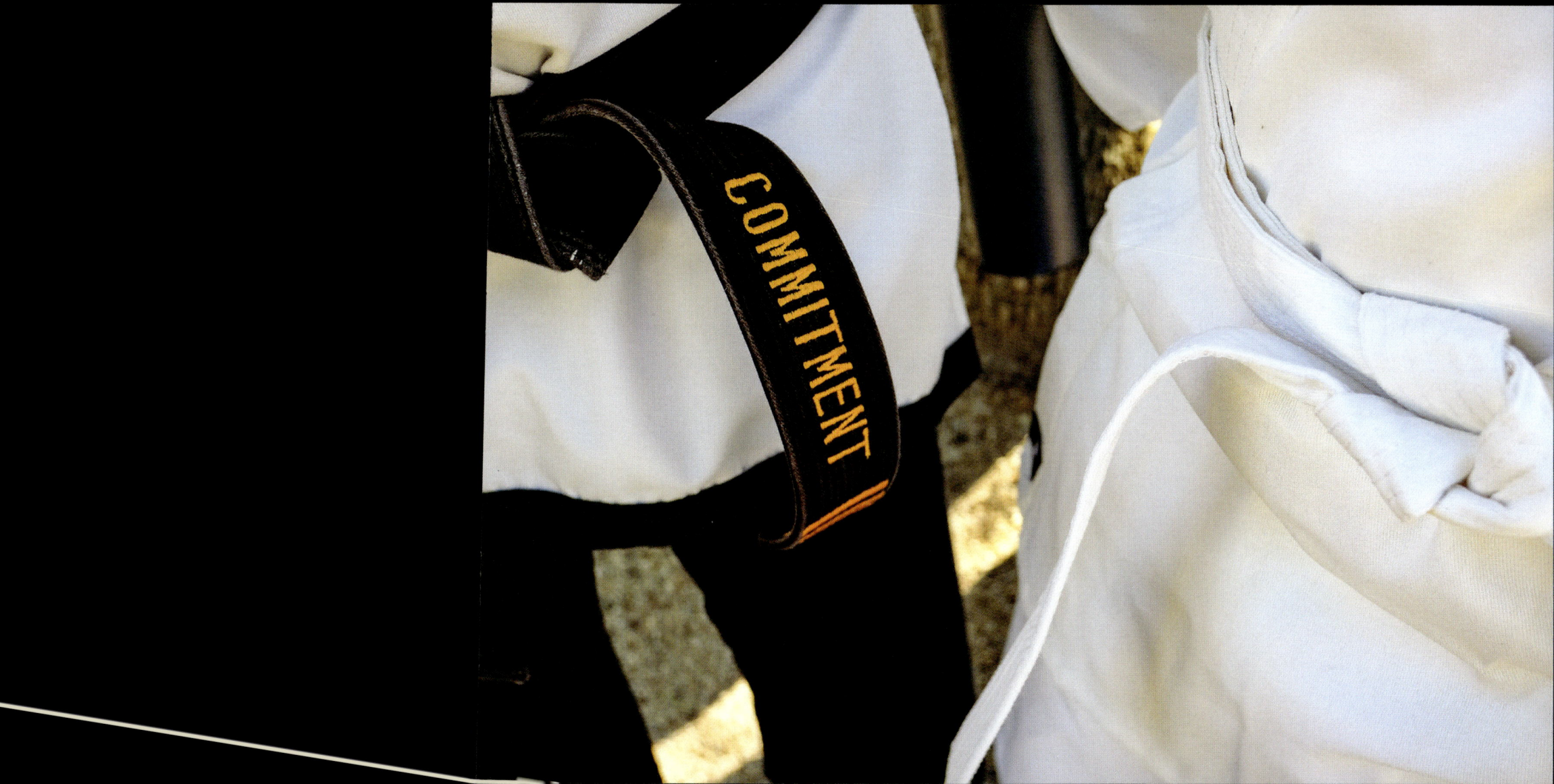

Conflict emerges when we focus more on our *differences* than we do on what we have in *common*.

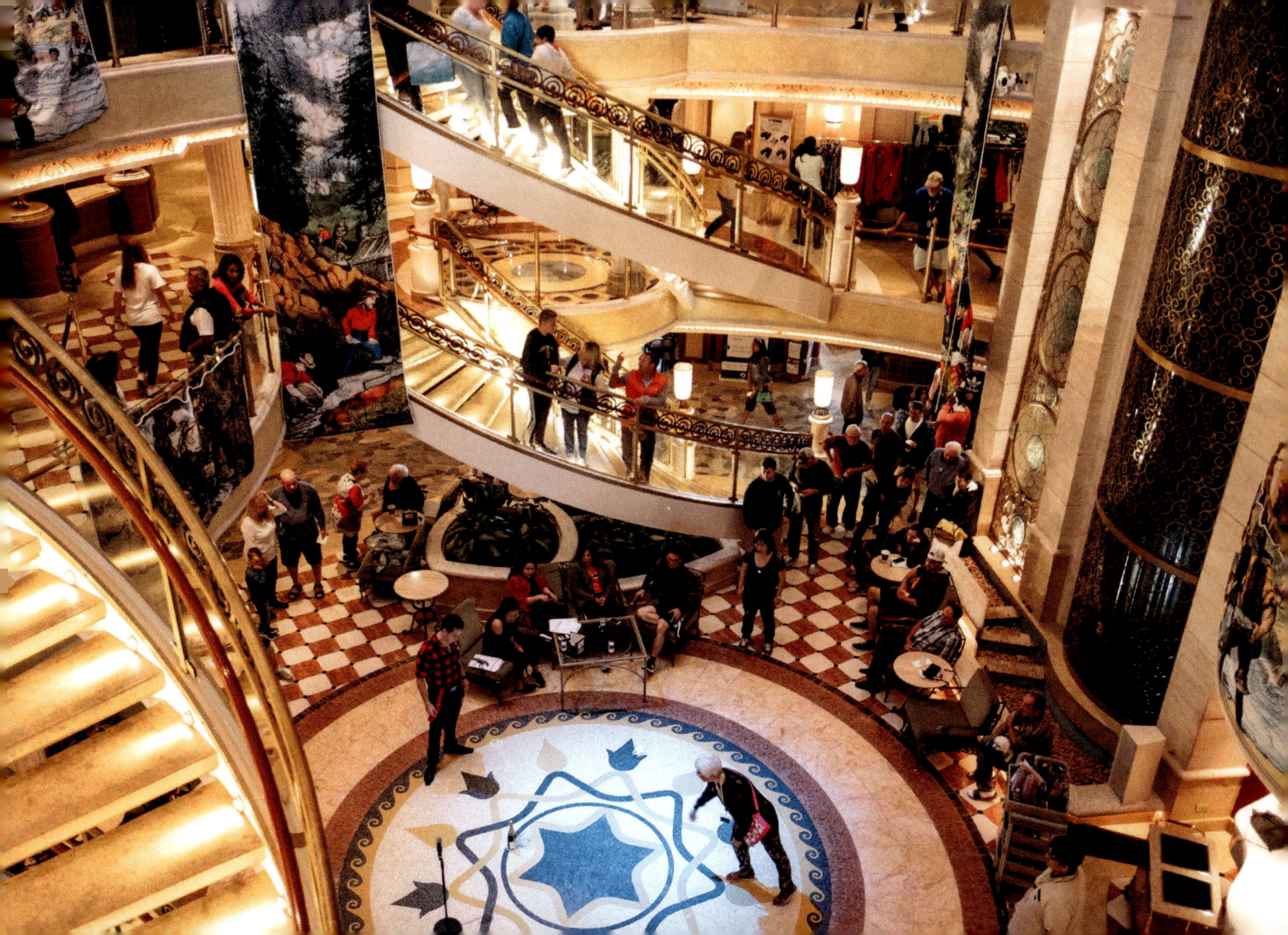

We can bend rebar throat-to-throat…..

We can break slabs of cement with our bare hands and feet….

**We can – we can – we can!**

We have the capacity to do extraordinary things. Transformation occurs when we trust and believe in ourselves!

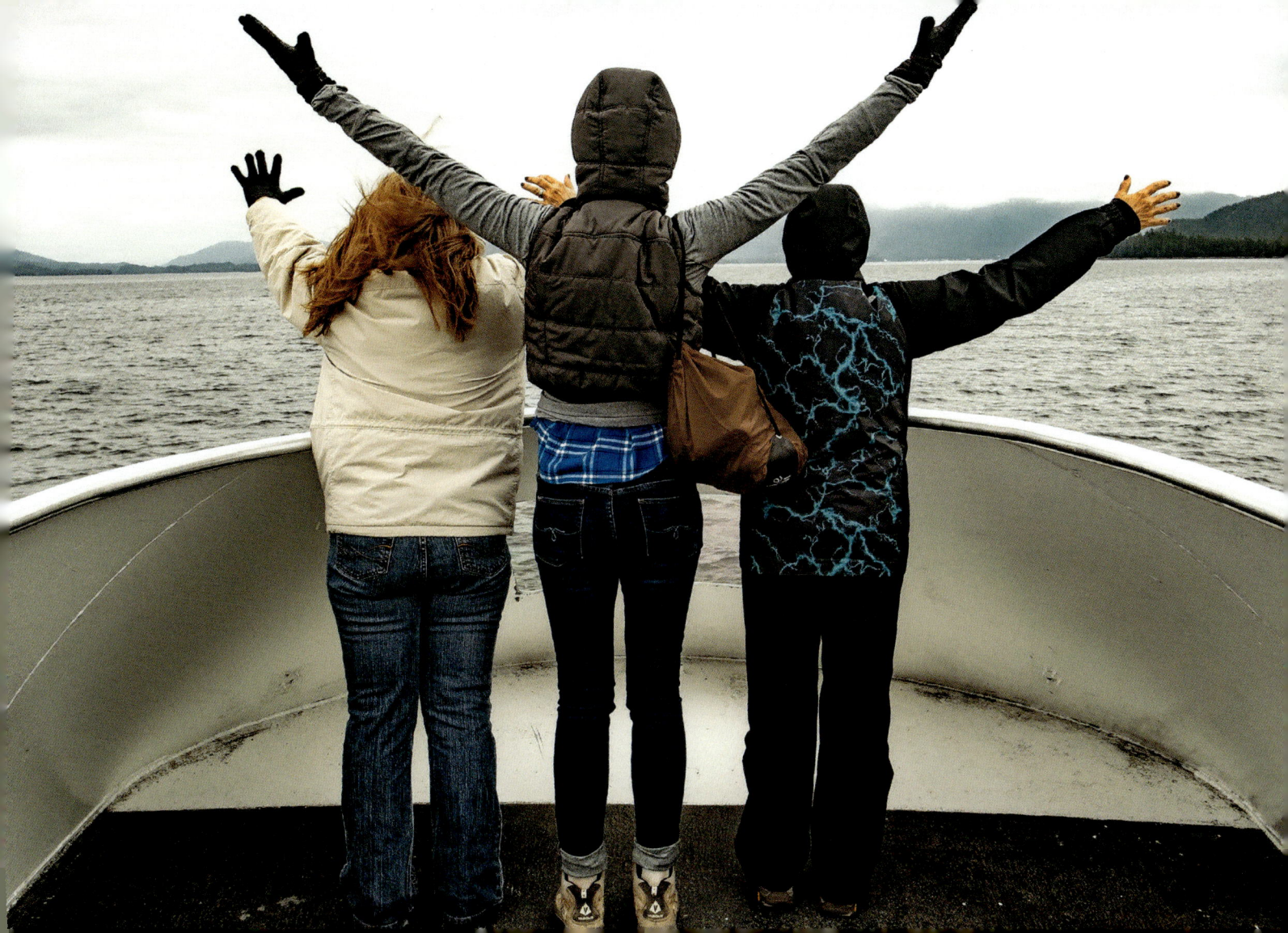

At the end of our life's journey, we will discover our deepest fulfillment will come from sharing our strengths and skills with others to improve their life circumstances.

**This is true transcendence and self-actualization.**

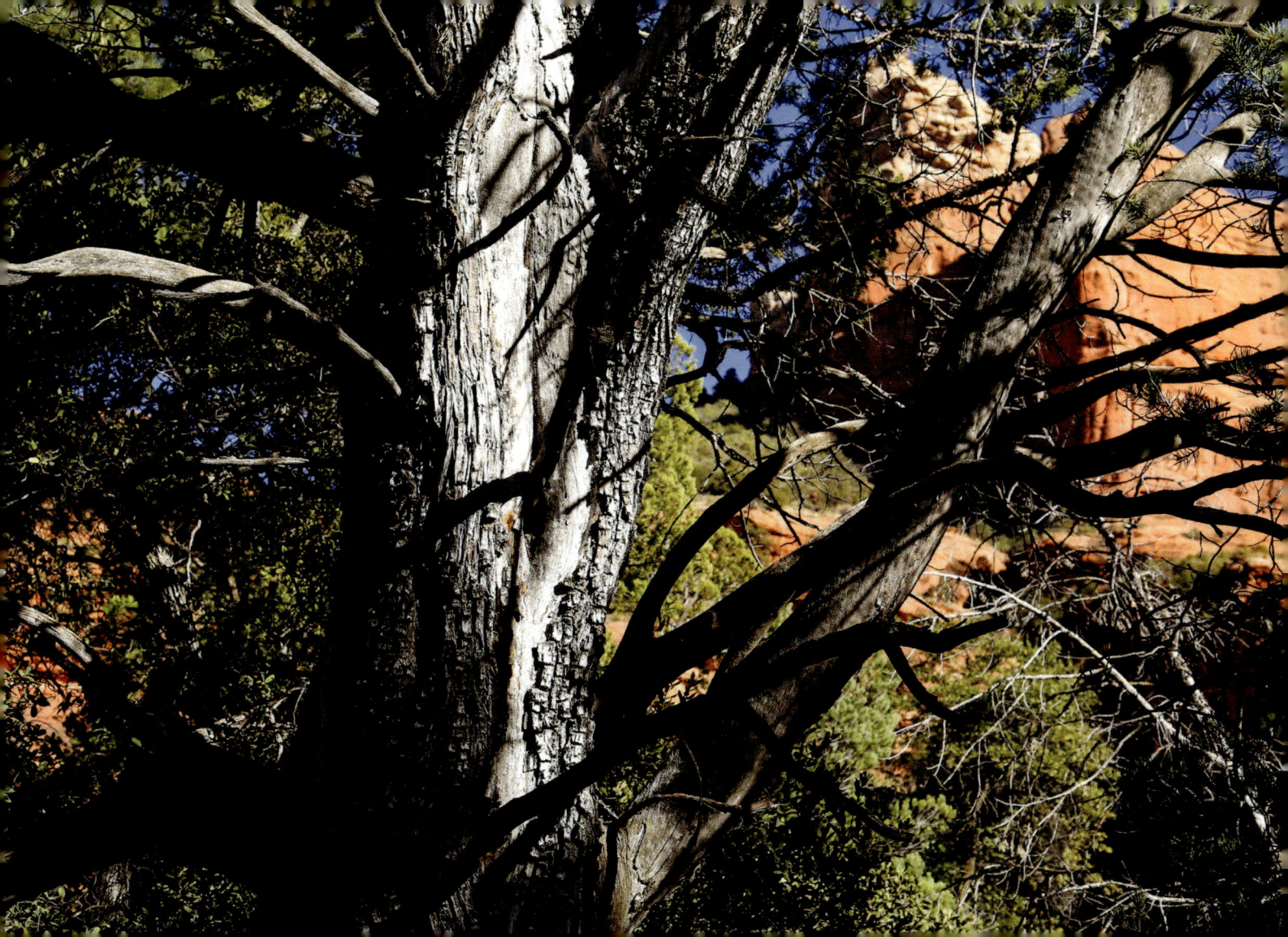

As human beings, we must realize we are all interconnected through a greater power propagating *peace, compassion* and *love*.

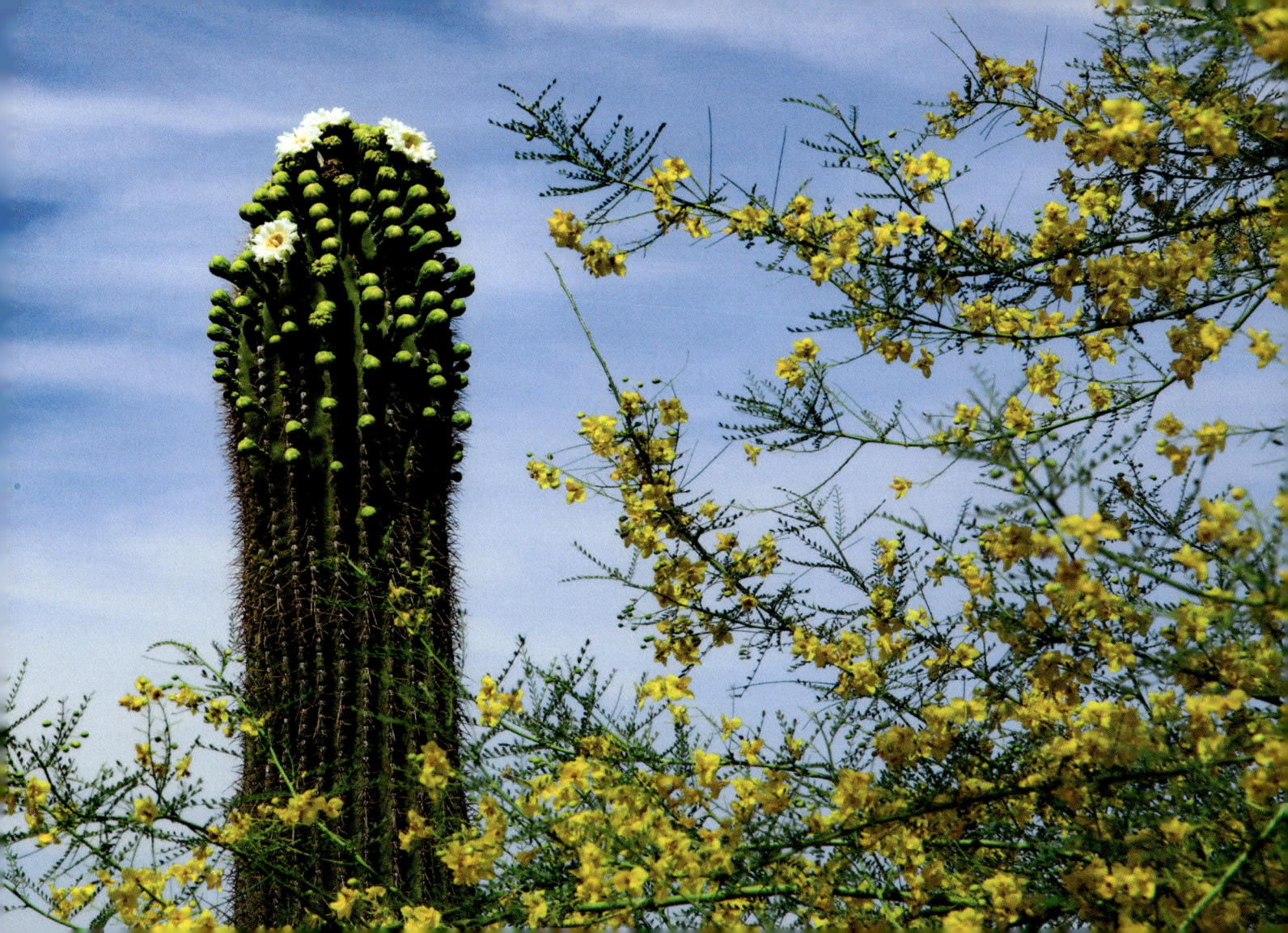

Training in the martial arts exposes and puts you face-to-face with your innermost fears. From that understanding, *peacemakers are born*.

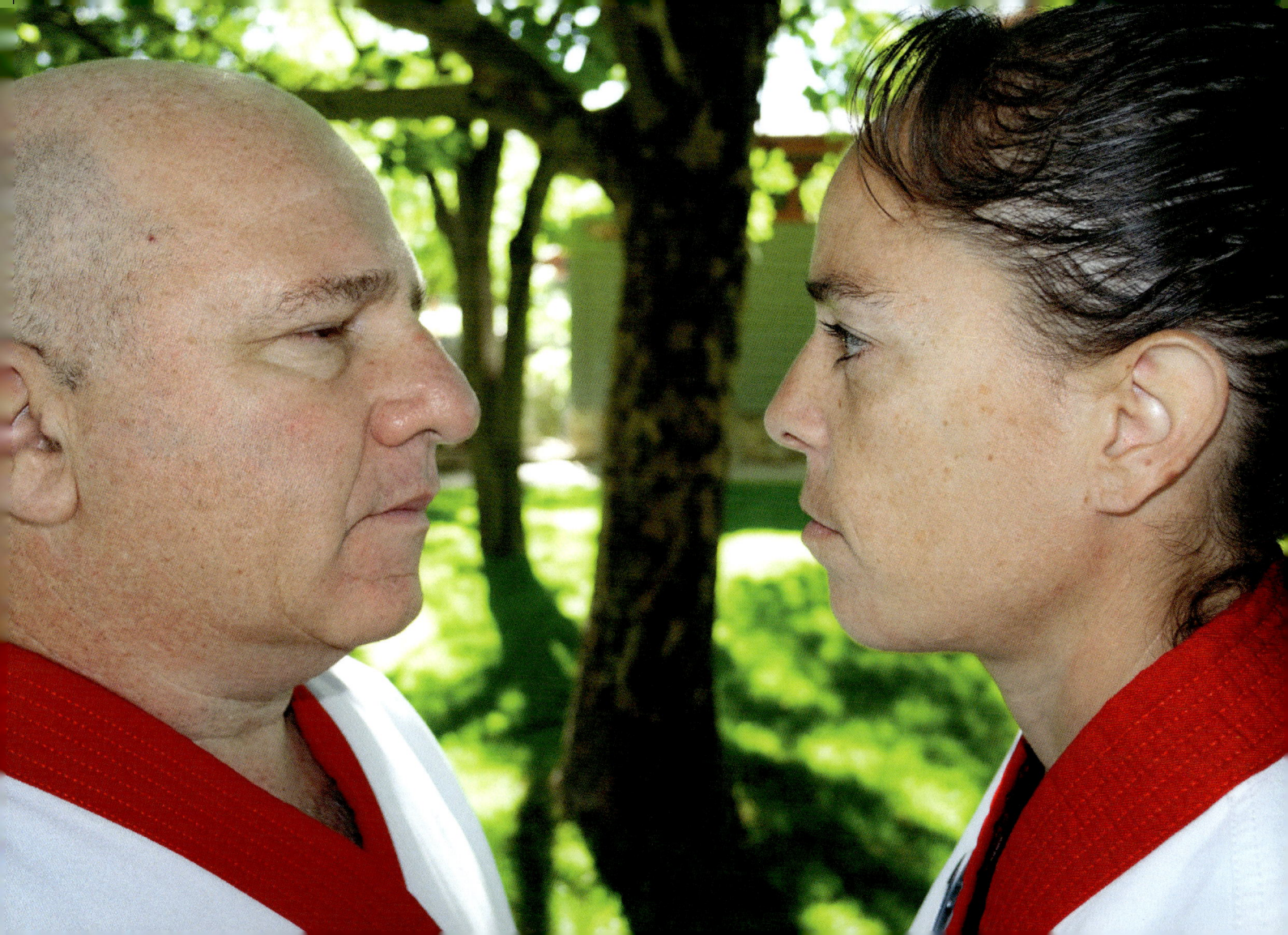

Investing in and accumulating memorable life experiences *provides more happiness* and fulfillment than amassing material possessions.

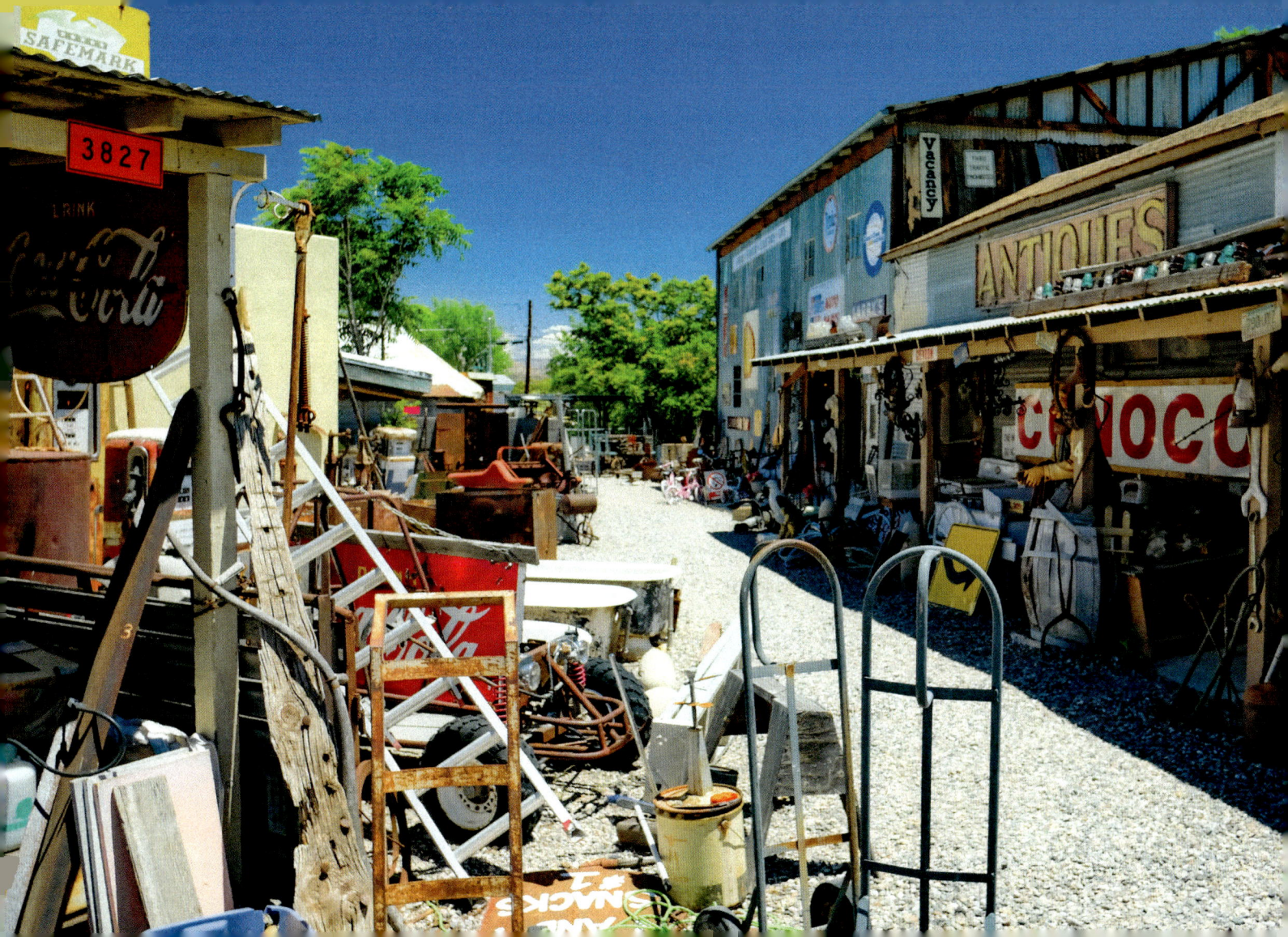

By following a sentence with the word **"but,"** we negate the preceding message. Instead, use the word **"and"** to preserve the correct intent.

Fulfilling relationships and supportive cultures emerge from a **"Yes-And"** philosophy.

*Be receptive to the ideas of others.*

*Be positive.*

*Make others look good!*

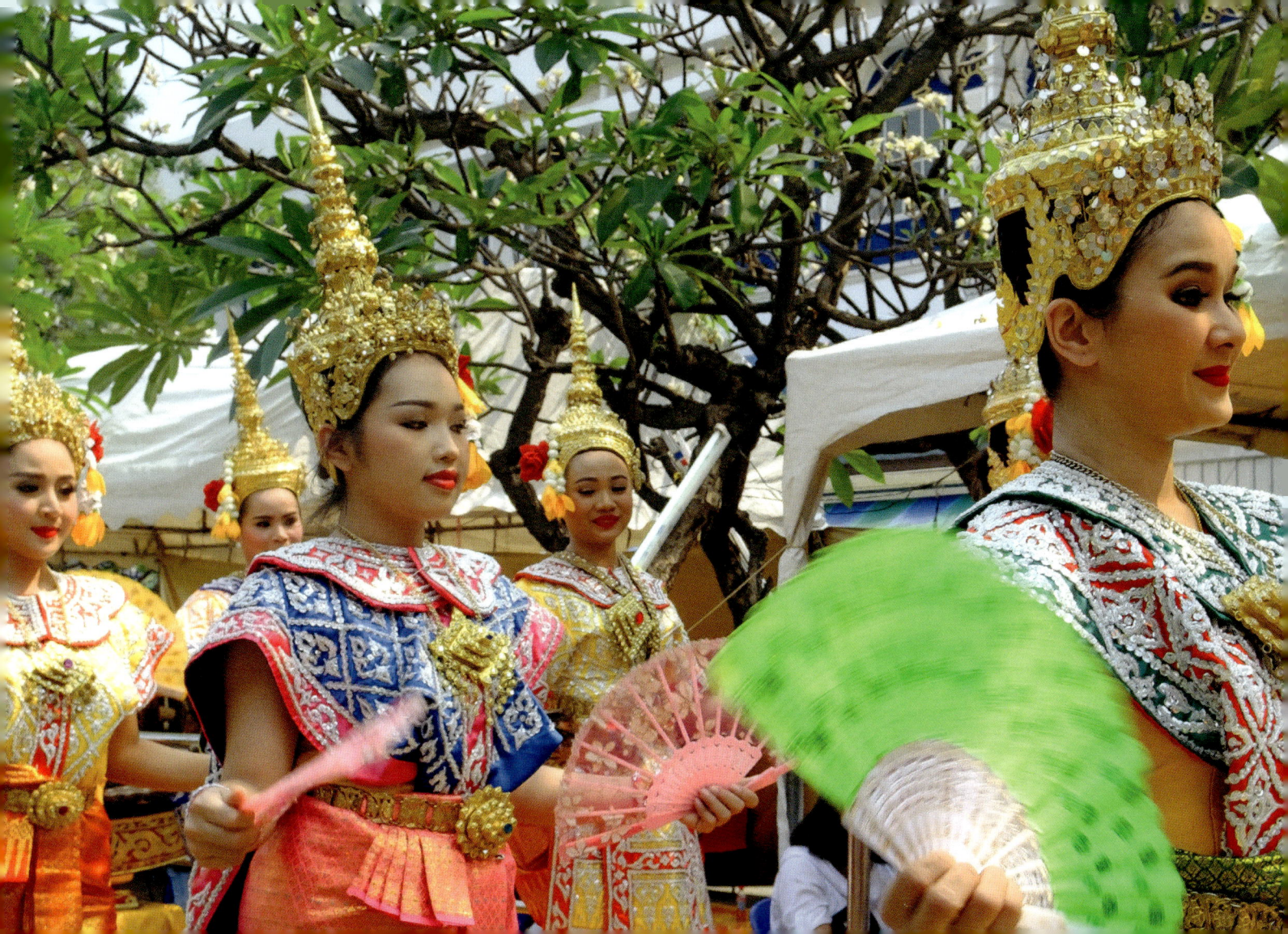

**Walk through life with enough ego to be confident, yet not too much to be arrogant.**

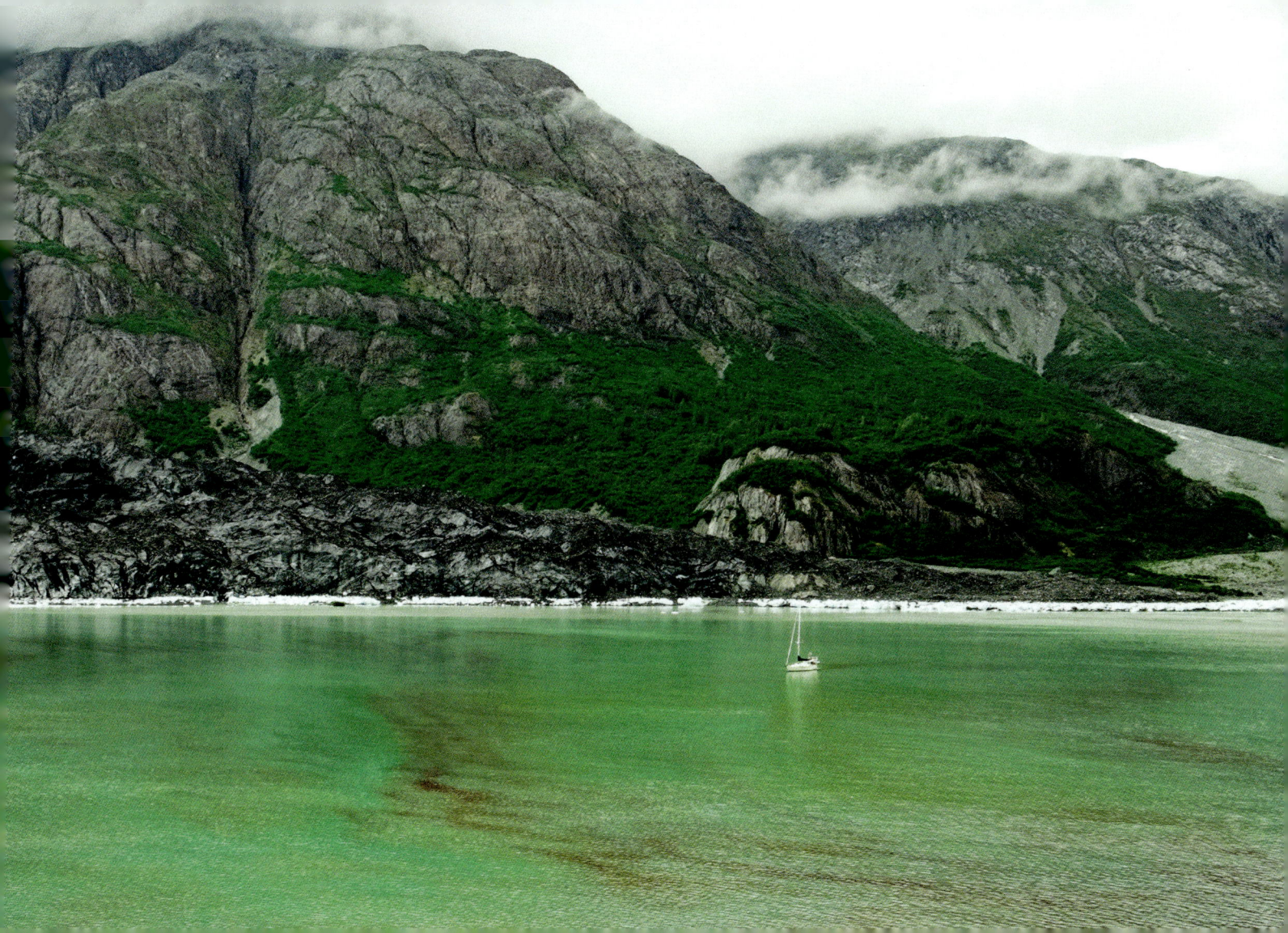

To transform "small talk" into "a good talk," *be an active listener and ask about them.*

Most people feel exceptionally engaged when they talk about themselves.

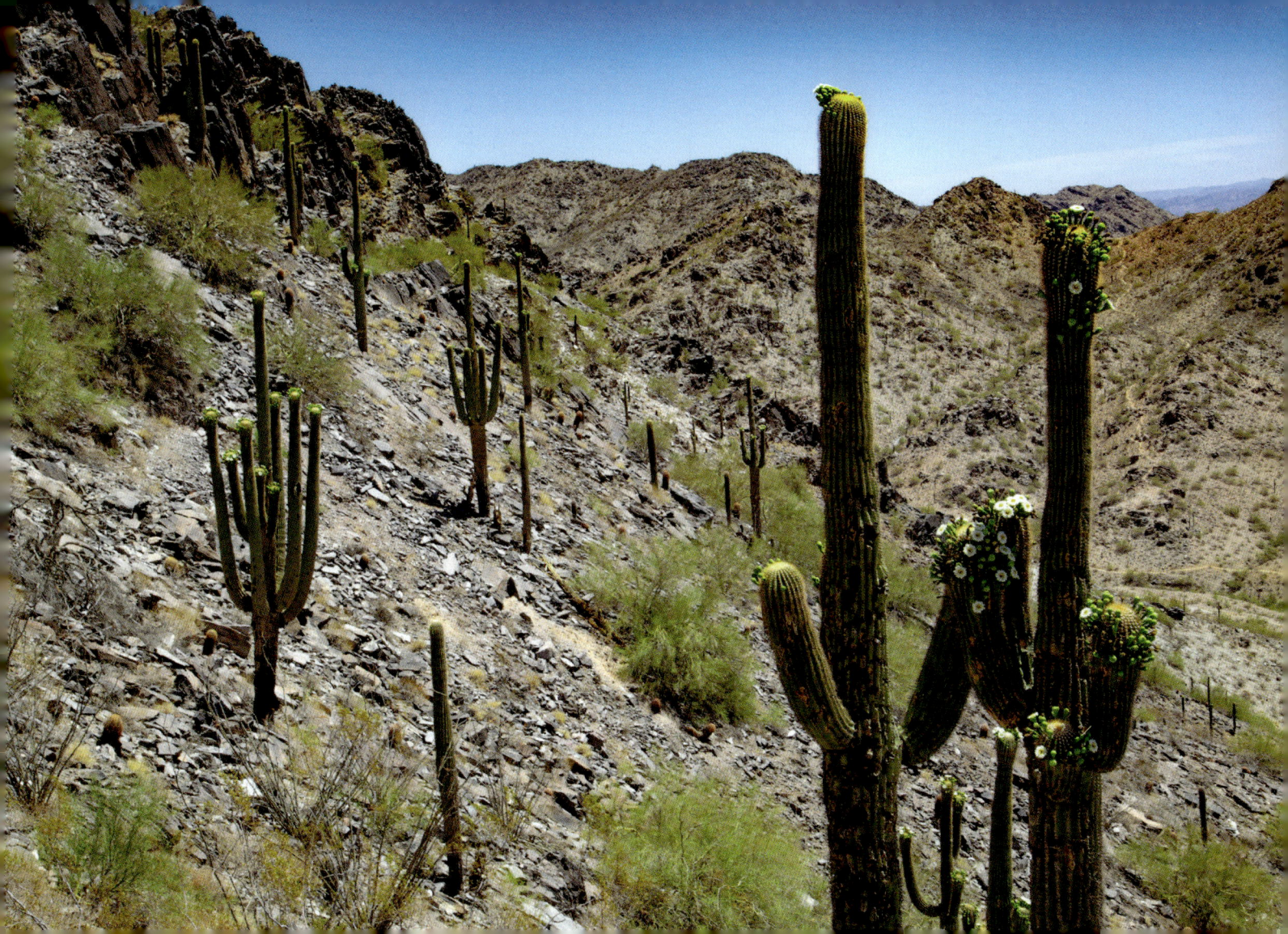

To develop trusting, loving and meaningful relationships — actions *definitely* speak louder than words.

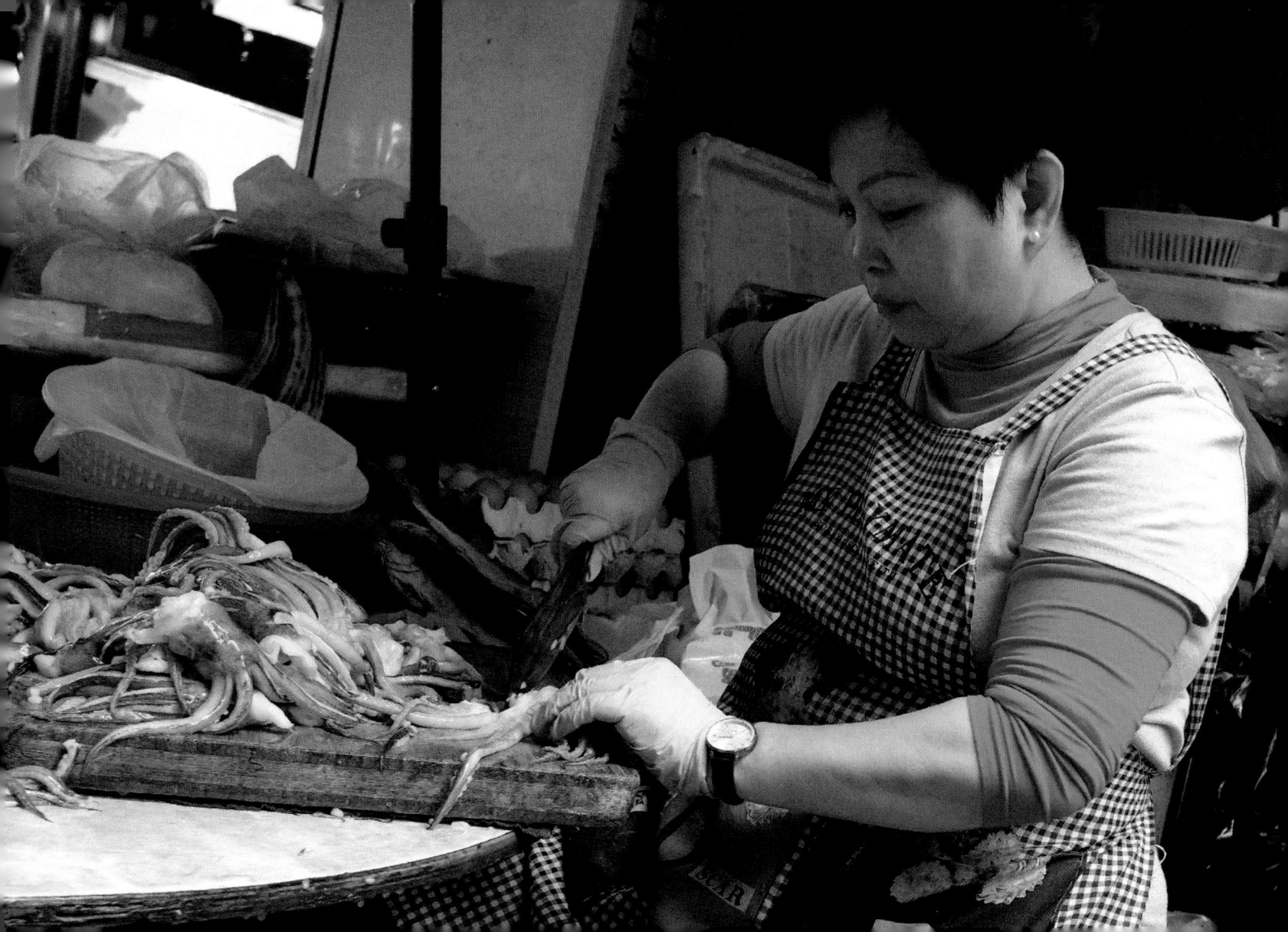

Traditional ancient wisdom coupled with contemporary leadership theory provides the foundation for the eclectic teaching at The Center for Humane Living.

CenterforHumaneLiving.org

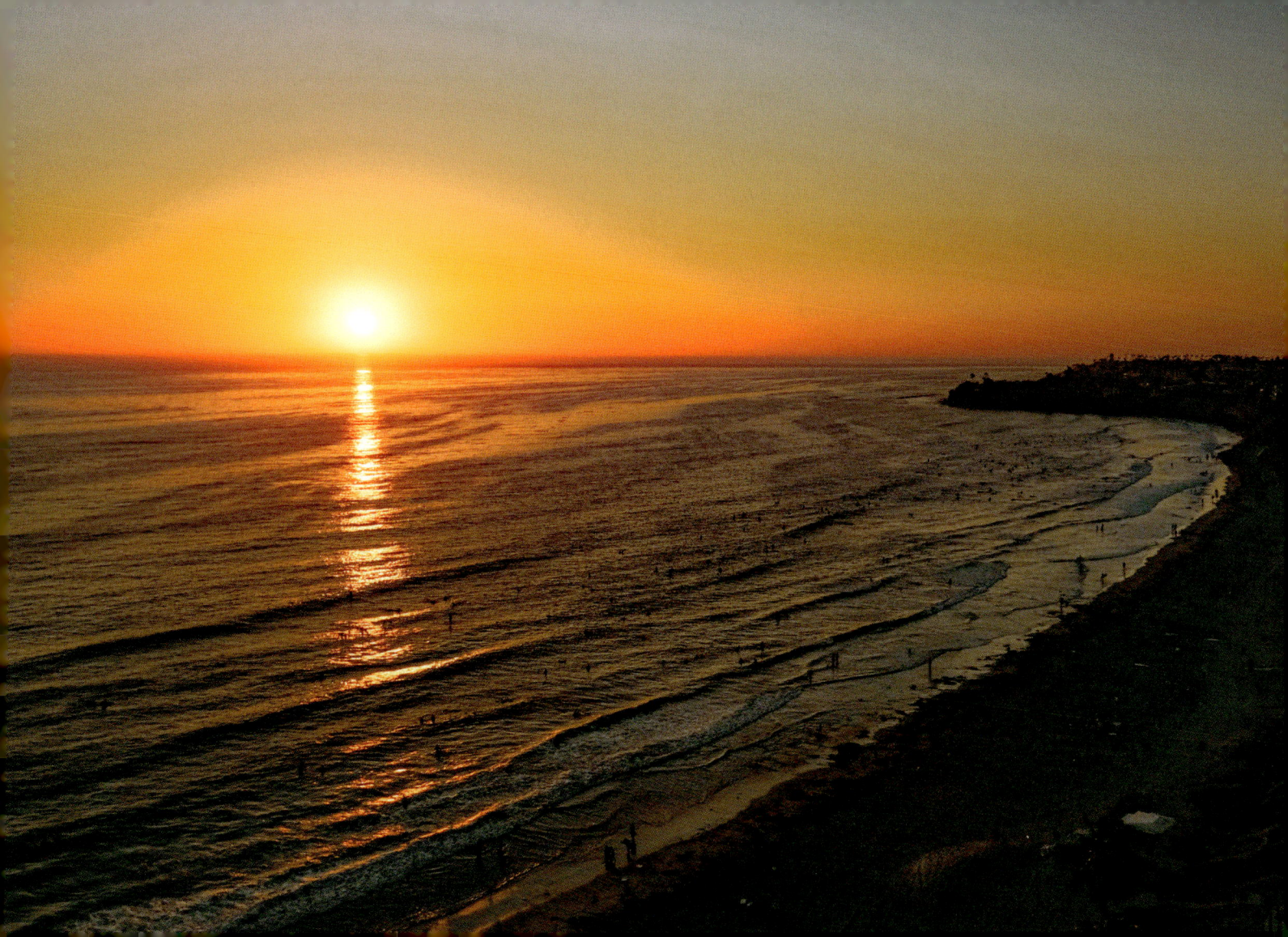

Recognize that the same "fight or flight" primitive survival response may occur with both life-threatening and non-life-threatening stimuli.

*Train your thinking and your behavior accordingly.*

**Don't overreact.**

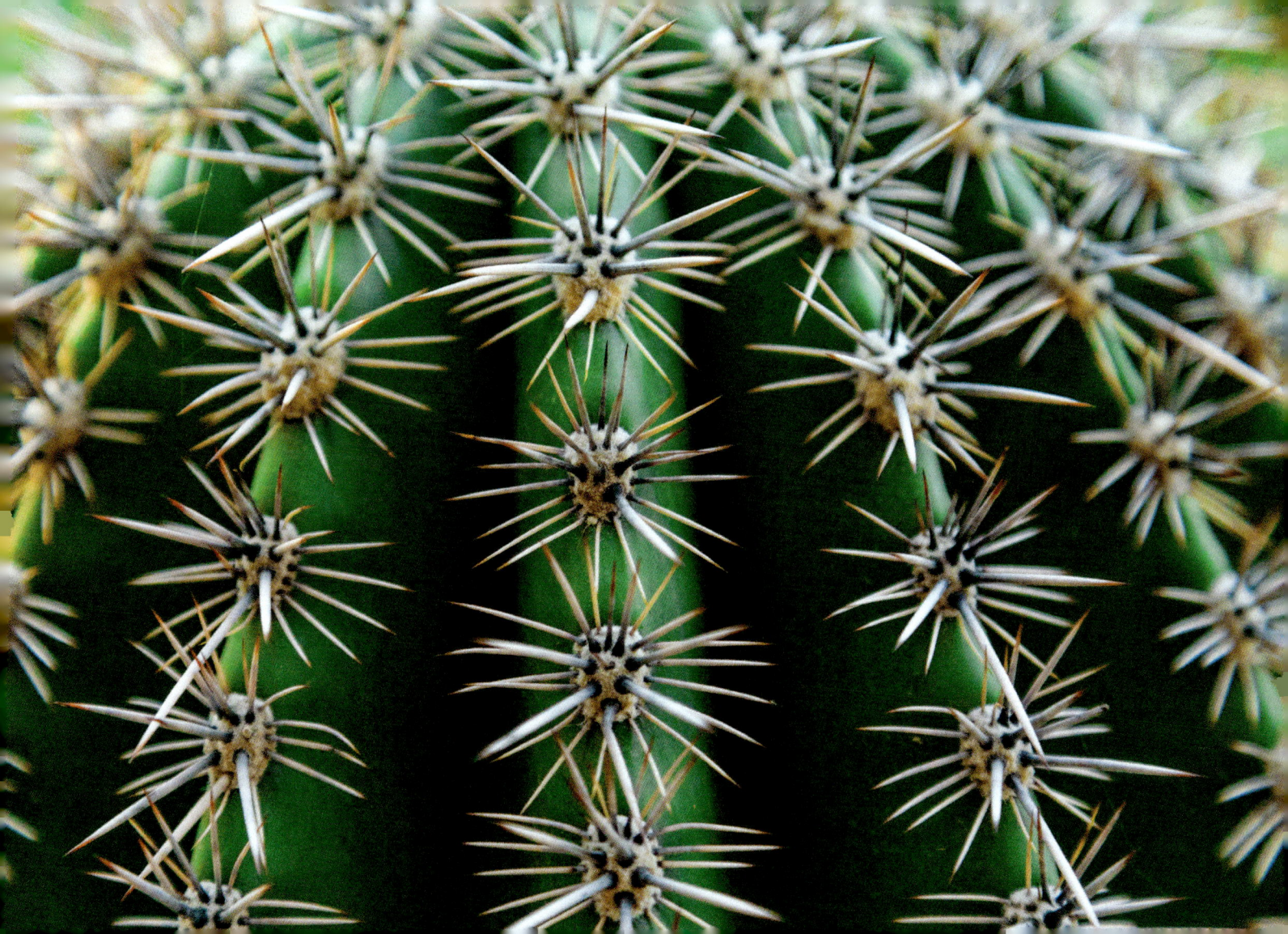

When the student is truly ready,

the teacher suddenly appears.


*Be ready* to be a lifelong learner.

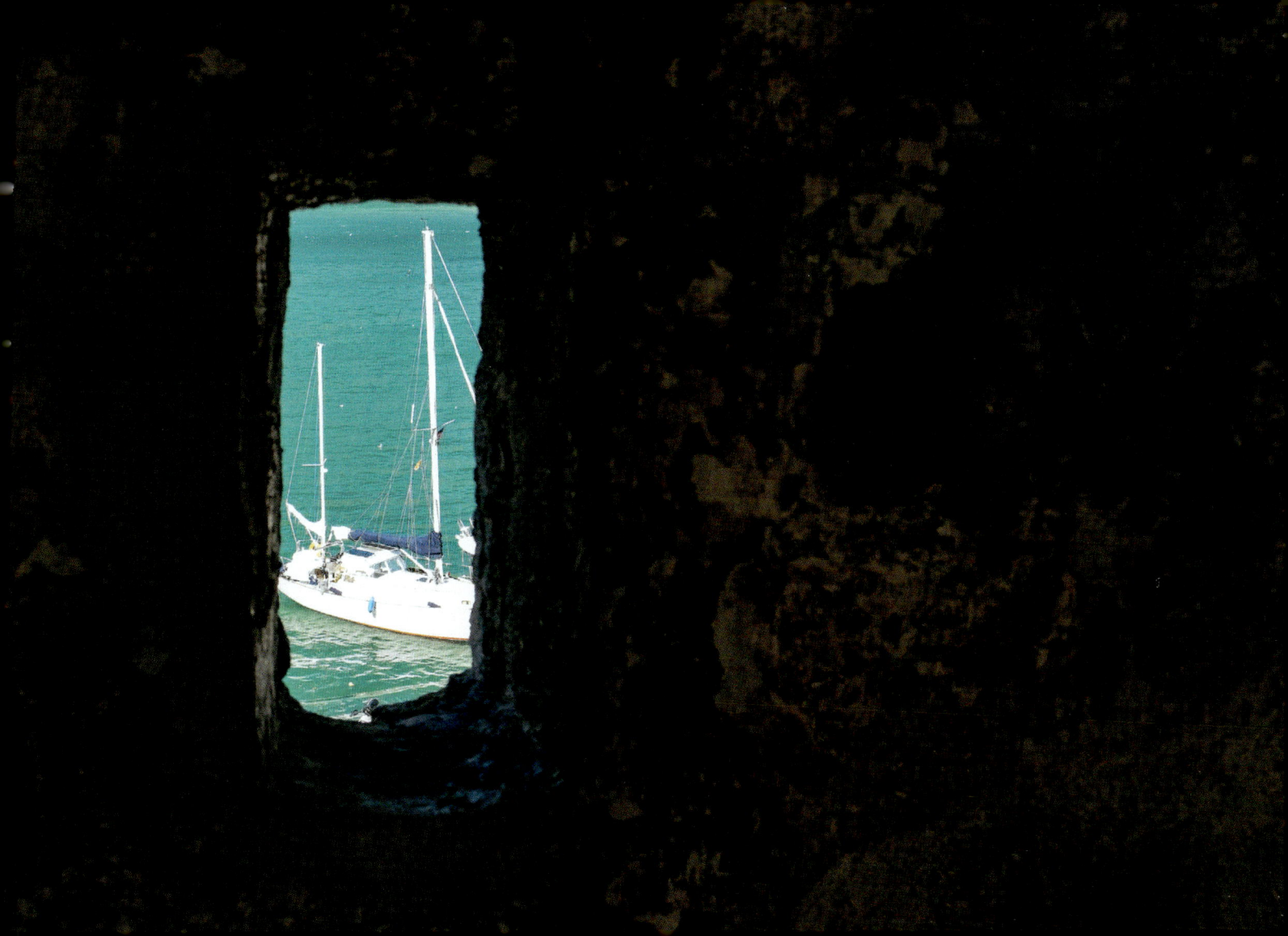

Traditional martial arts training is repetitive and mundane.

The warrior mindset must be awakened to the reality that "boring" is *both productive and essential for a disciplined life*.

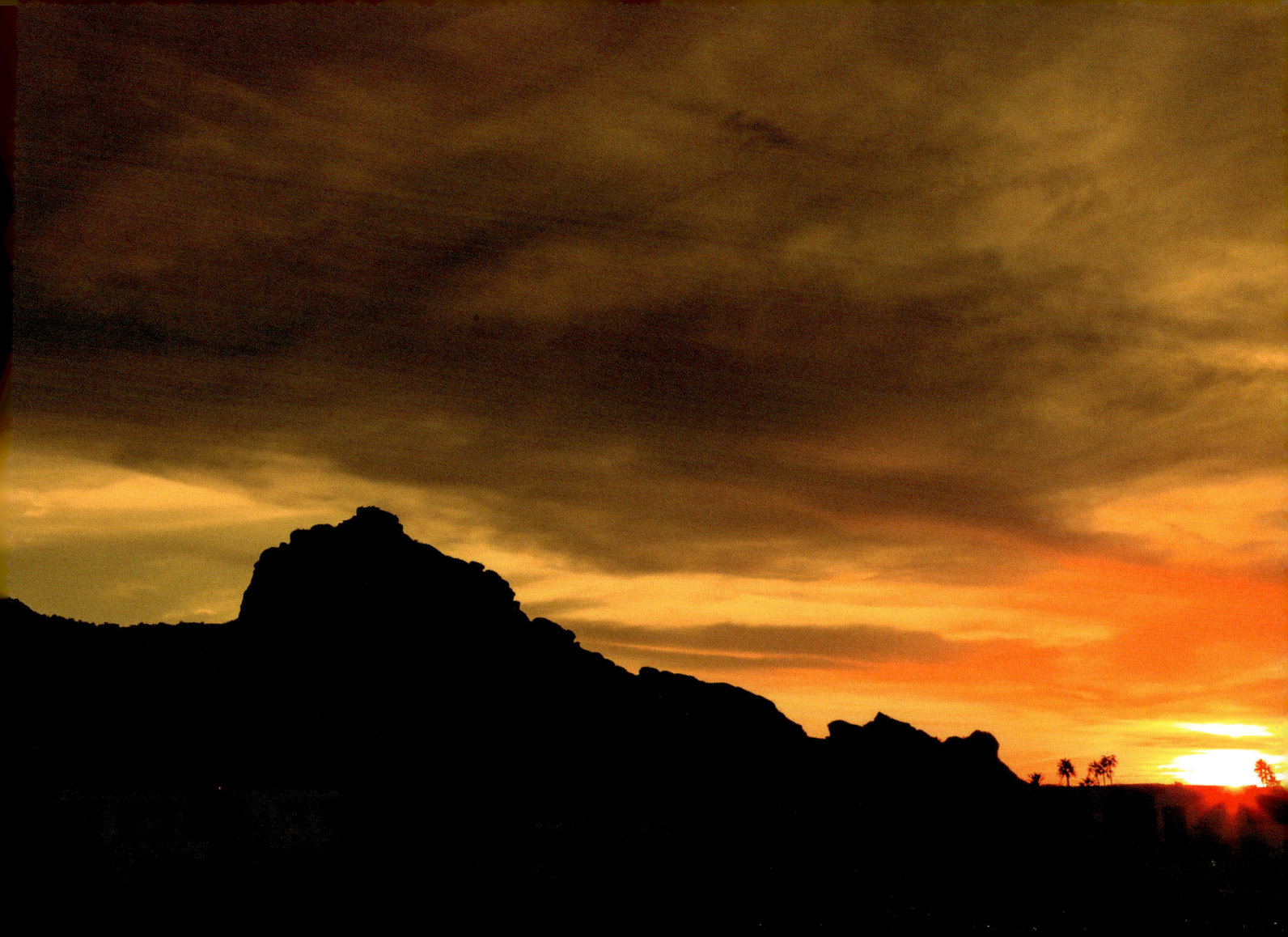

*Resilience* allows us to emerge unchanged from harsh life circumstances.

*Anti-fragility* is the capacity to absorb harshness to change, grow and become stronger.

# Longevity
wains with resilience and flourishes with anti-fragility.

Bangkok, Thailand
ISO 200 f/5.6 1/110 sec

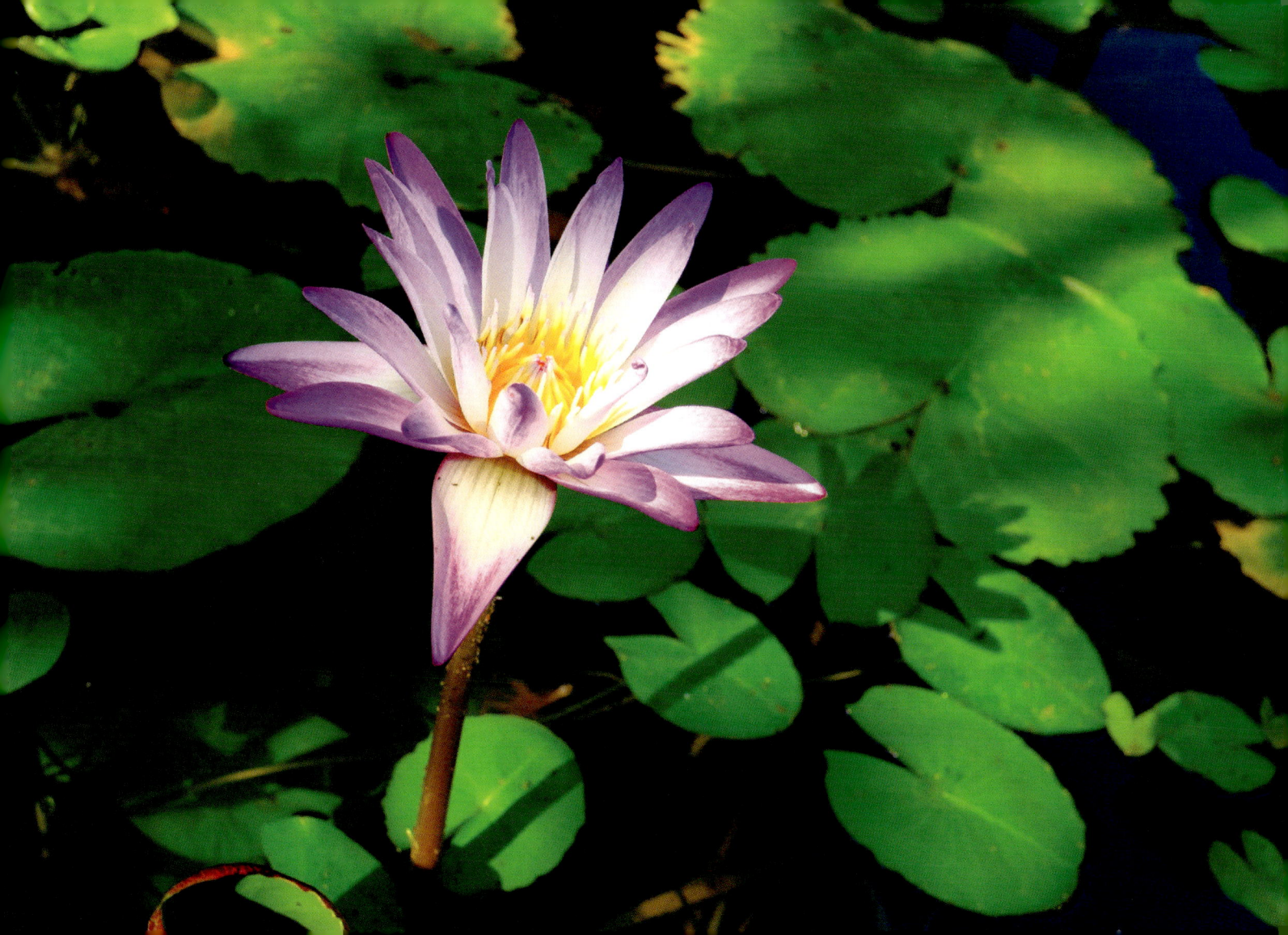

Our **primitive brain** ensures our survival through a protective "fight or flight" response.

Our **cognitive brain** demonstrates our evolving humanity with a capacity for thinking and complex problem solving.

In conflict, we must manage our primitive reactive brains and engage our humanity by silently asking ourselves,

***"What do we really want out of this encounter for ourselves, for others and for our entire team?"***

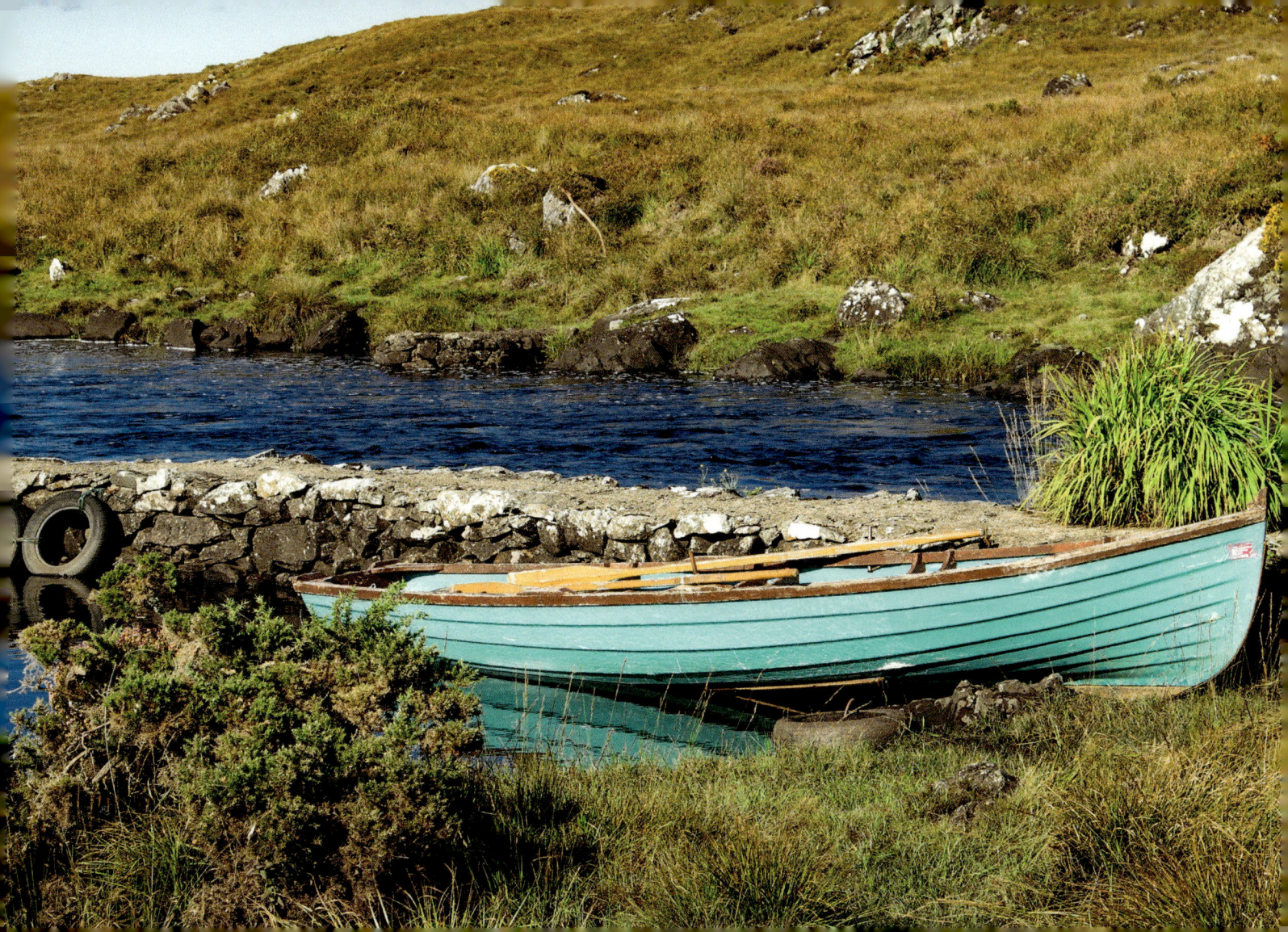

The best self-defense is to listen

to our inner voice of instinct and insight.

*Avoid the perils of cognitive rationalization.*

Pay attention to the feelings of fear

— they are there to protect us!

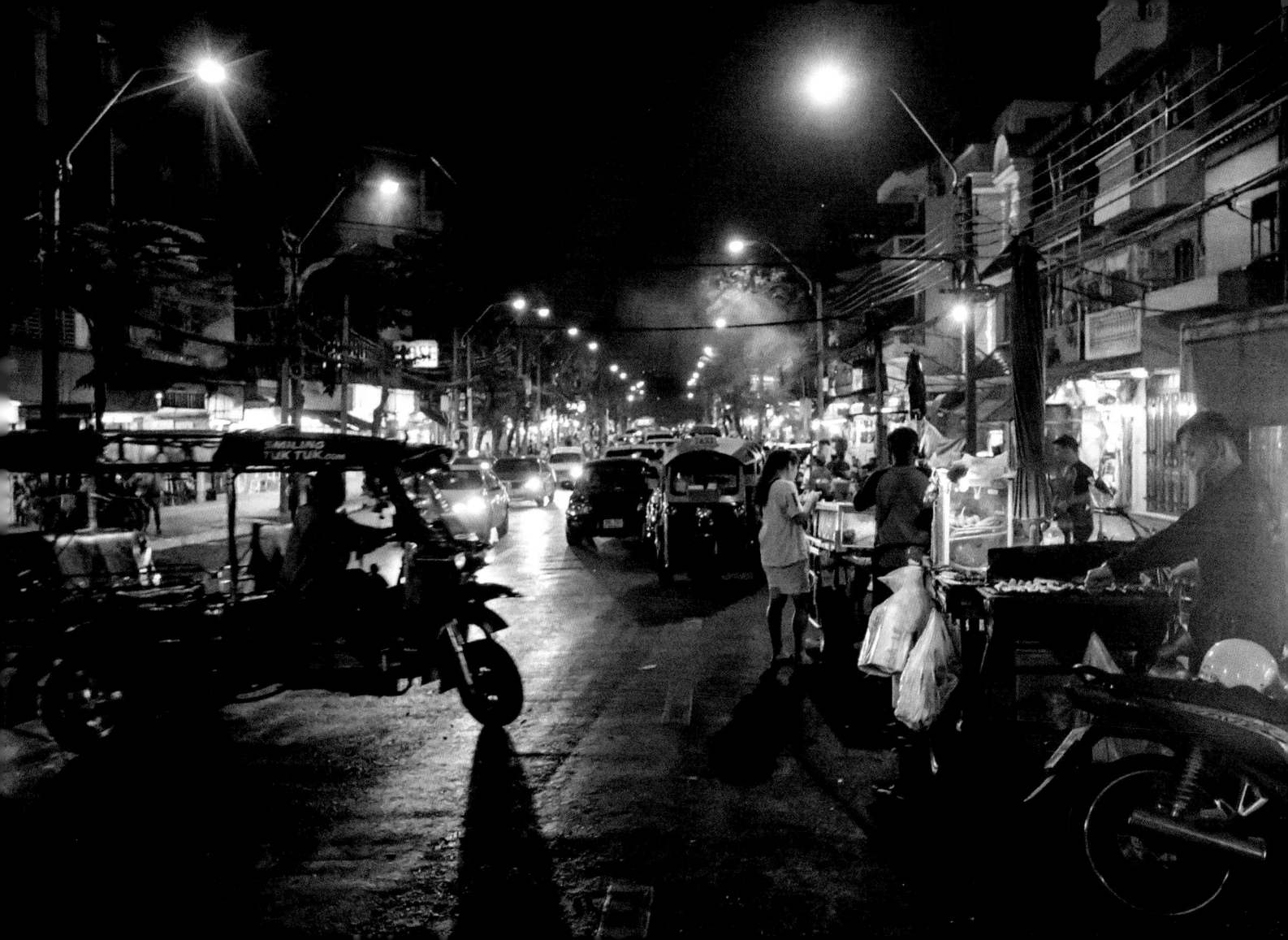

Chaos is the place where we all first look foolish to the crowd.

**Order always follows.**

Only with this sequence will true brilliance emerge.

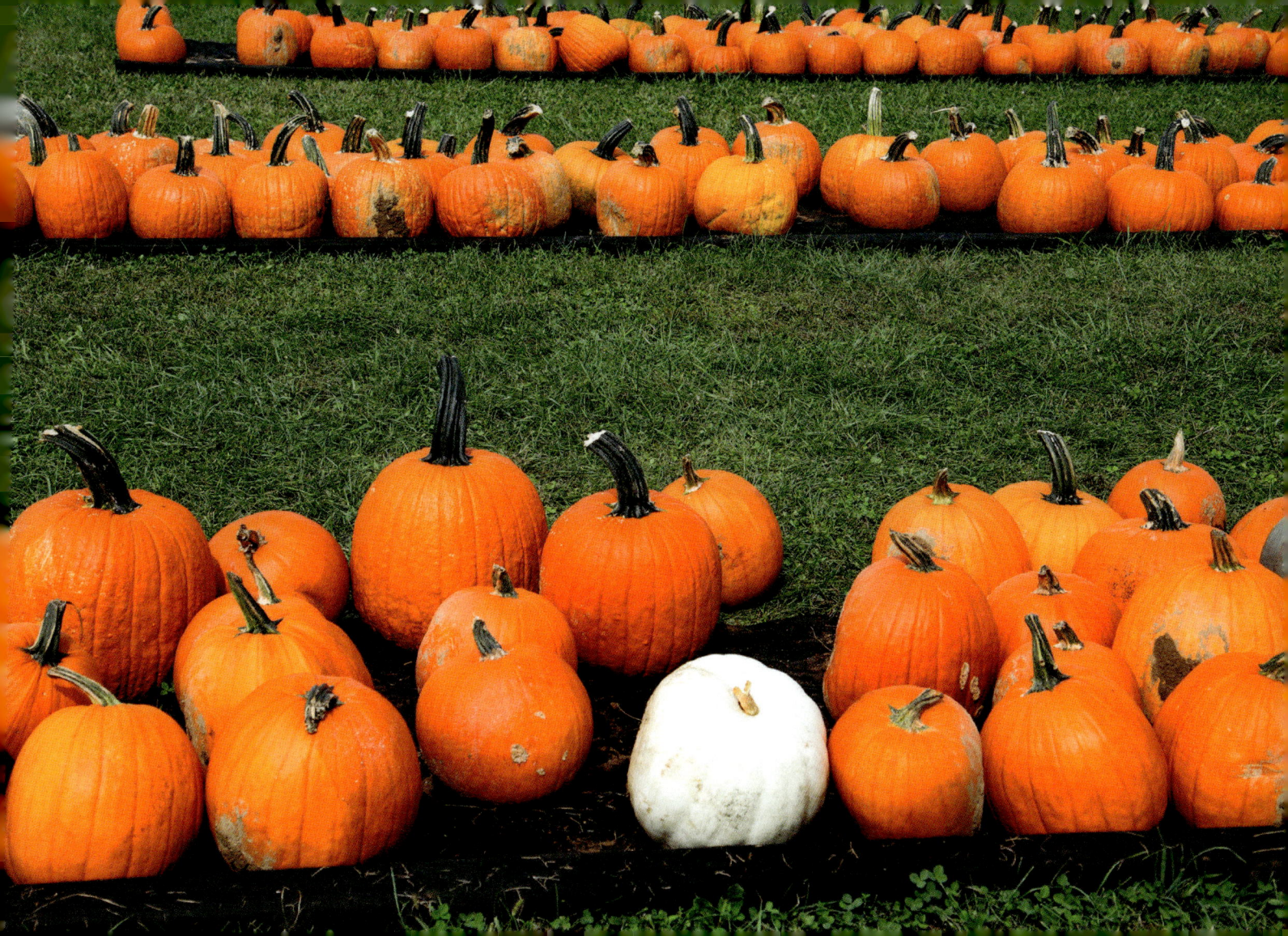

Once we understand that we *cannot* **attack emptiness** and *cannot* be **attacked from nothingness**, we can create *peace*.

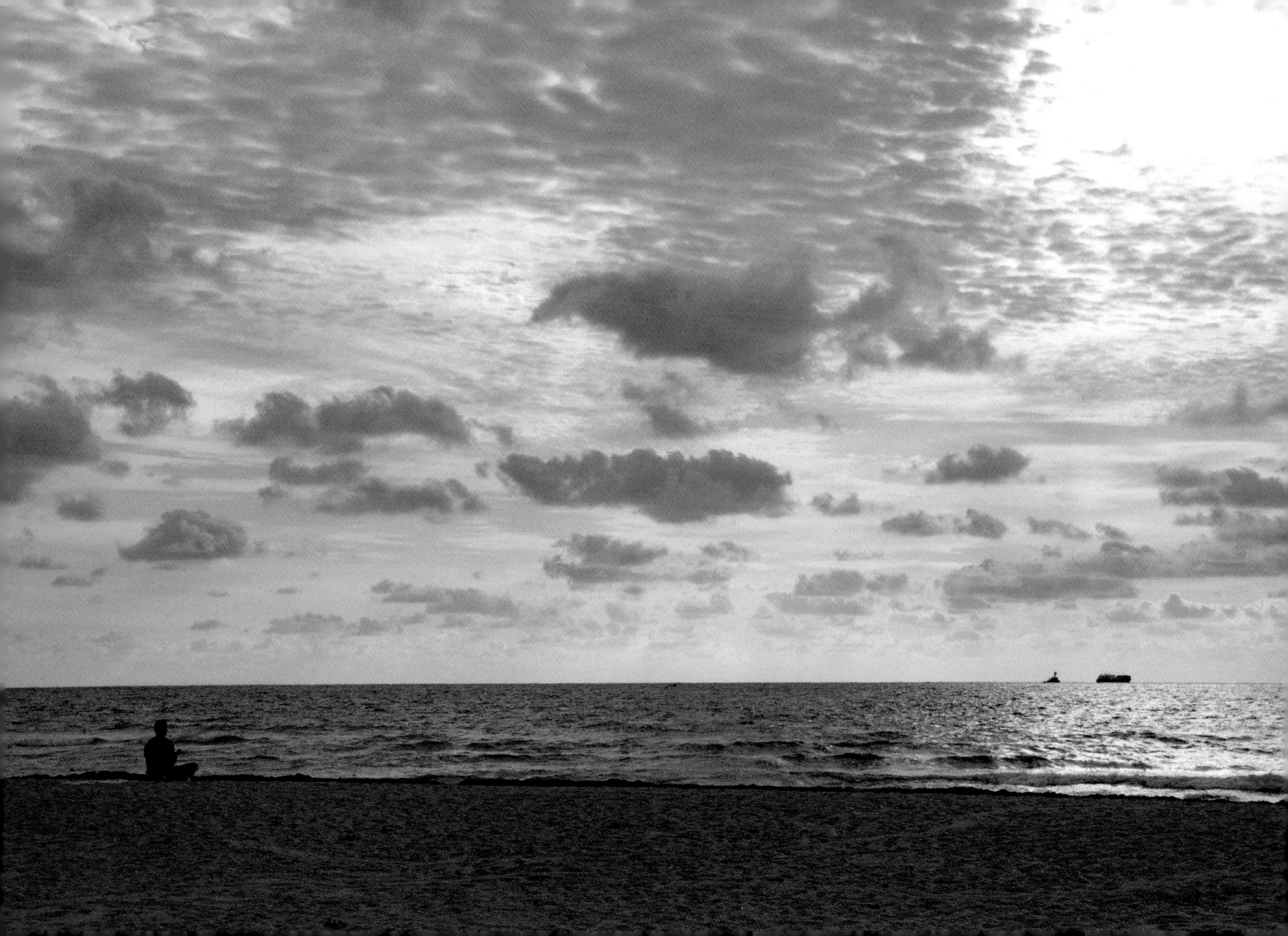

A true warrior endures the incapacitating struggles of pain, fear and anxiety by *bringing forth* unparalleled

## courage, energy and positivity

to defeat any opponent, perceived or real.

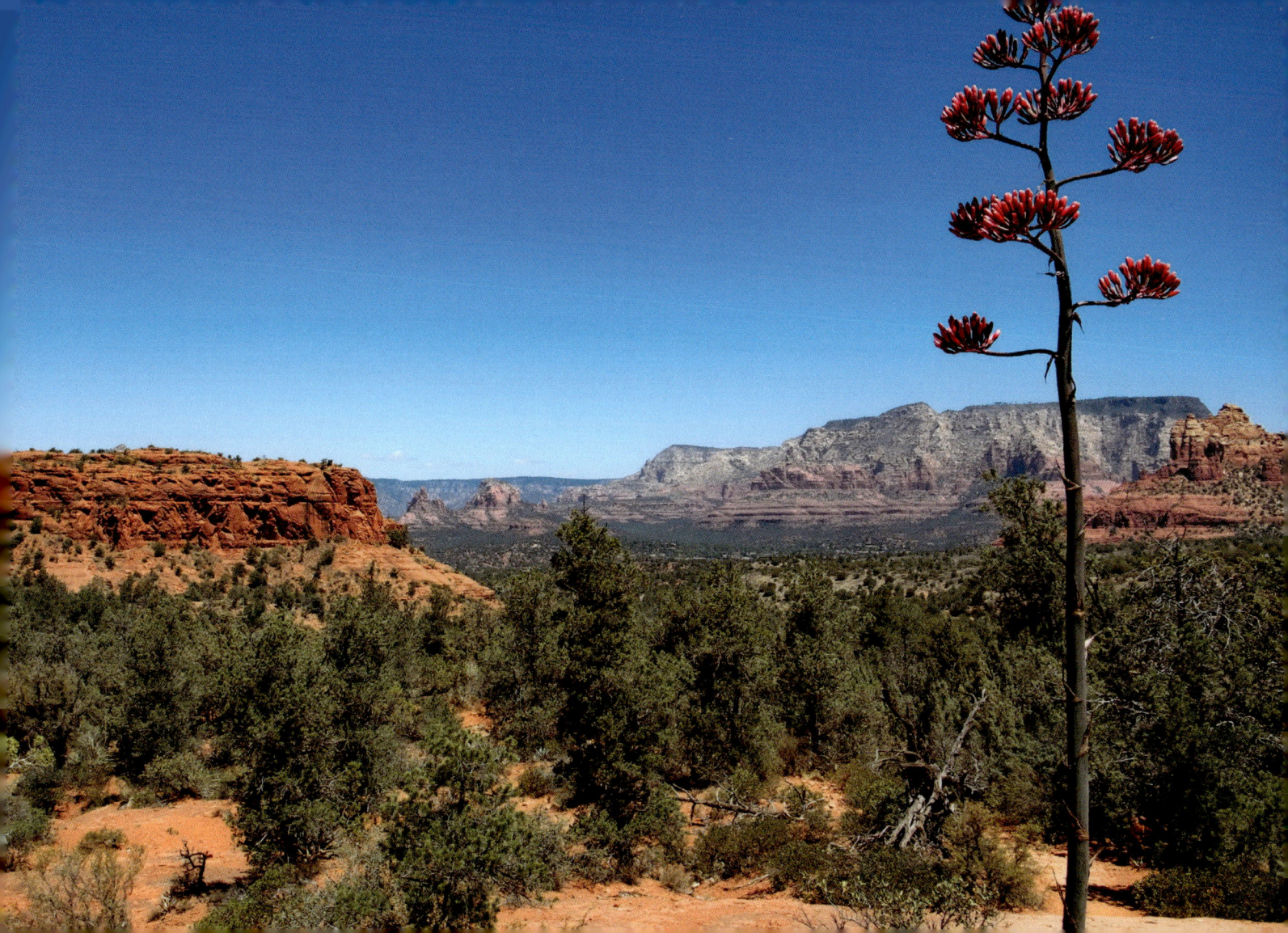

**Humility opens the door for pride,**

**arrogance, conceit and hubris to**

*respectfully make an exit.*

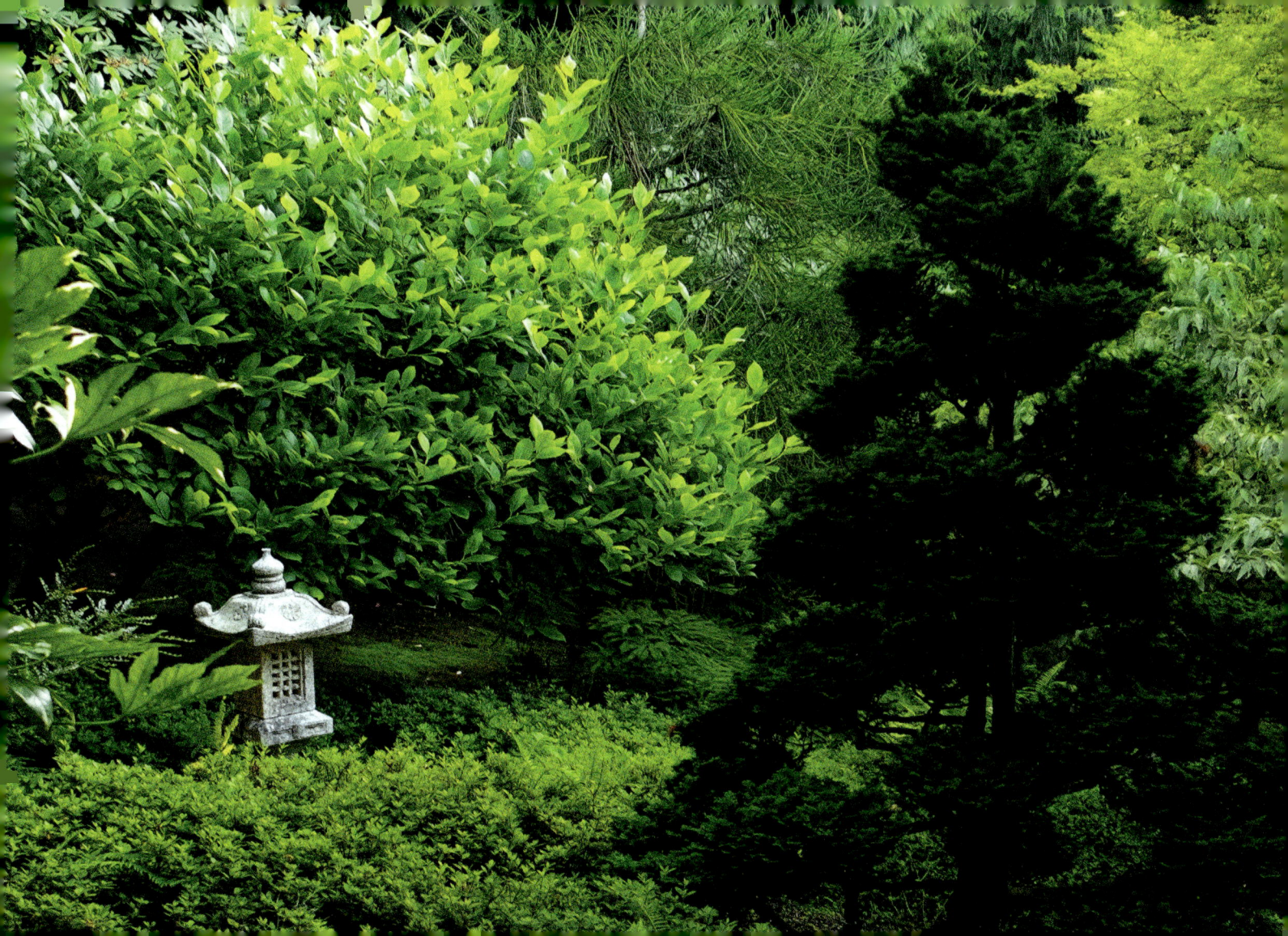

There are those we will encounter who are *"hot heads"* or *"head strong"* in how they move through life.

By leading with their heads like hot air balloons, they are not grounded to the earth. They are *unstable* and *off balance*, moving only where the *air currents of life* take them.

To be **grounded** and **centered**, the focus must come from our **"one point"** located a **few inches below our navel** and extended through the **soles of our feet**,

**grounding us to the earth with every step.**

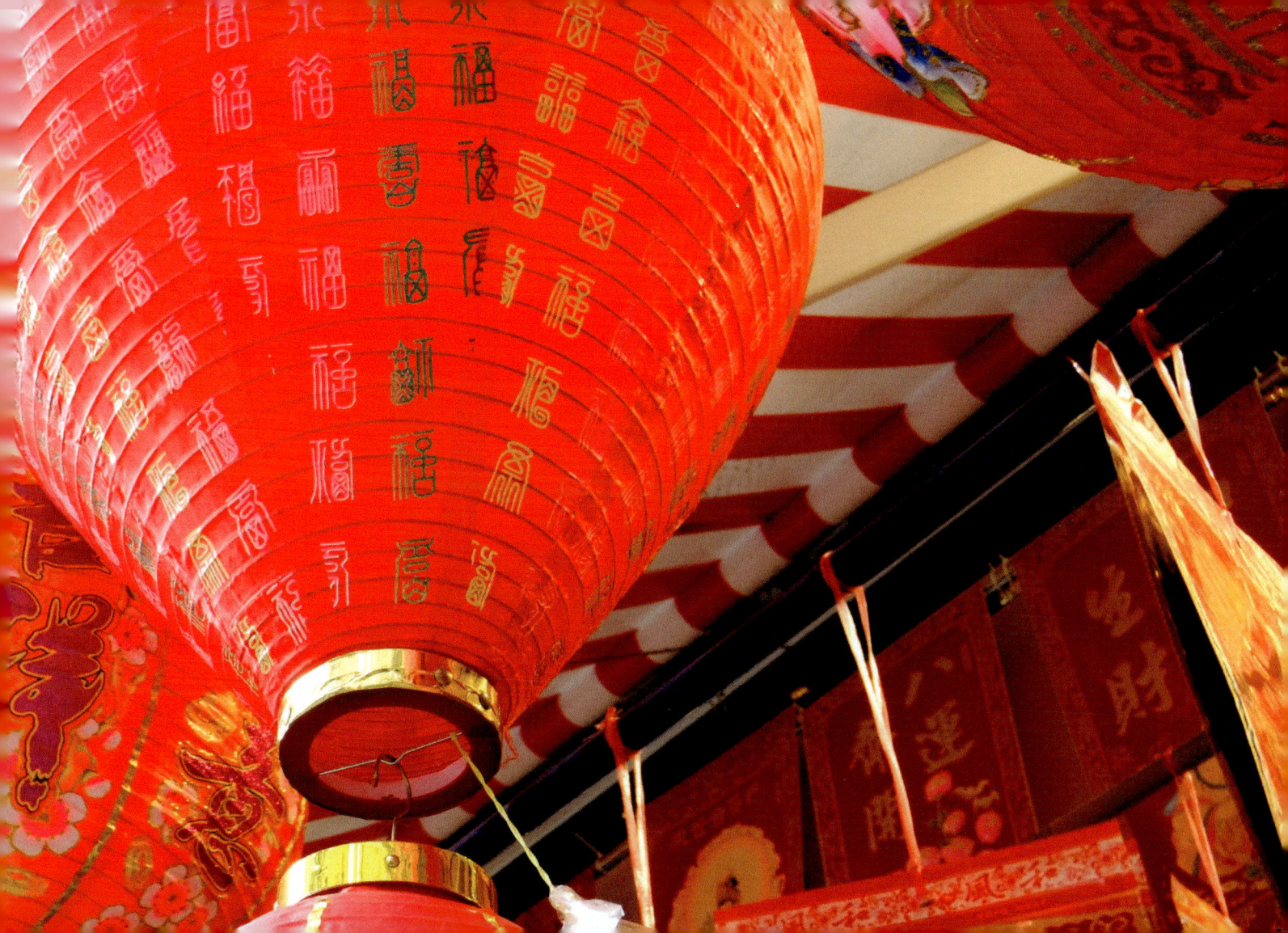

There is a battle of two wolves in all of us.
The good wolf of peace, empathy, love, humility and kindness battles the bad wolf of envy, greed, anger, pride and self-pity.

*Which one wins, you ask?*

**That's easy. The one you feed.**

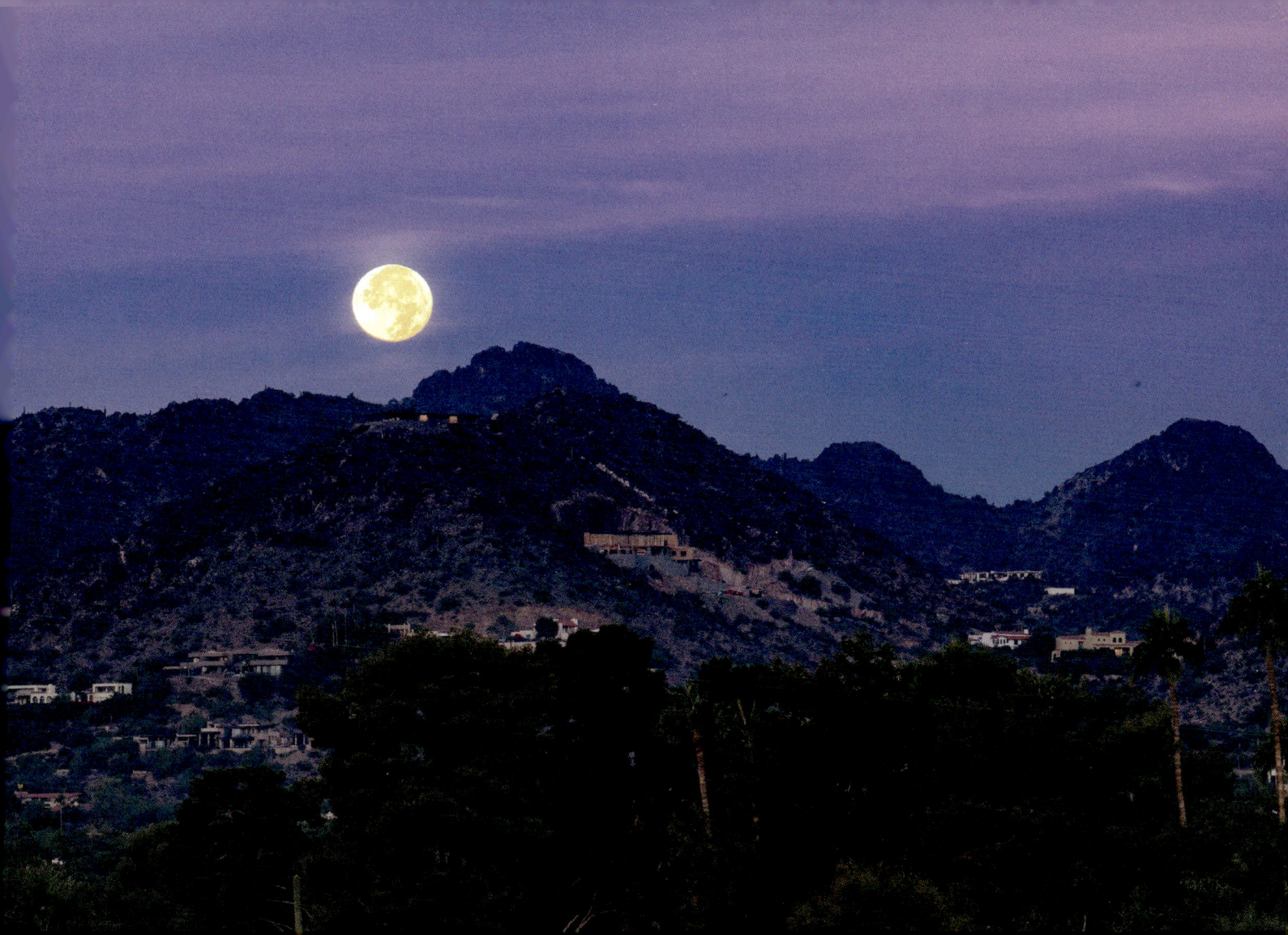

**When we stop learning, we die.**

**If we maintain a *"beginner's mind,"***

**we will nourish our inner-most vitality.**

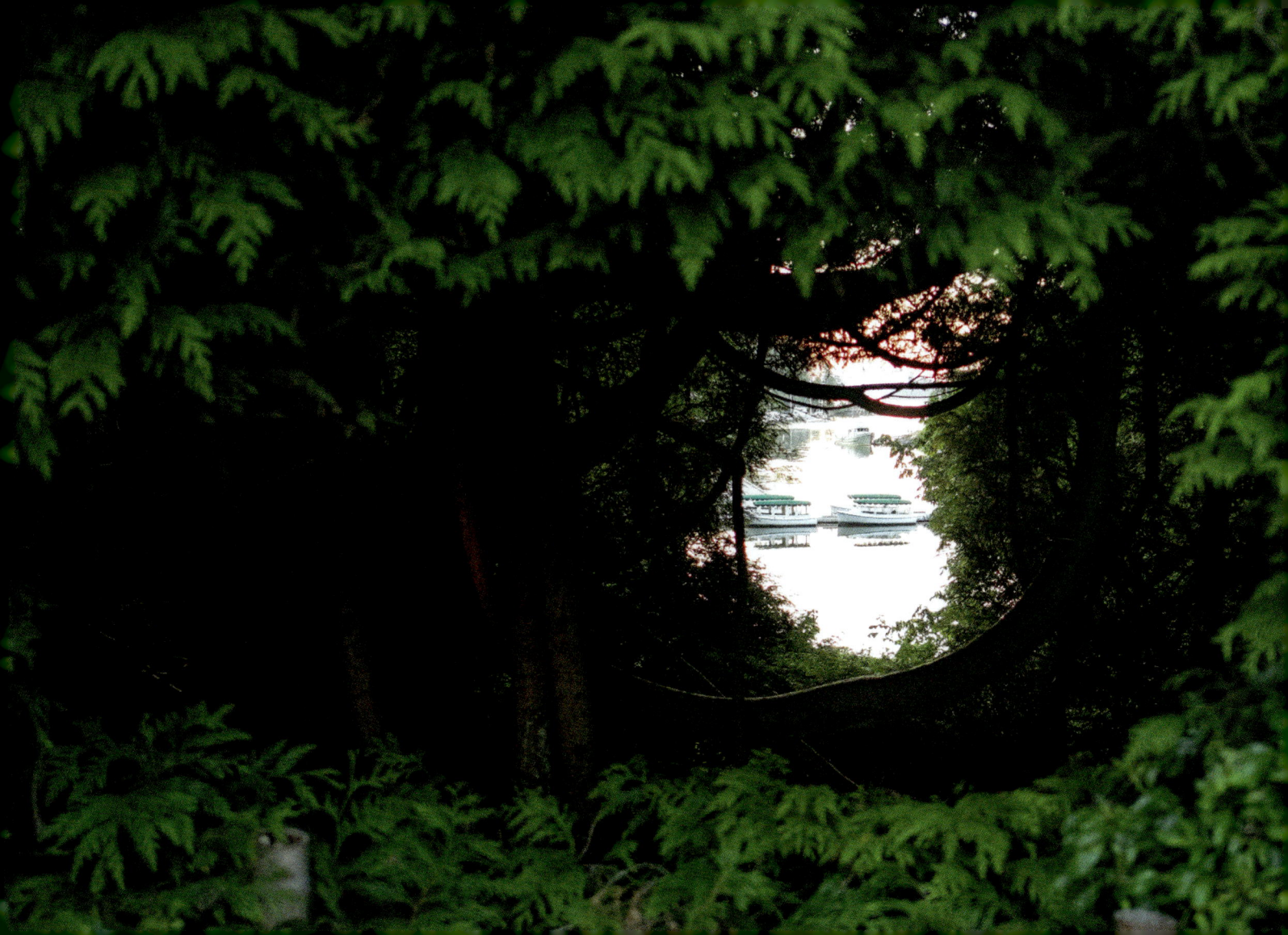

One of the most valuable lessons learned during my martial arts training was written on the stepping stones leading to the dojo.

*"Please-leave-your-ego-at-the-door."*

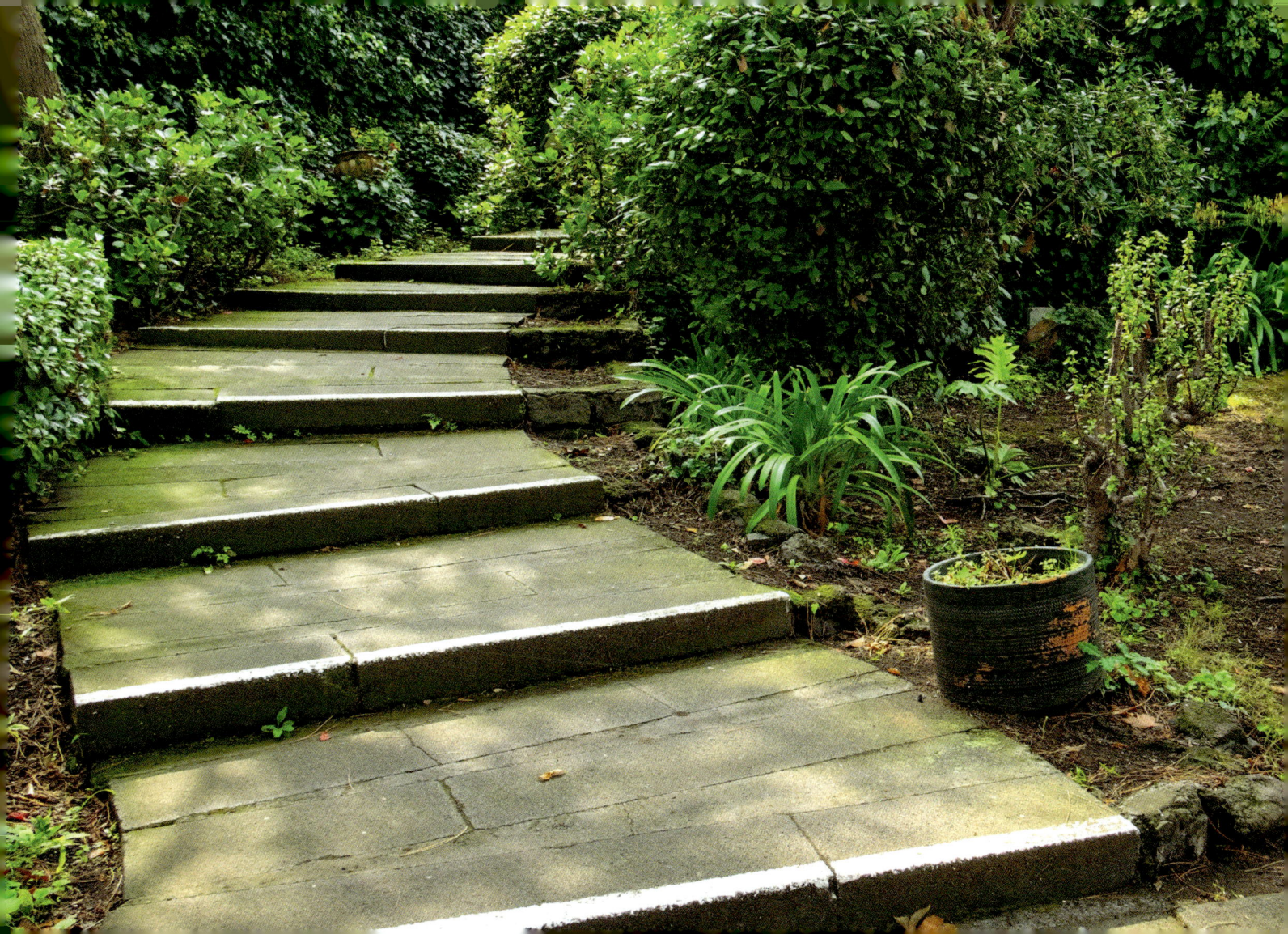

Humility occurs when we purposely choose **avoidance** and **acceptance** over domination and control.

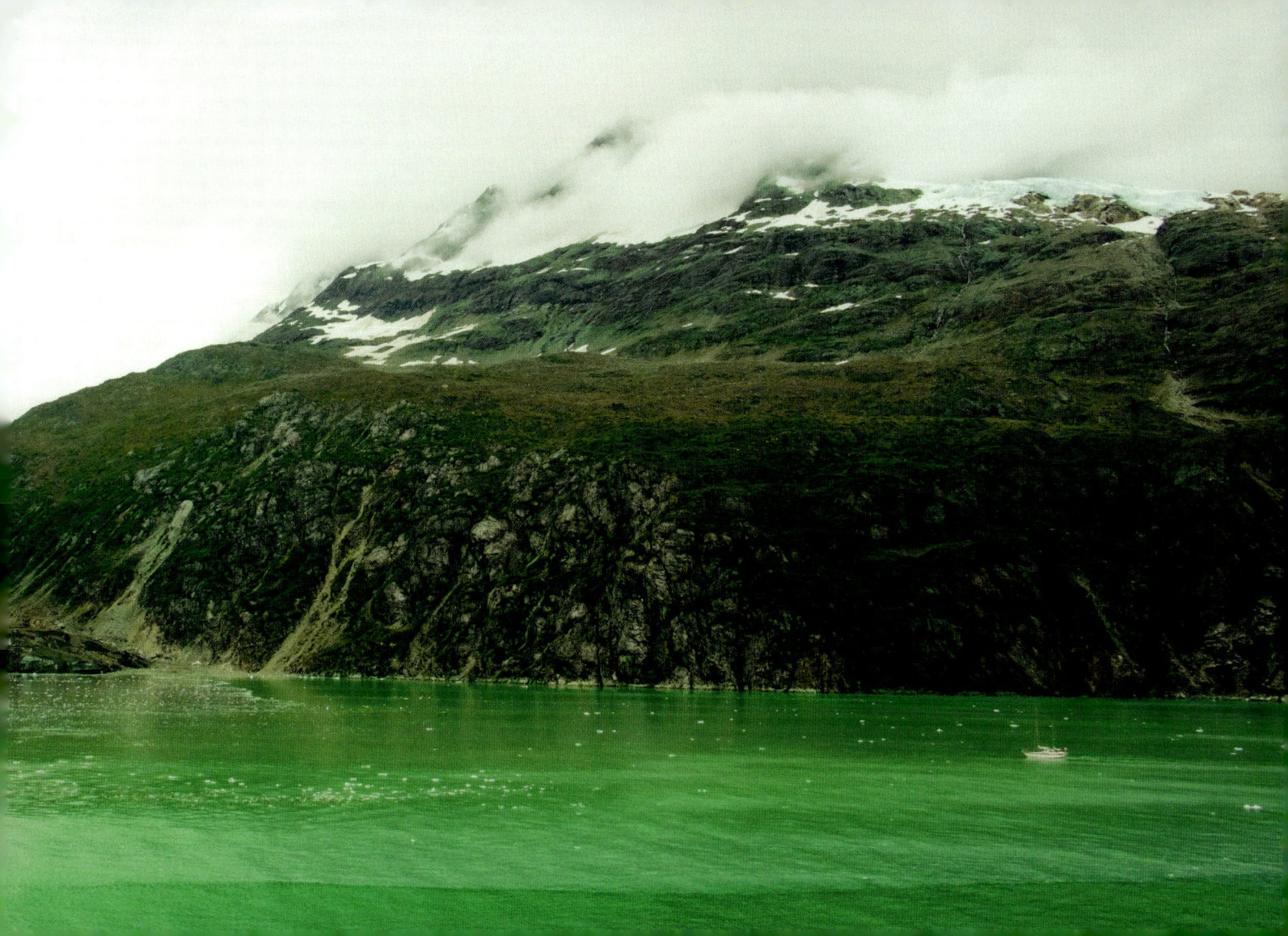

Respond to social bullying by seeking a peer group where you will be **genuinely accepted and loved** for who you really are.

Discover how it feels to truly *"belong"* instead of having to conform to be accepted.

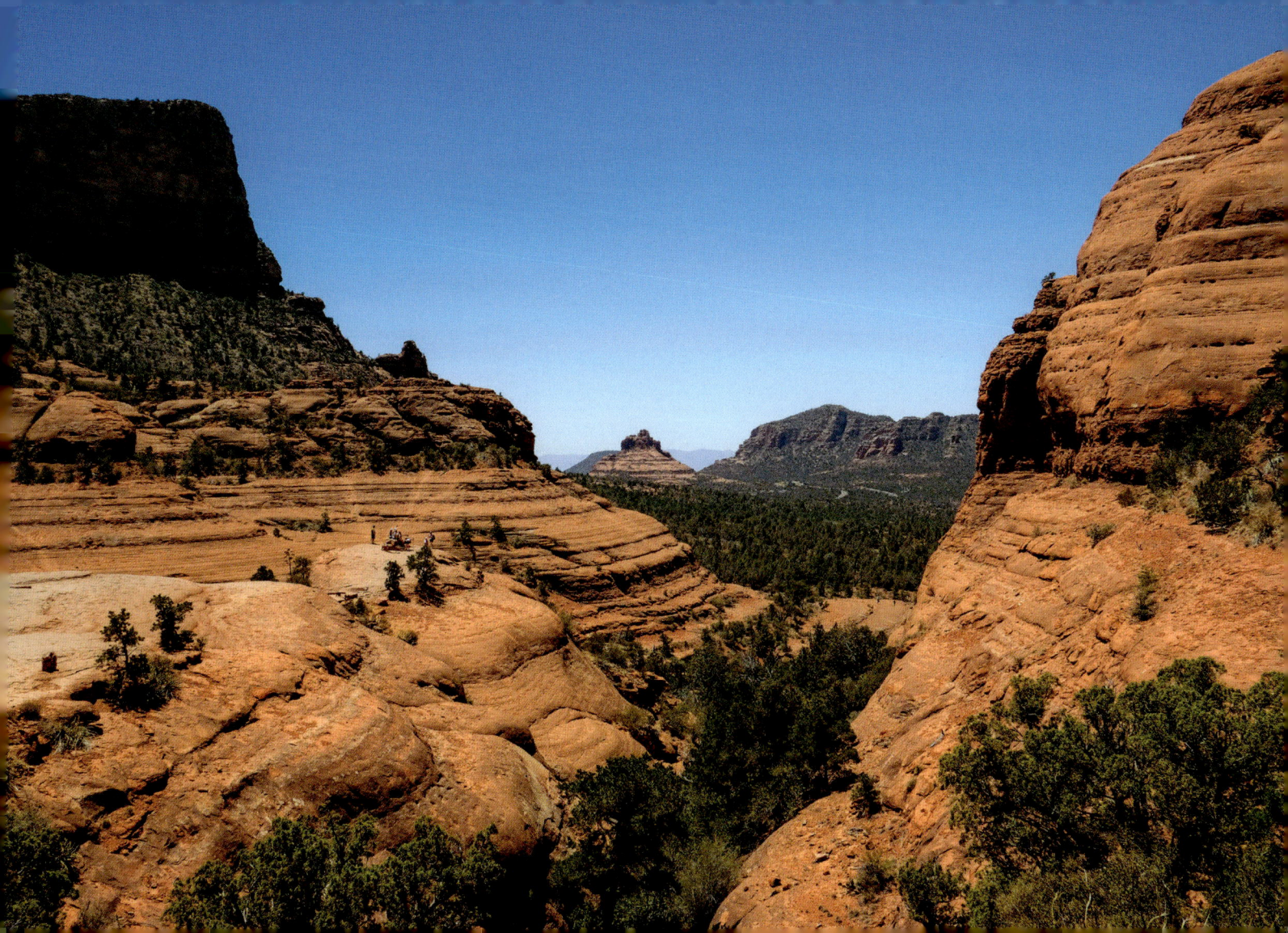

**Our family is like a garden and our children, the flowers.**

For each flower to take root and grow to its potential, it requires **individual care** and **nurturing** from a caring gardener.

With patience and unconditional love, each flower will *radiantly blossom*, adding its unique beauty to the garden.

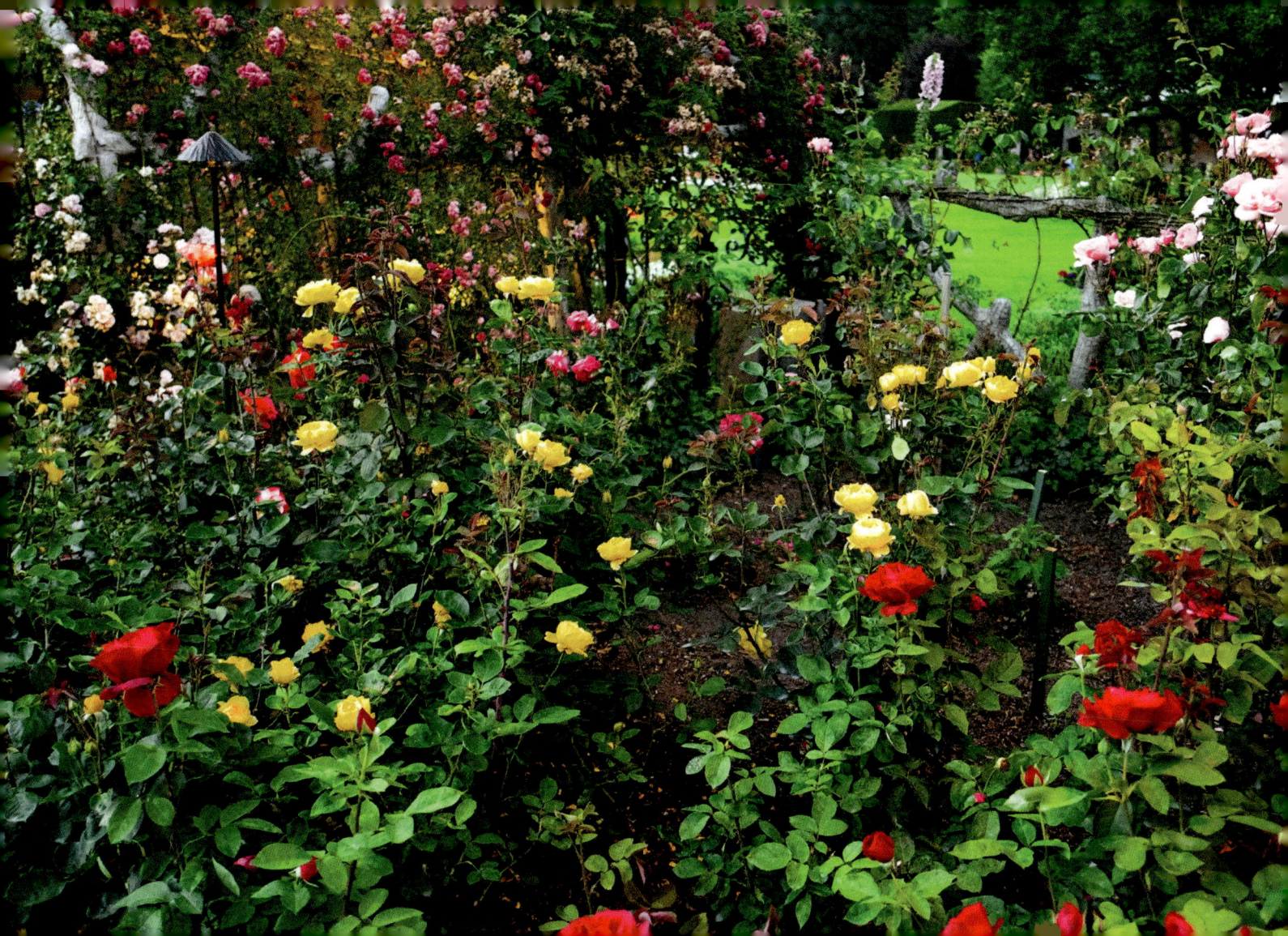

Recognize that while having "thick skin" may *prevent* the negatives from getting in, it will also

*restrict* the positives from getting out.

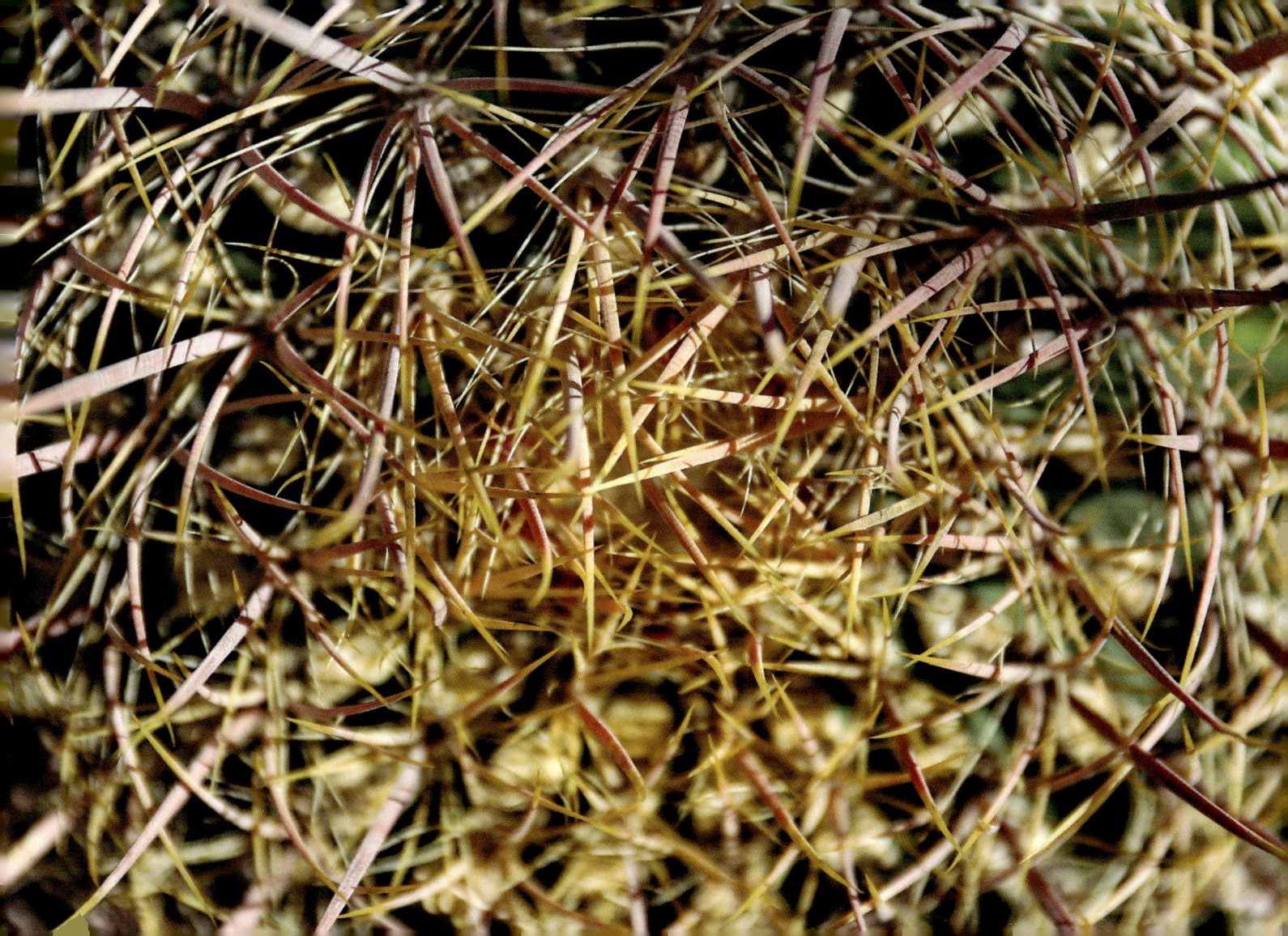

Remember that while drugs and alcohol may *attenuate* the pain of life's atrocities, they also attenuate the **joy**.

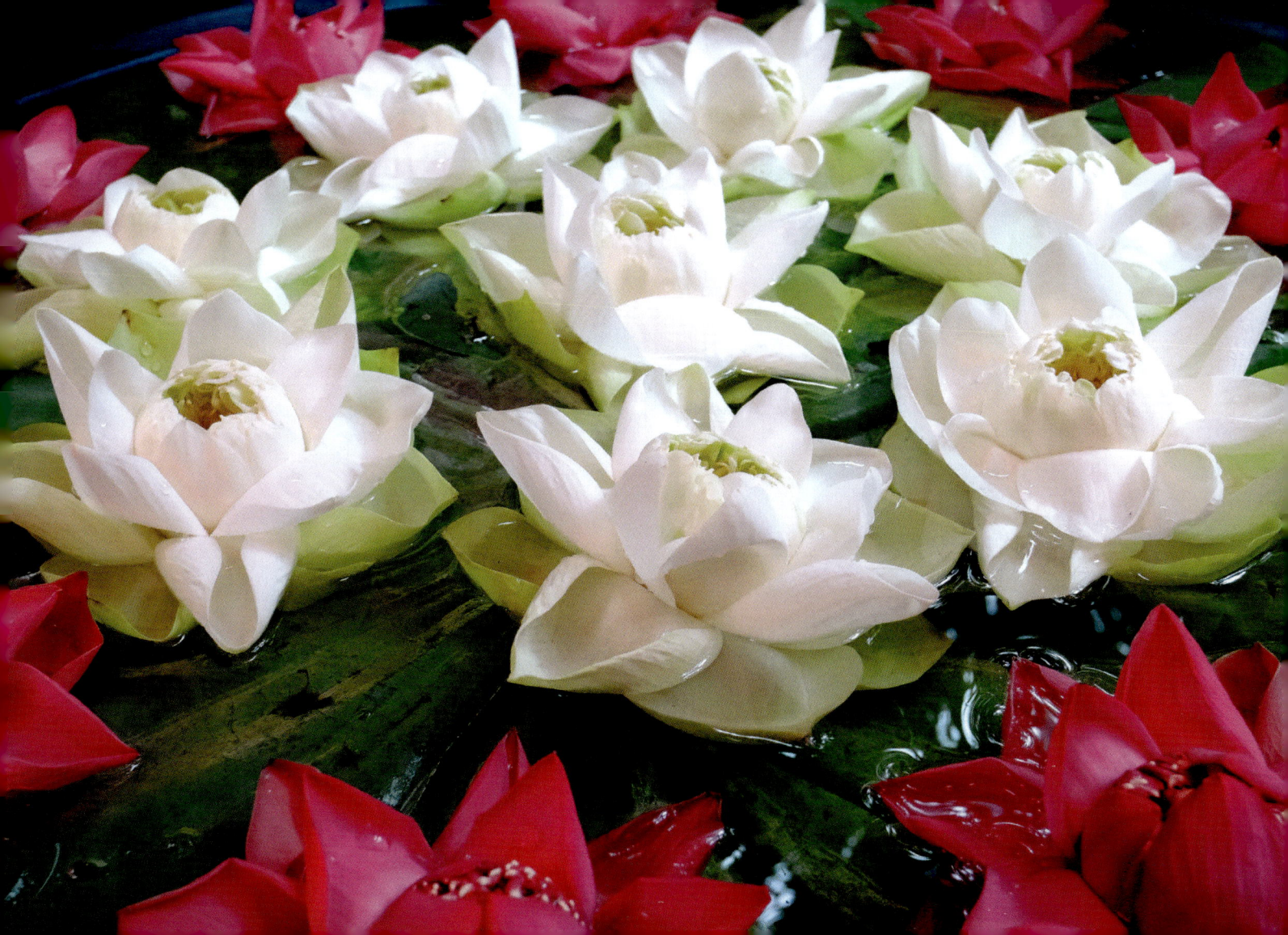

*"I love you with all my heart."*

*"I speak from the heart."*

*"My heart belongs to you."*

Notice how we as human beings, identify the heart as the center of human emotions. The heart influences the brain far more than the brain influences the heart.

Through a self-directed meditative process of deep breathing and guided imagery, the feelings of love, gratefulness and compassion guide the brain and body to a unified state of physical and emotional well-being.

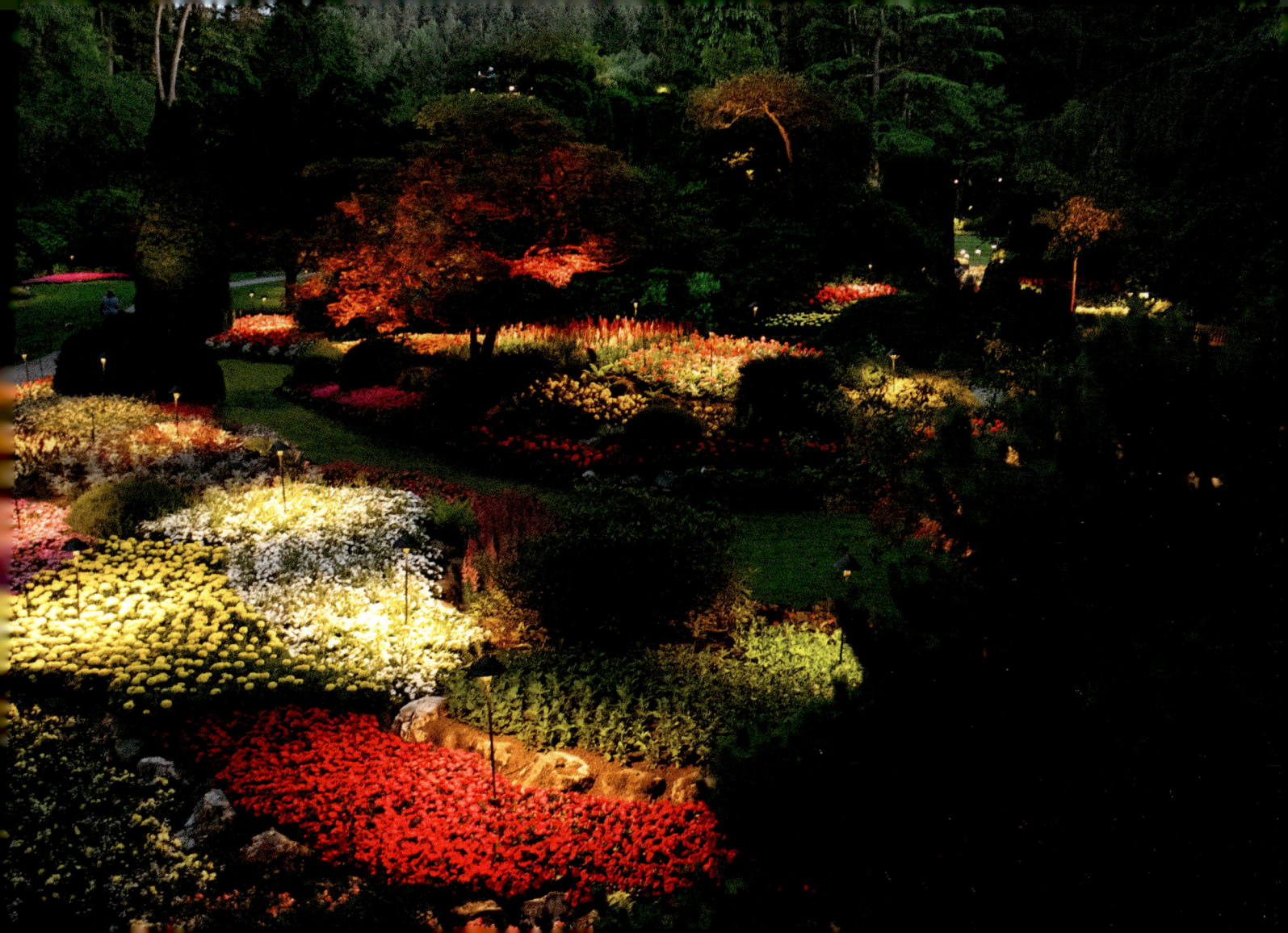

*Empathy* is the capacity to understand and feel what another person experiences.

It represents the inner sphere of a relationship that is *both* personally rewarding and emotionally fatiguing.

*Compassion* is the aptitude to show concern, love, tenderness and sensitivity without necessarily sharing an experience.

It is the outer sphere of a relationship which becomes more *sustainable* than empathy.

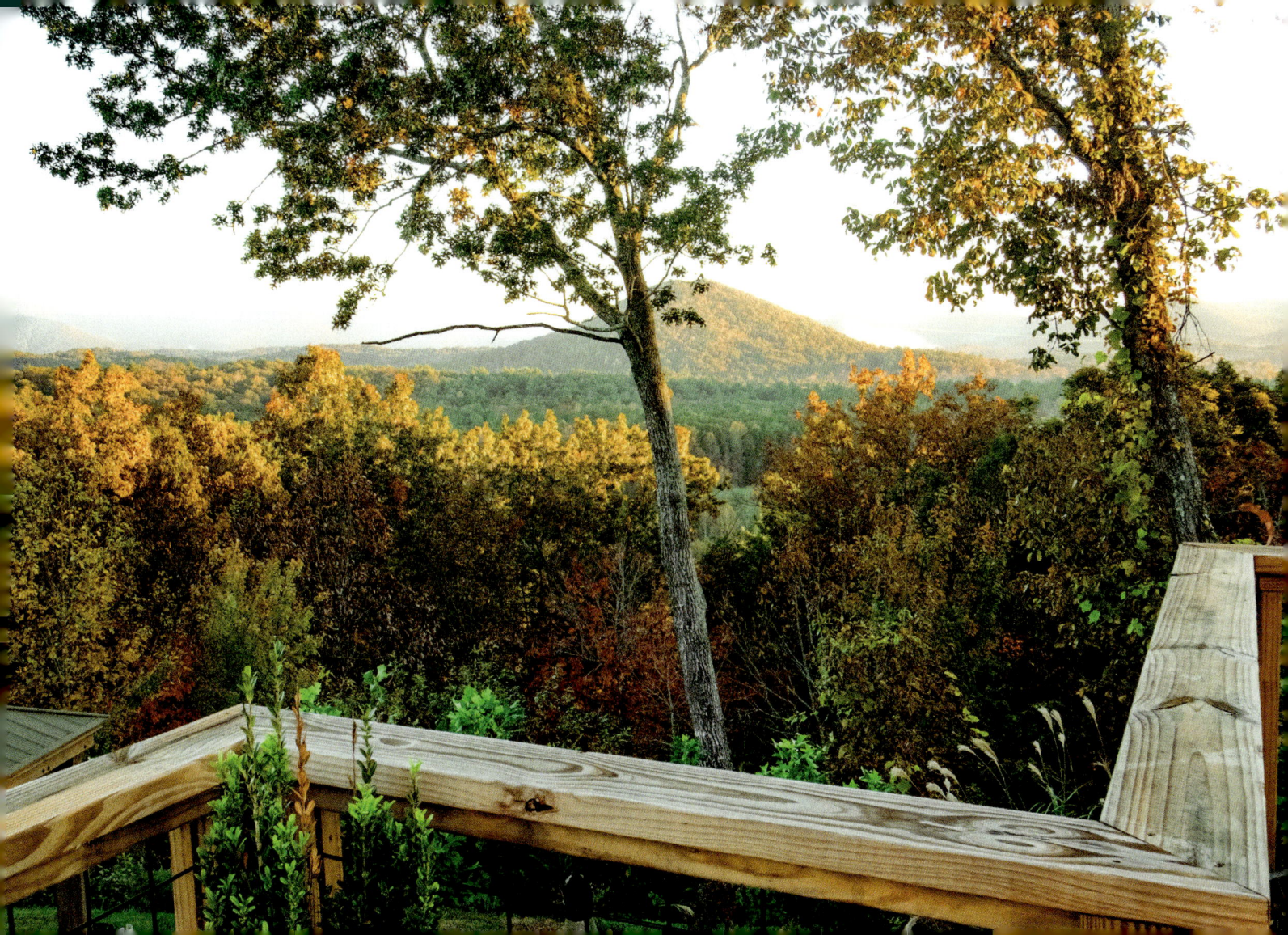

Isn't it revealing that the words

"listen" and "silent"

share exactly the same letters?

Paradise Valley, AZ
ISO 400 f/18 1/30 sec

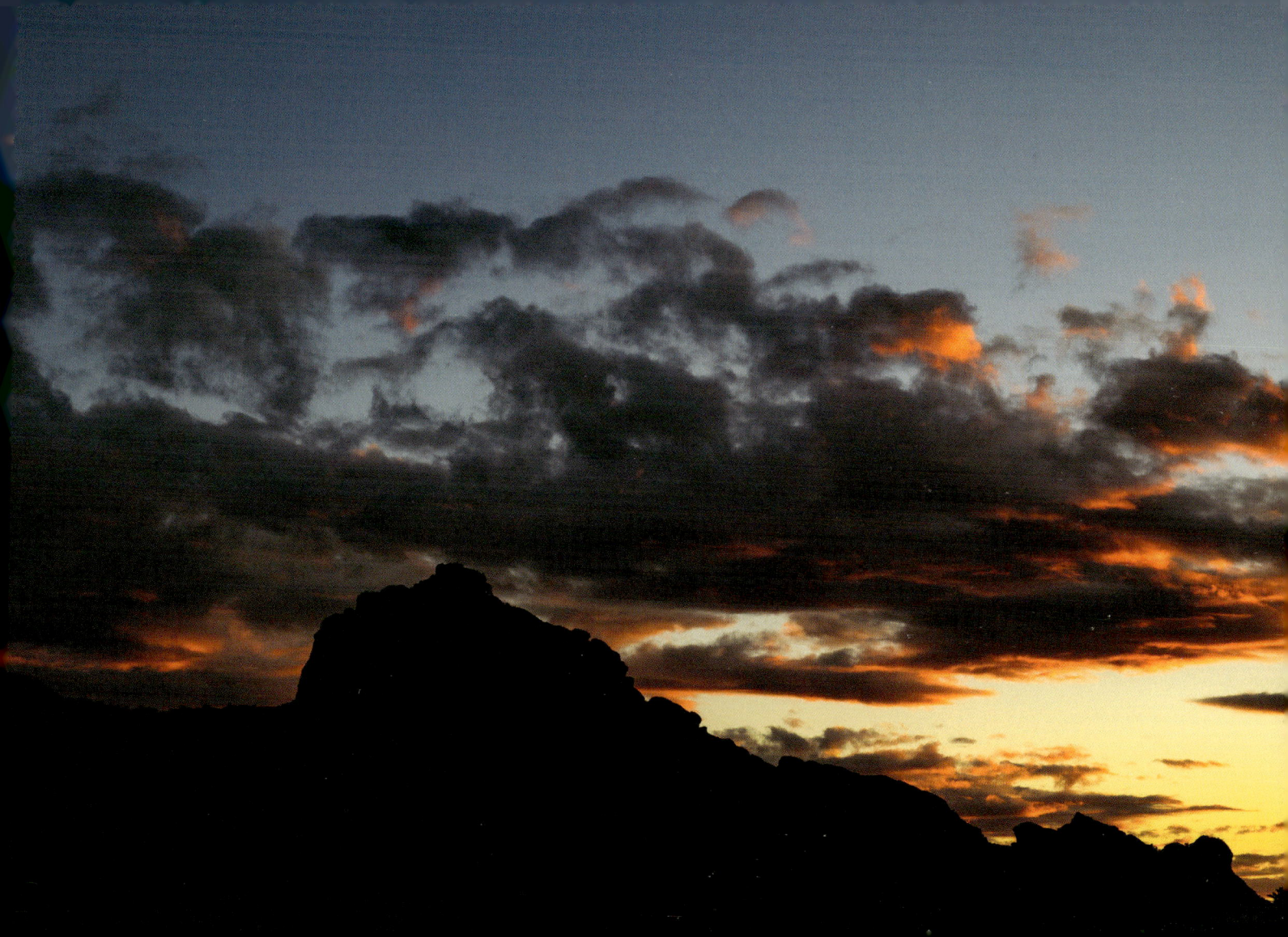

We must not be afraid of reinventing ourselves as we move through life.

**The fear of transition can be re-channeled as positive energy that leads to new expressions of joy and fulfillment.**

By stepping into the realm of change and embracing the opportunities for new learning, we open ourselves to *experience transformational vitality*.

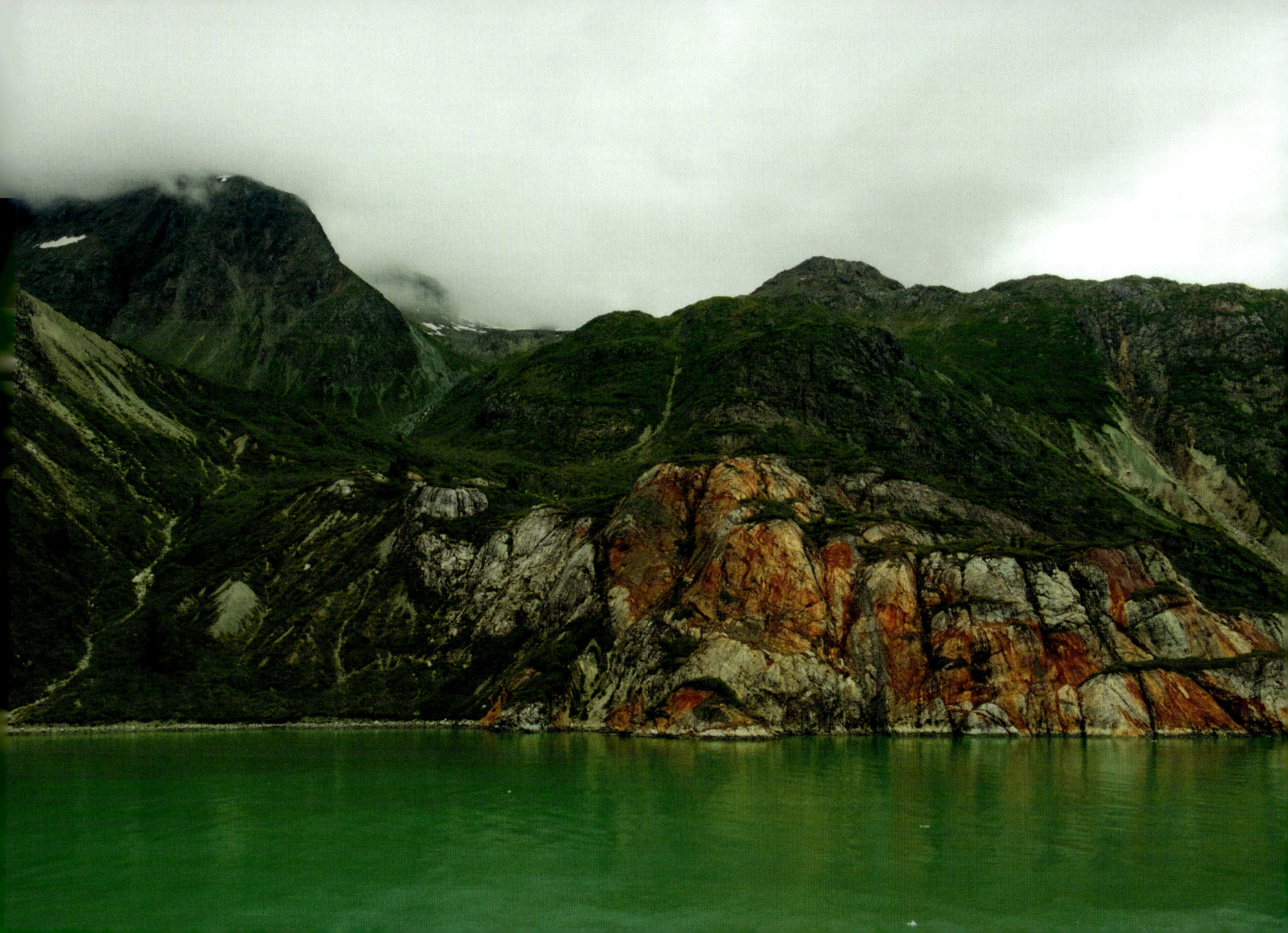

The foundation of a warrior's mindset is built from the bricks and mortar of an **unwavering commitment** to living a life that is *courageous, honorable, loyal, just* and *respectful of obligation*.

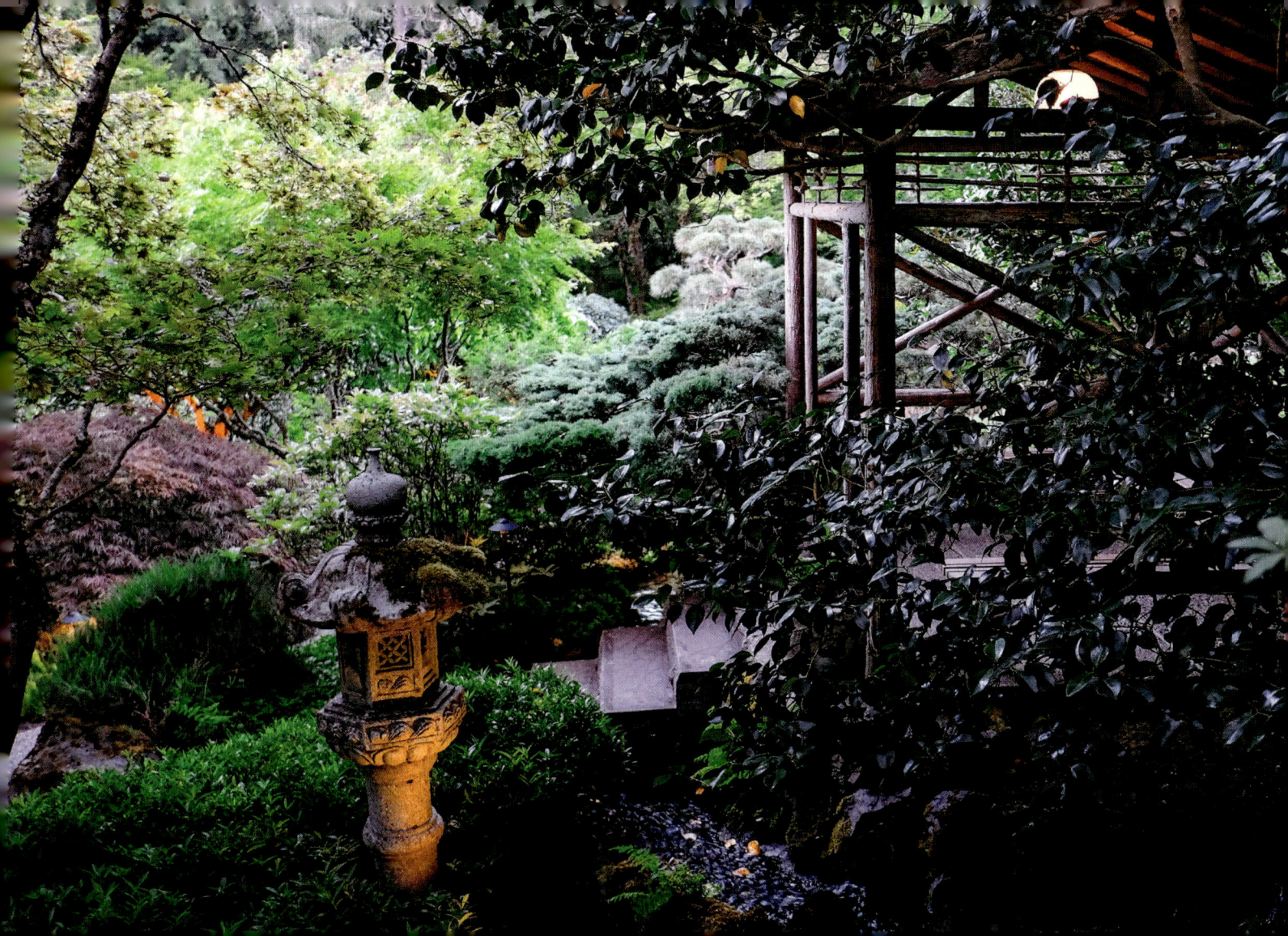

When leading change, we must first focus on *establishing a trusting culture* before attempting to launch a strategy of action

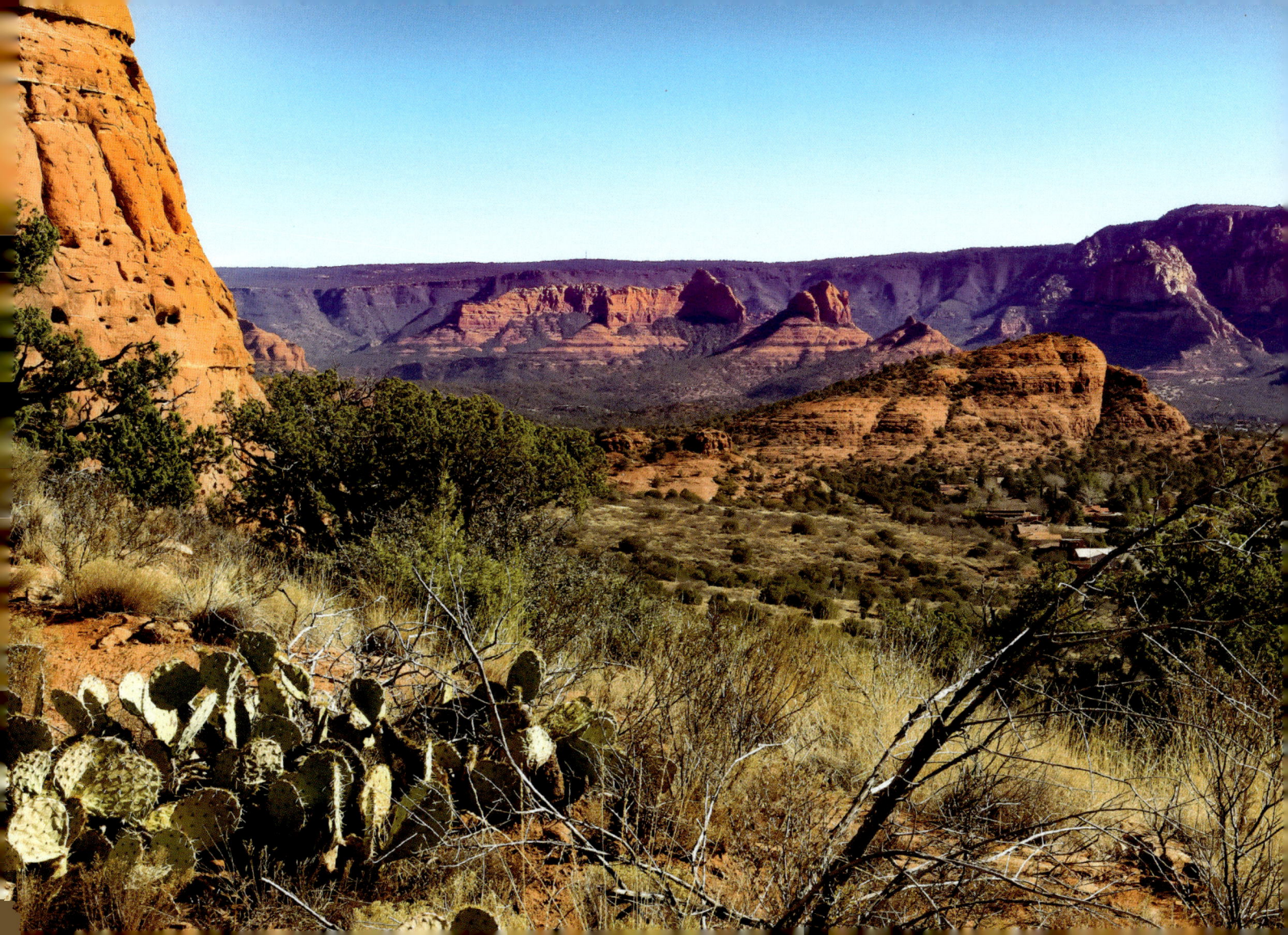

By beginning every important discussion or meeting with *three-to-five positive affirmations*, the problems or challenges subsequently discussed will have much *less sting*.

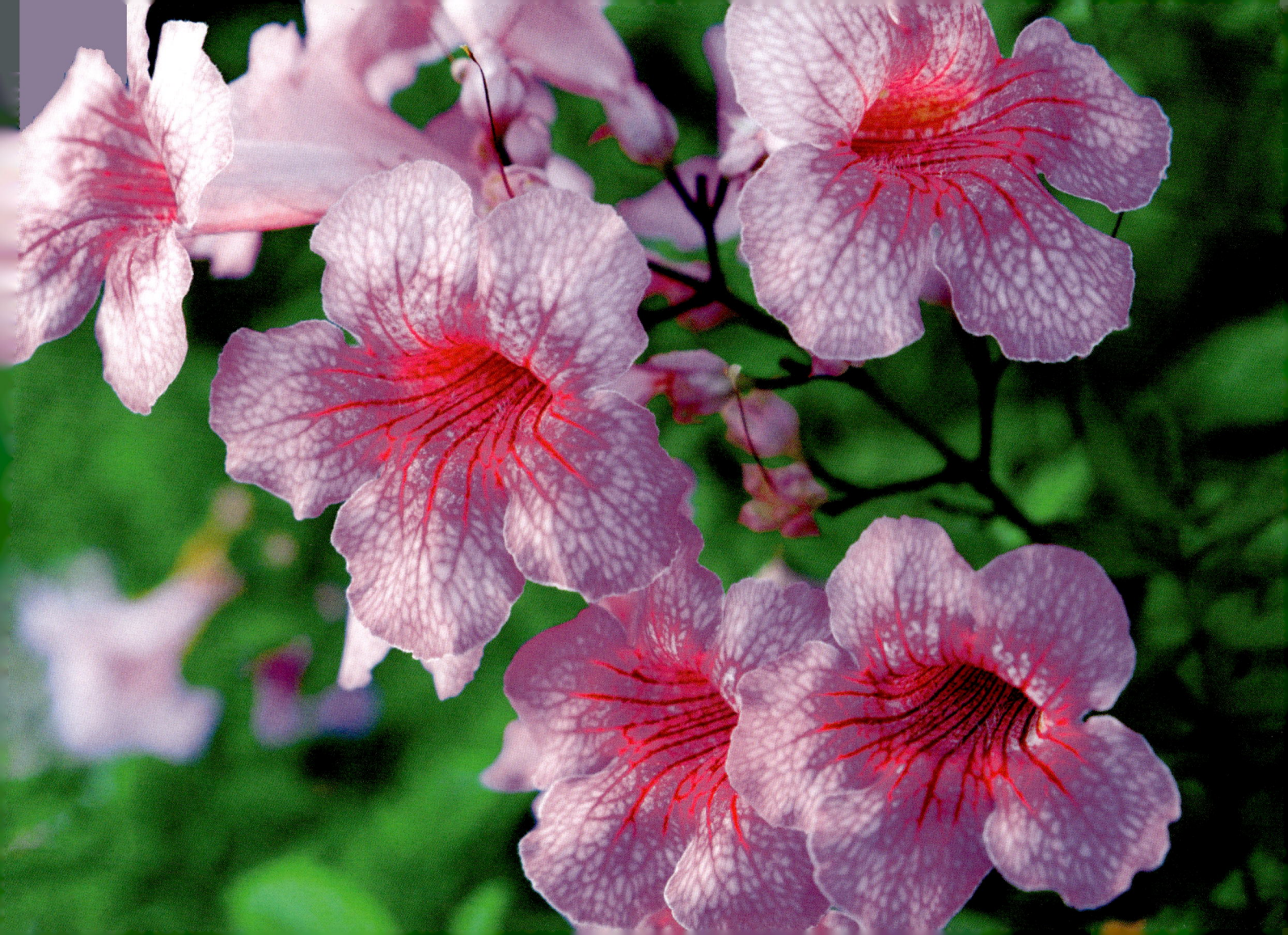

"Attack the process—support the people."

In managing conflict, we must focus our initial efforts on supporting the people involved in order to preserve relationships. Collectively thereafter, we can thoughtfully address failures in process that led to the conflict or breakdowns.

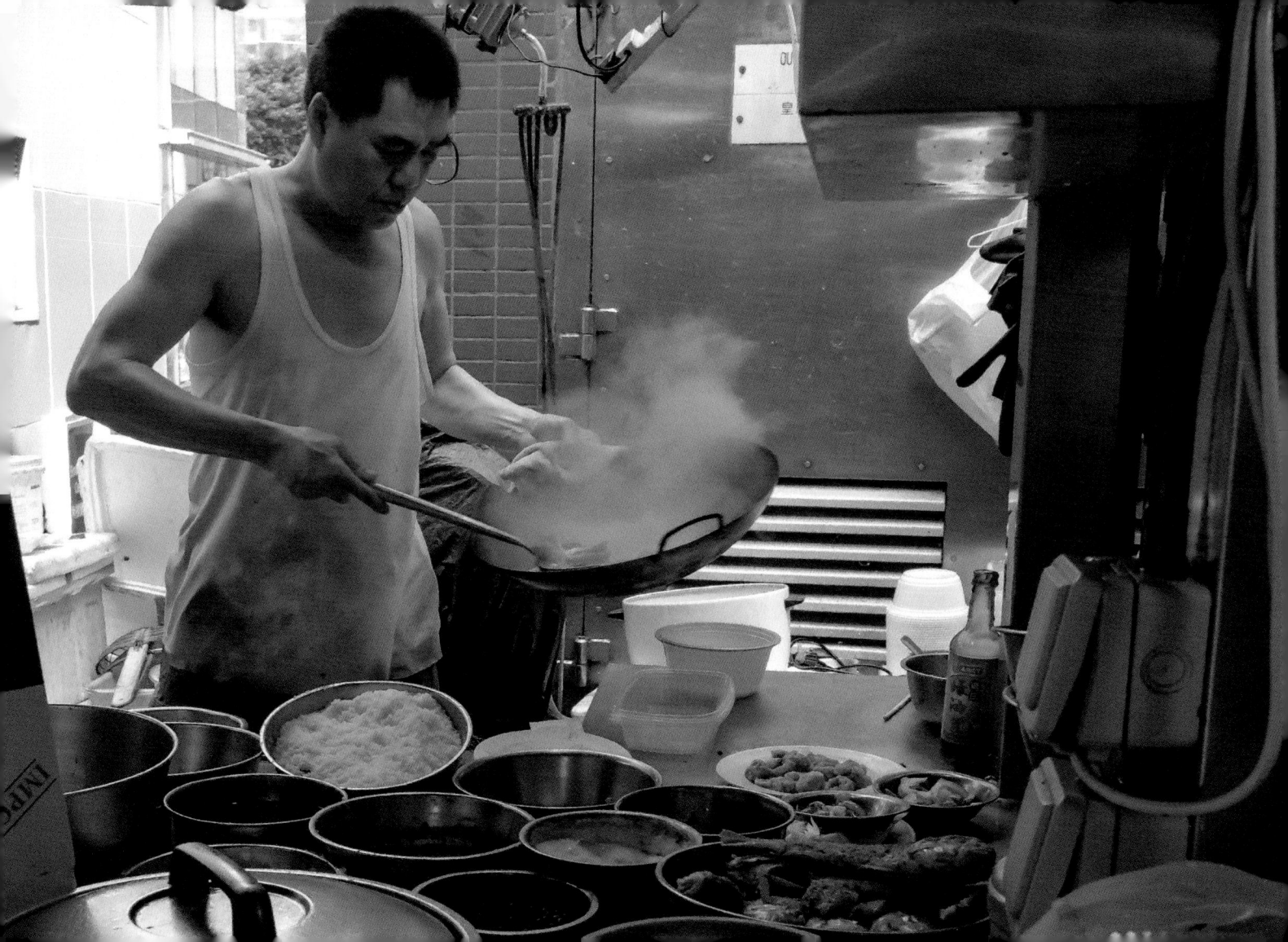

As a society, we must focus less on breakdowns or negatives and more on opportunities or positives to enhance our collective happiness.

*Learn the valuable skill of positive reframing.*

Stop watching the nightly news!

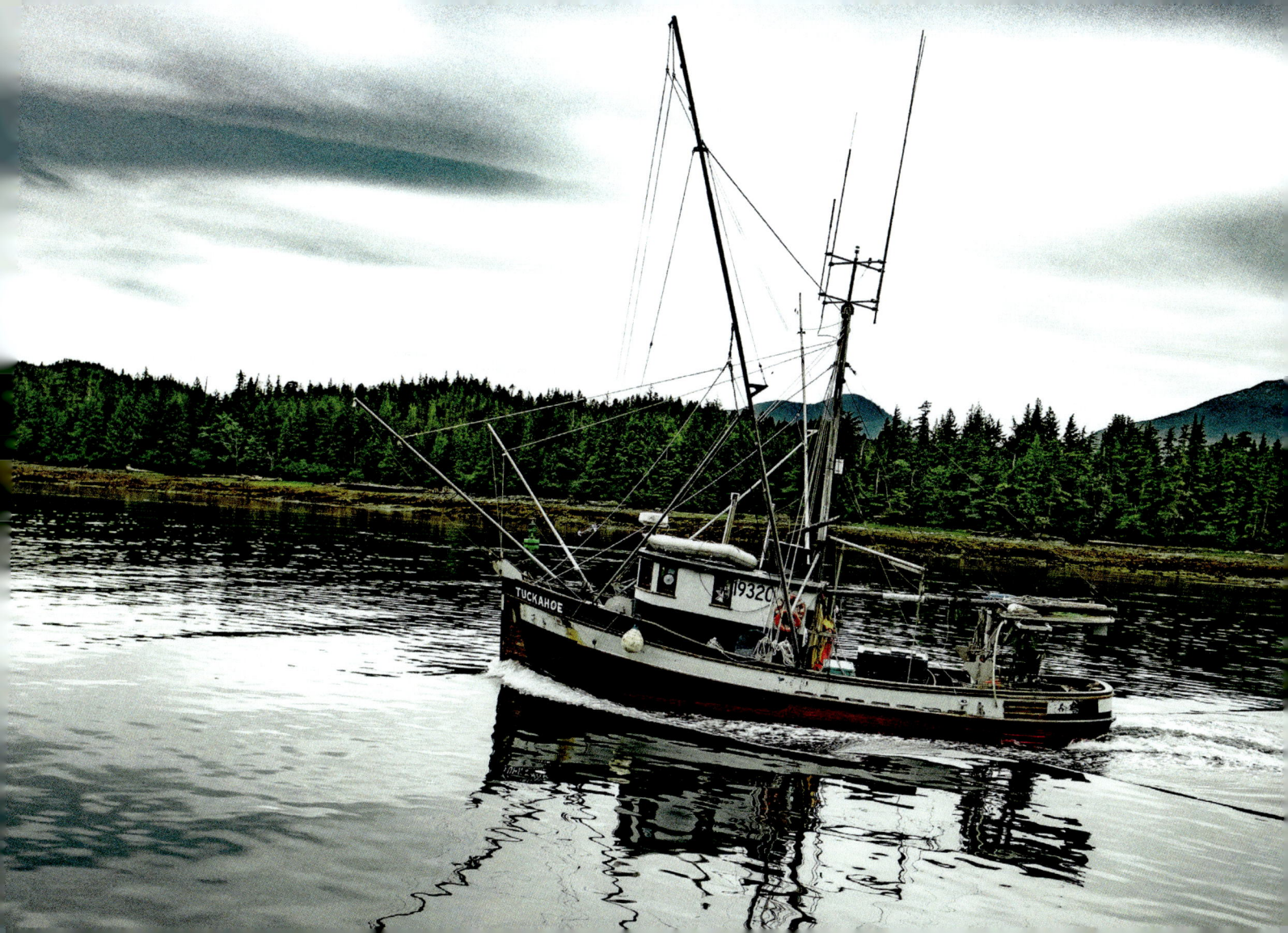

In the famous book "All I Need to Know, I Learned in Kindergarten," the author, Robert Fulghum, discussed that the life skills of sharing, playing fair, saying you're sorry and cleaning up after yourself are learned in kindergarten.

The brutal reality, unfortunately, is that many people don't remember these valuable life lessons.

*Don't punish them; teach them.*

Once you have set clear expectations for their behaviors, then, and only then, can you hold them **accountable**.

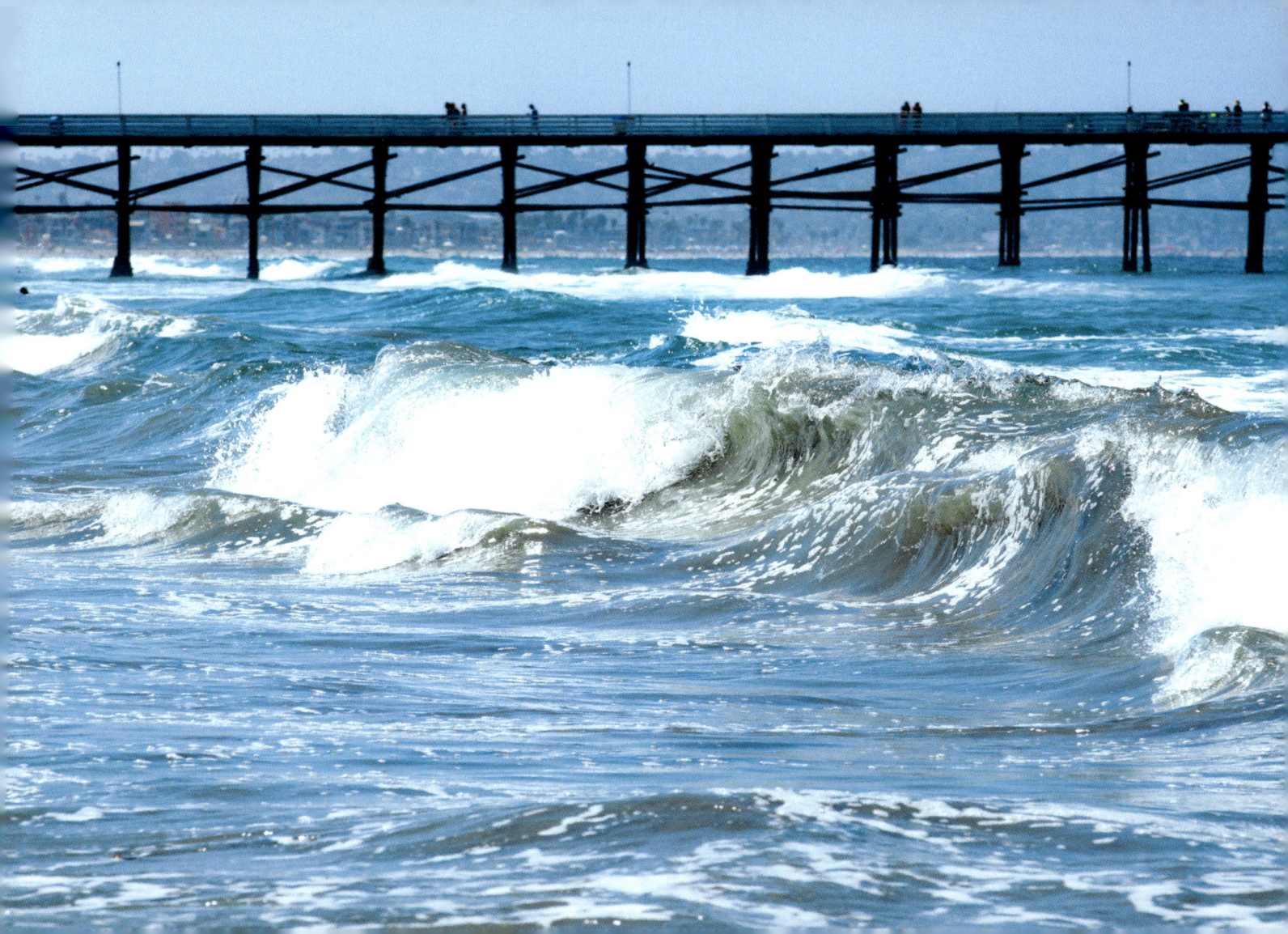

When choosing your life partner, **prioritize** both their *dedication to accepting you for who you are* and their *commitment to bringing out the potential of who you can be.*

**Listen to your inner voice** in this regard; it speaks with clarity and insight.

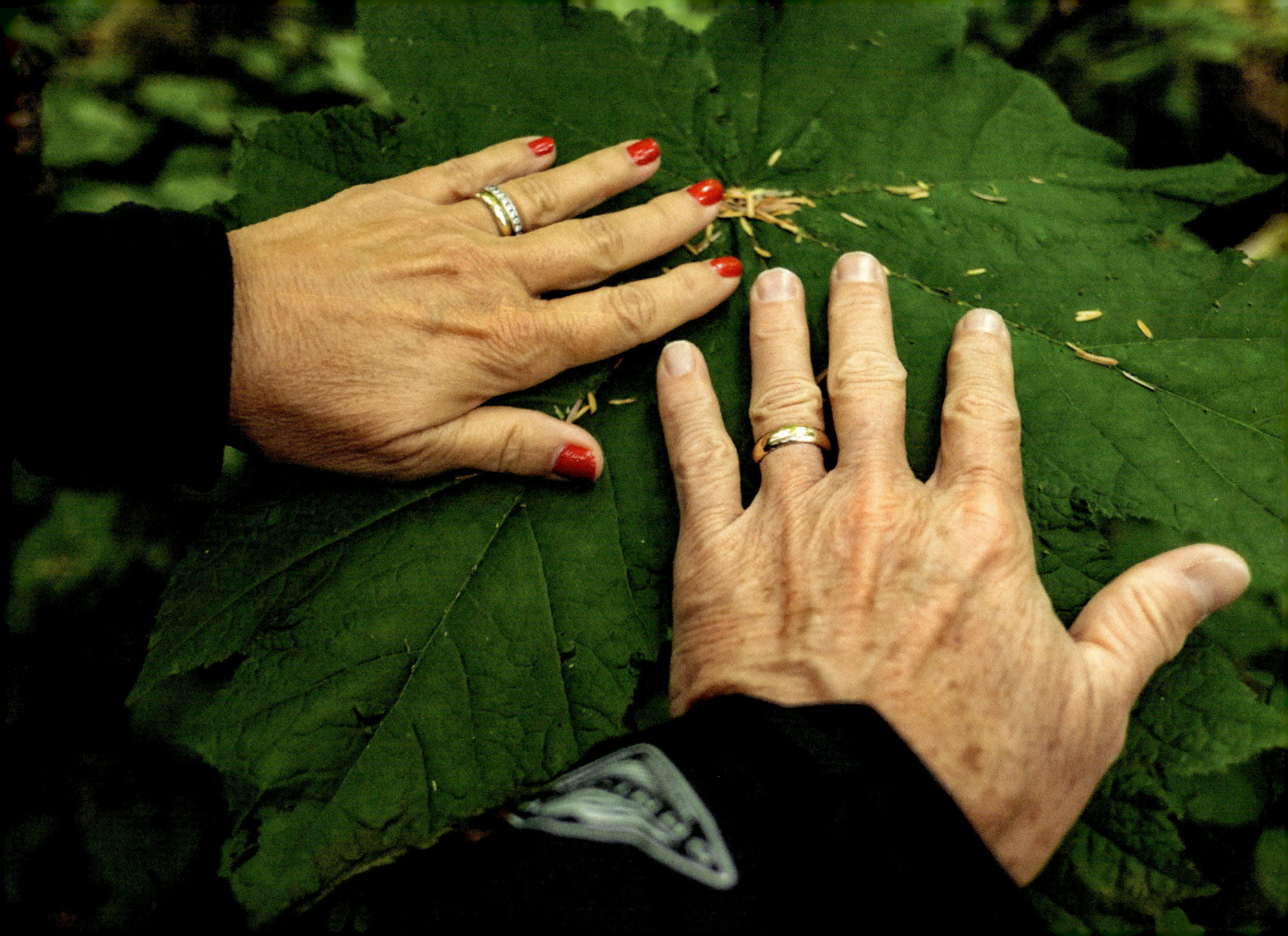

To successfully transform conflict, we must be clever and other times either courageous, vulnerable or innocent.

*The trick is to know which situation calls for each skillset.*

Our goal as peacemakers is to be able to adapt each seamlessly and appropriately.

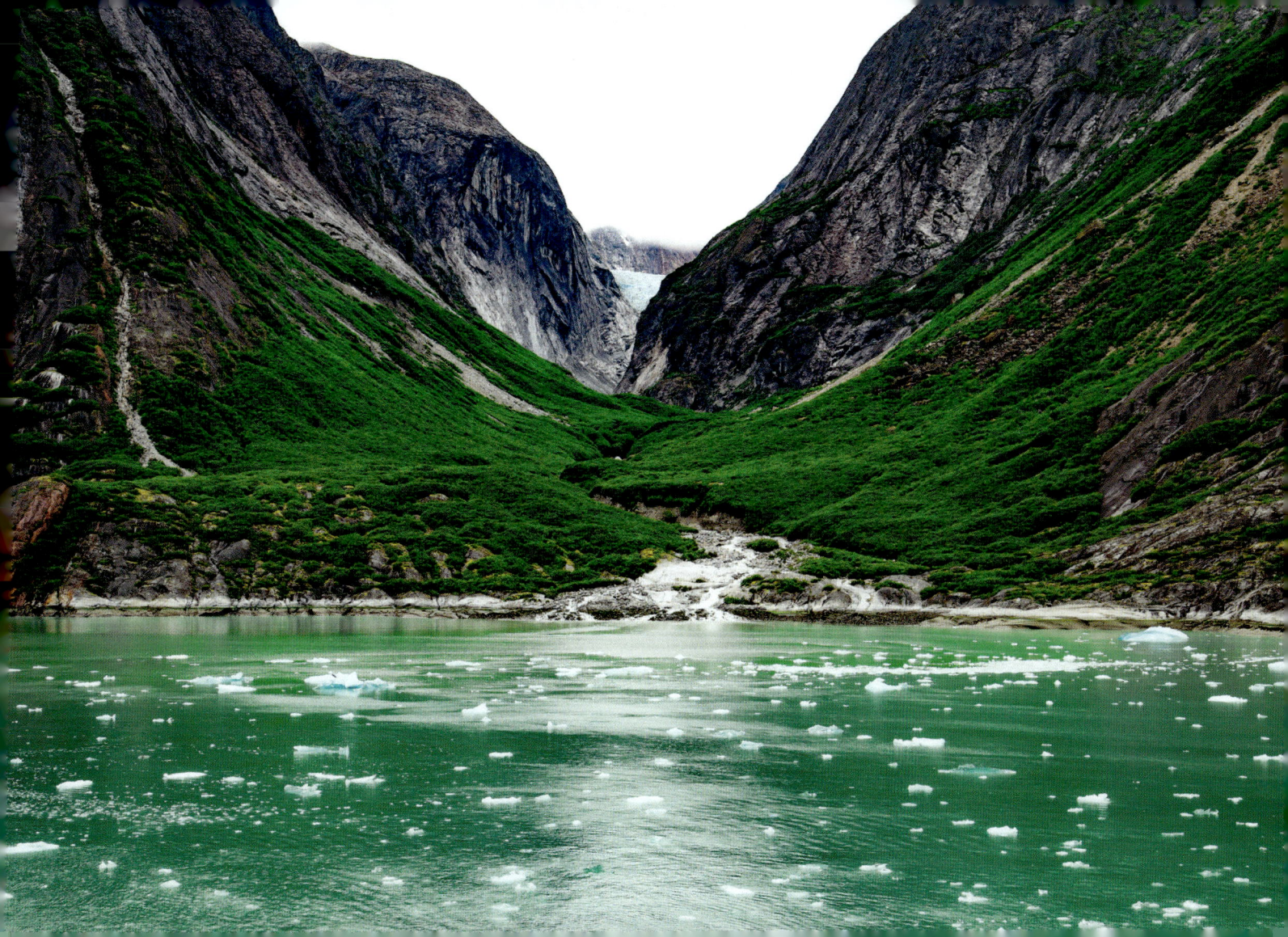

when speaking *truth to power* and *leading up* to your leader, begin by gifting to them all the wonderful leadership skills and attributes you believe they should already possess.

As your leader opens the gift,
they often want to keep it.

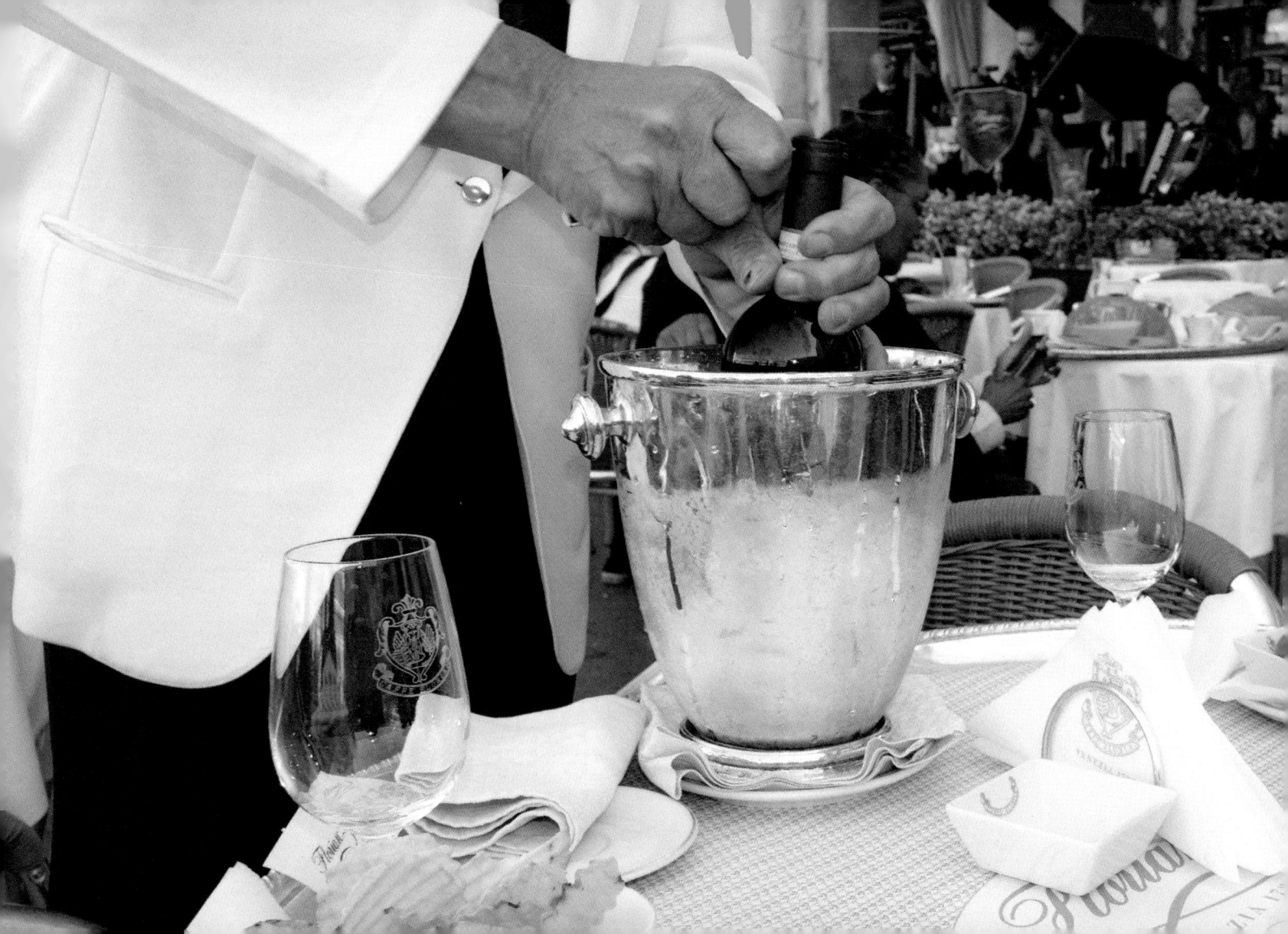

Plan time in your everyday schedule to *think*, *innovate* and *create*.

Don't fall into the trap of being too busy to *invent* your own **future**.

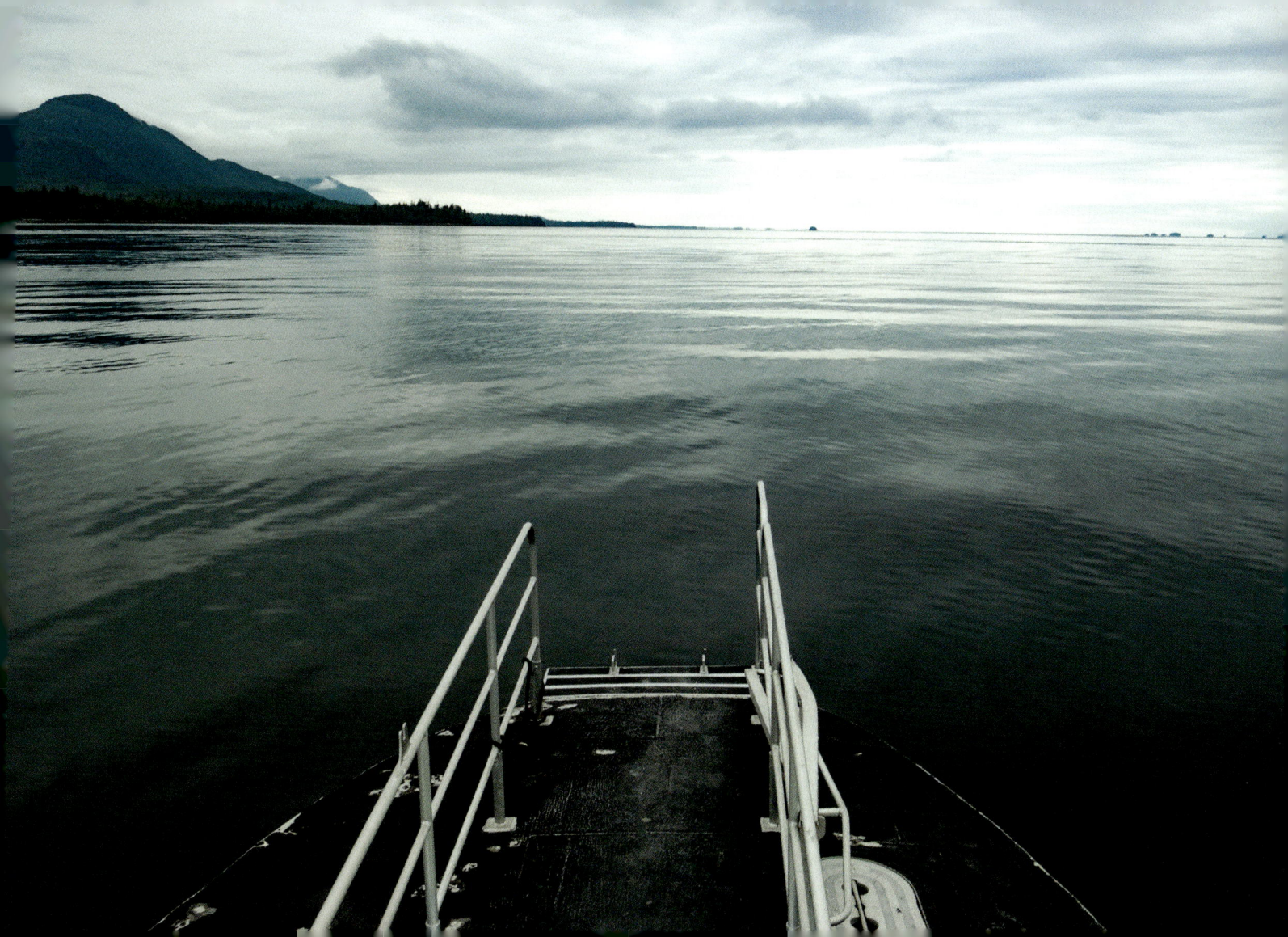

**Be present to appreciate the sweetness of the present moment**—*free from both*

the depressions of the past

and the anxieties of the future.

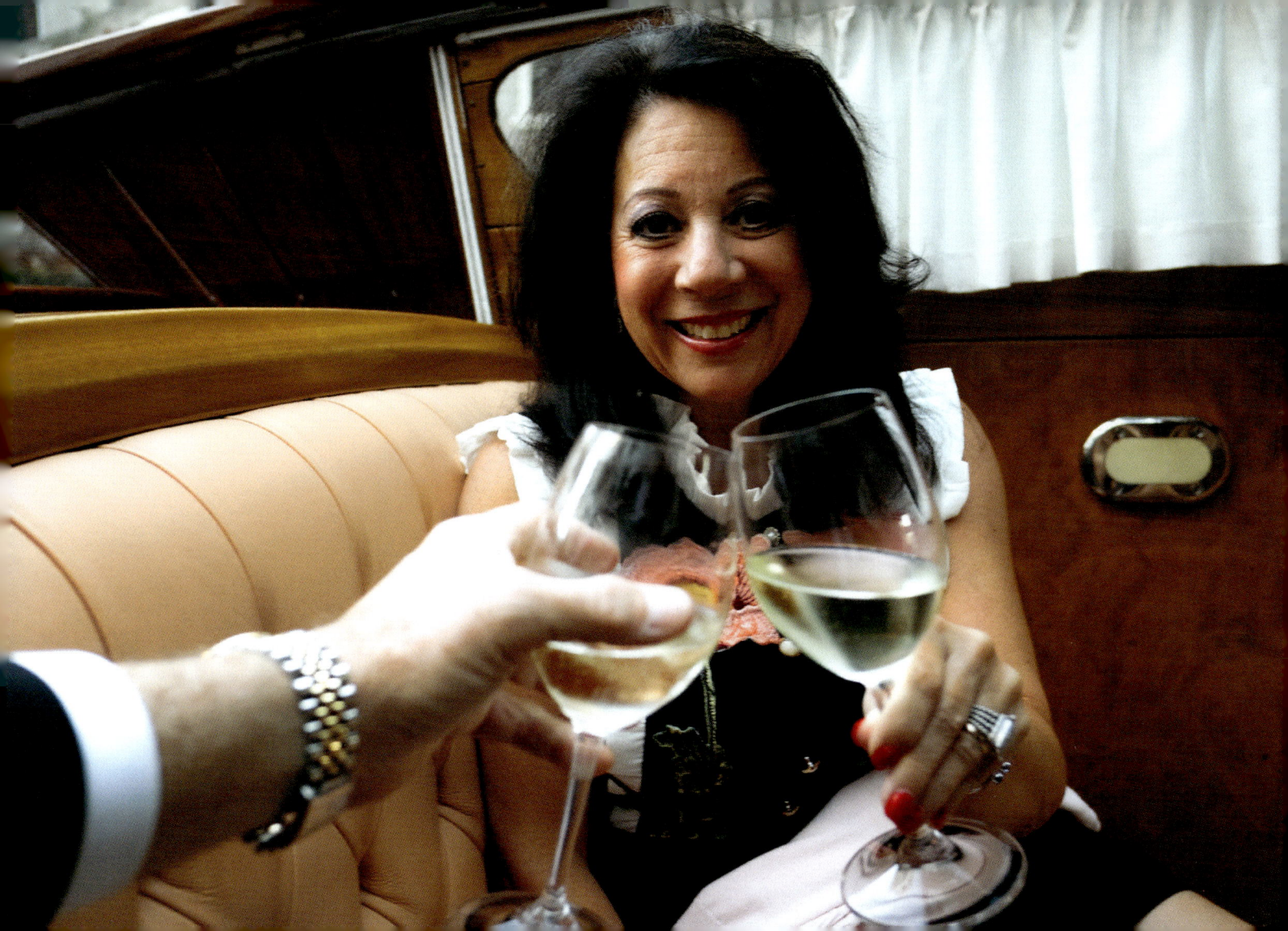

*"Grandfather dies, father dies then son dies."*

All that we need to know about true life prosperity is revealed in this sequence.

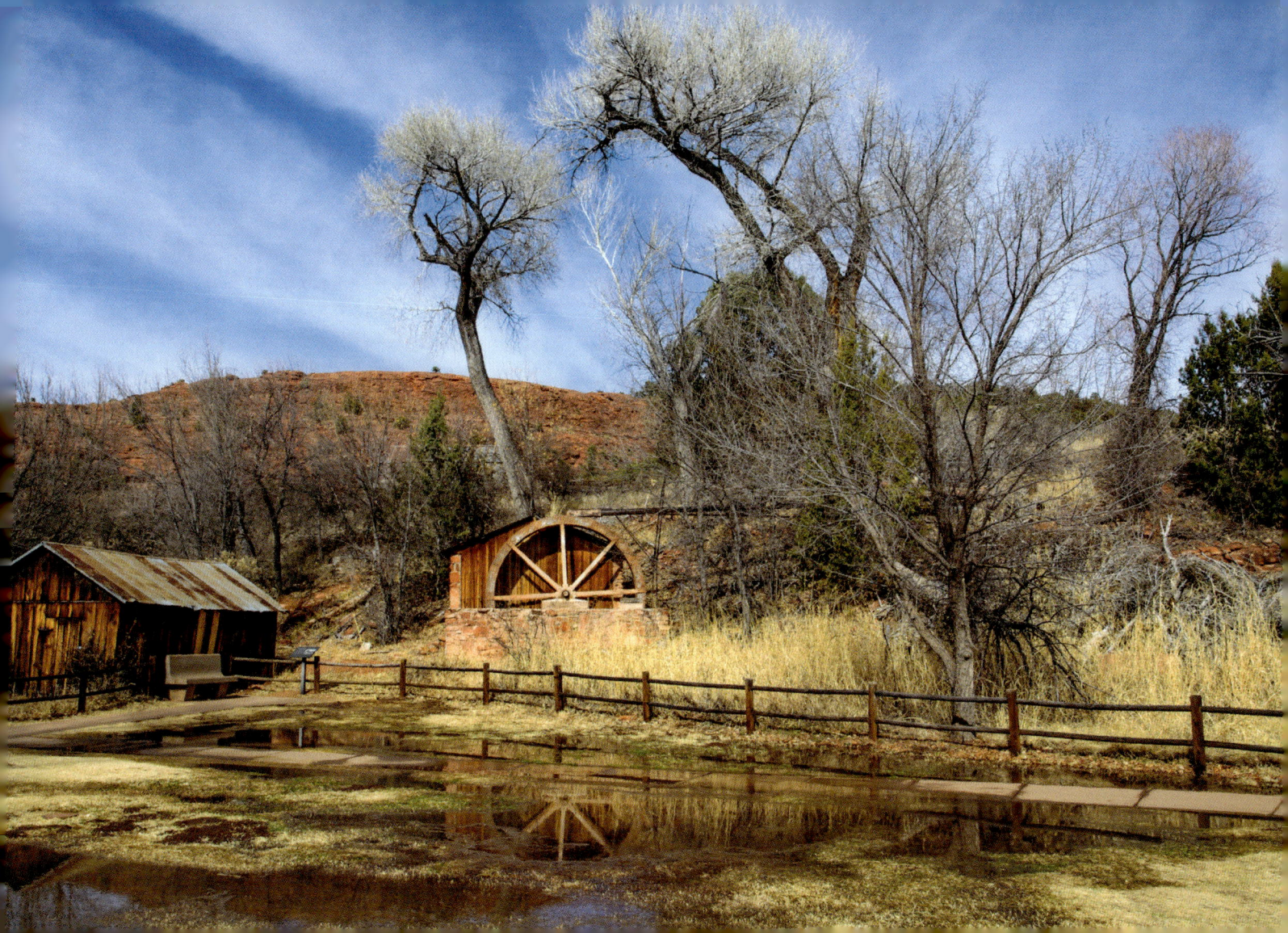

**Familiarity in a relationship may be a double-edged sword if not handled carefully.**

On one edge is the warmth and satisfaction that results from frequent interaction.

The other edge may cut sharply from failed expectations stemming from the notion that "they should know what I am thinking."

*Don't fall into the trap of familiarity;* **keep the dialogue going.**

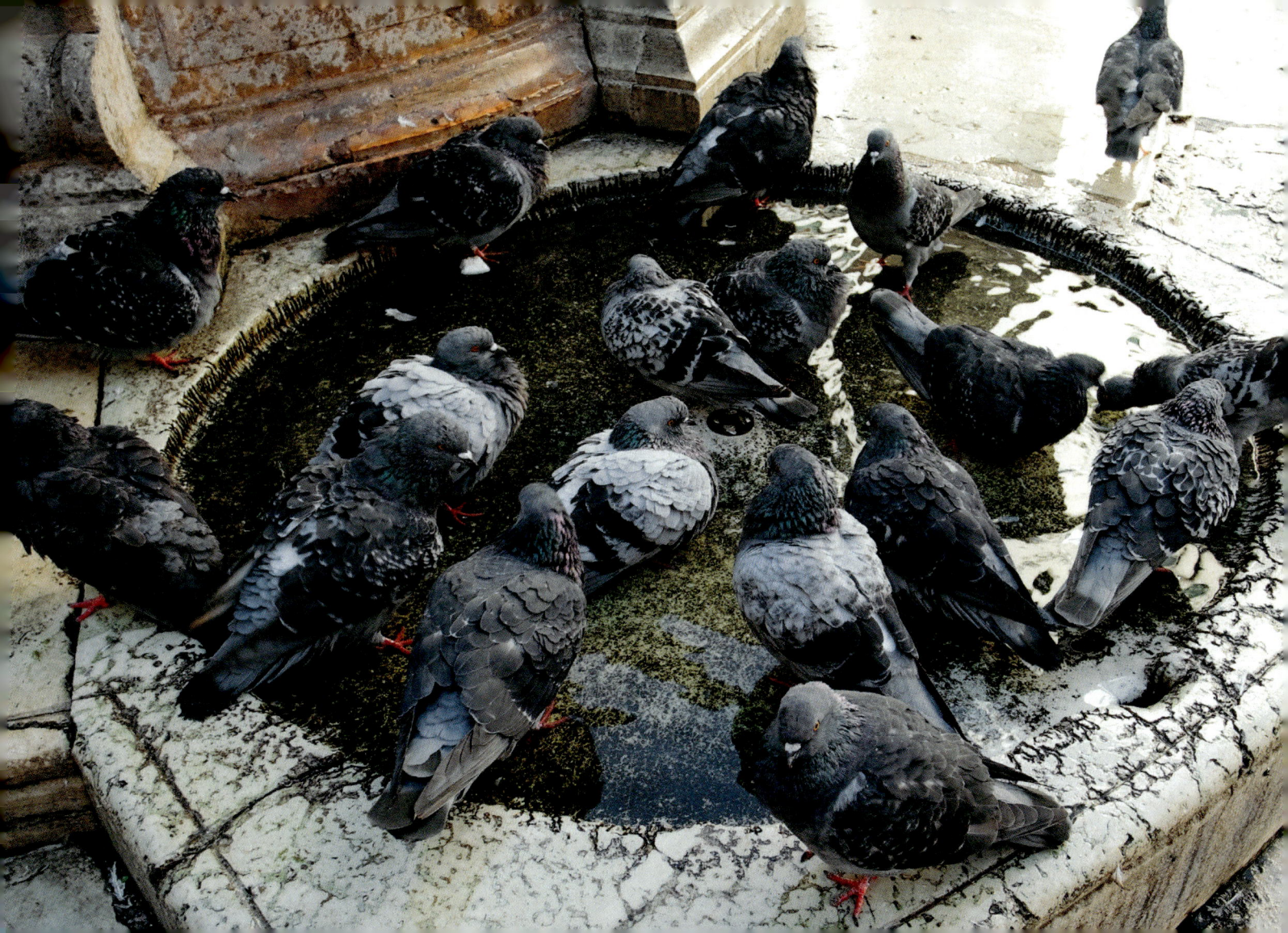

When you illuminate life's path with a candle of passion and energy, others will line up to follow you into the darkness of an uncertain future.

Should that candle burn out, however, you become *invisible to all other travelers*.

Discover what you need to **keep your candle lit**.

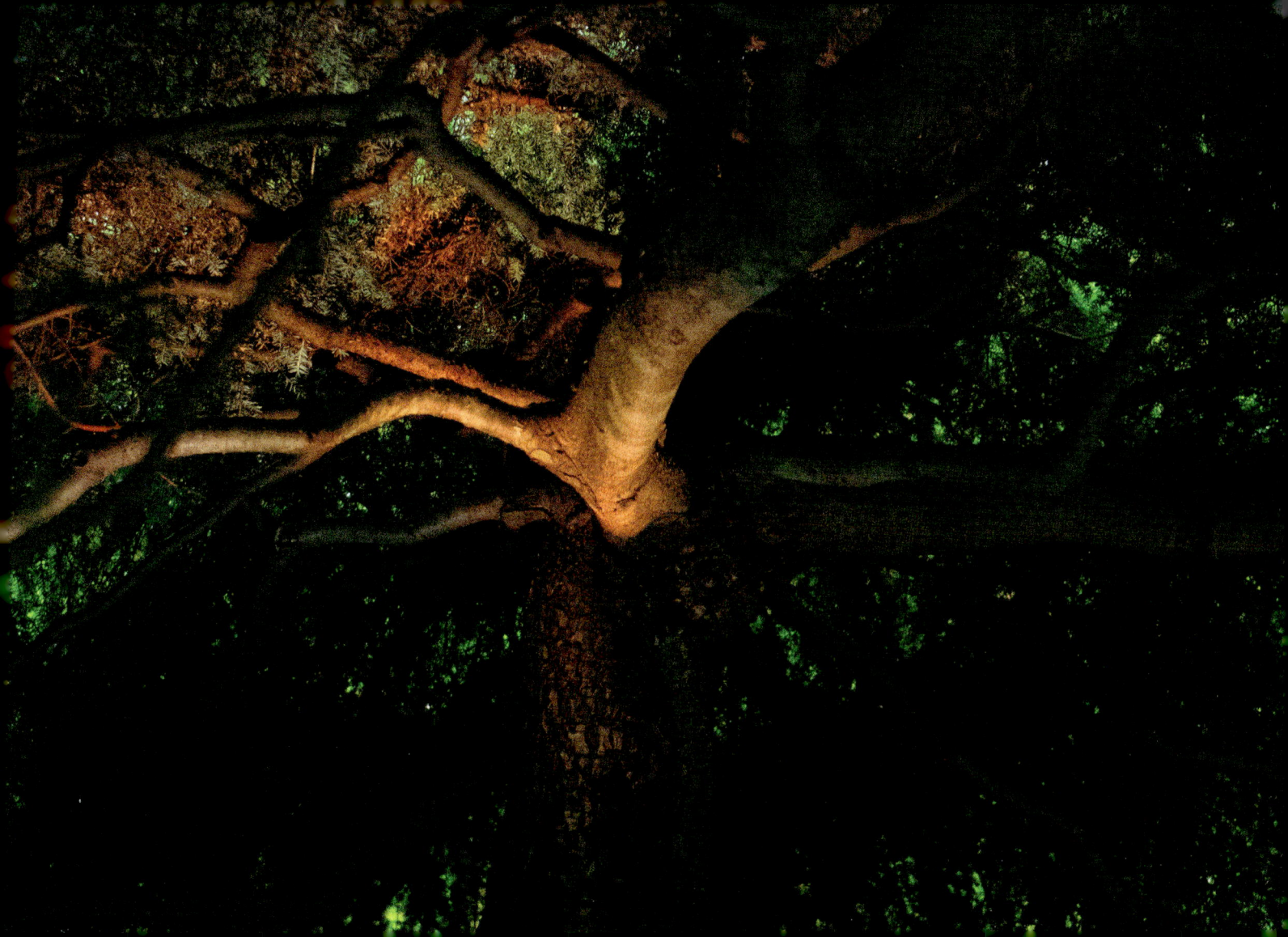

*Strive to have a "mind like moon"*
to provide light to the darkness,
shining on all equally.


*Strive to have a "mind like water"*
to reflect only what is there,
clear, pure and still.

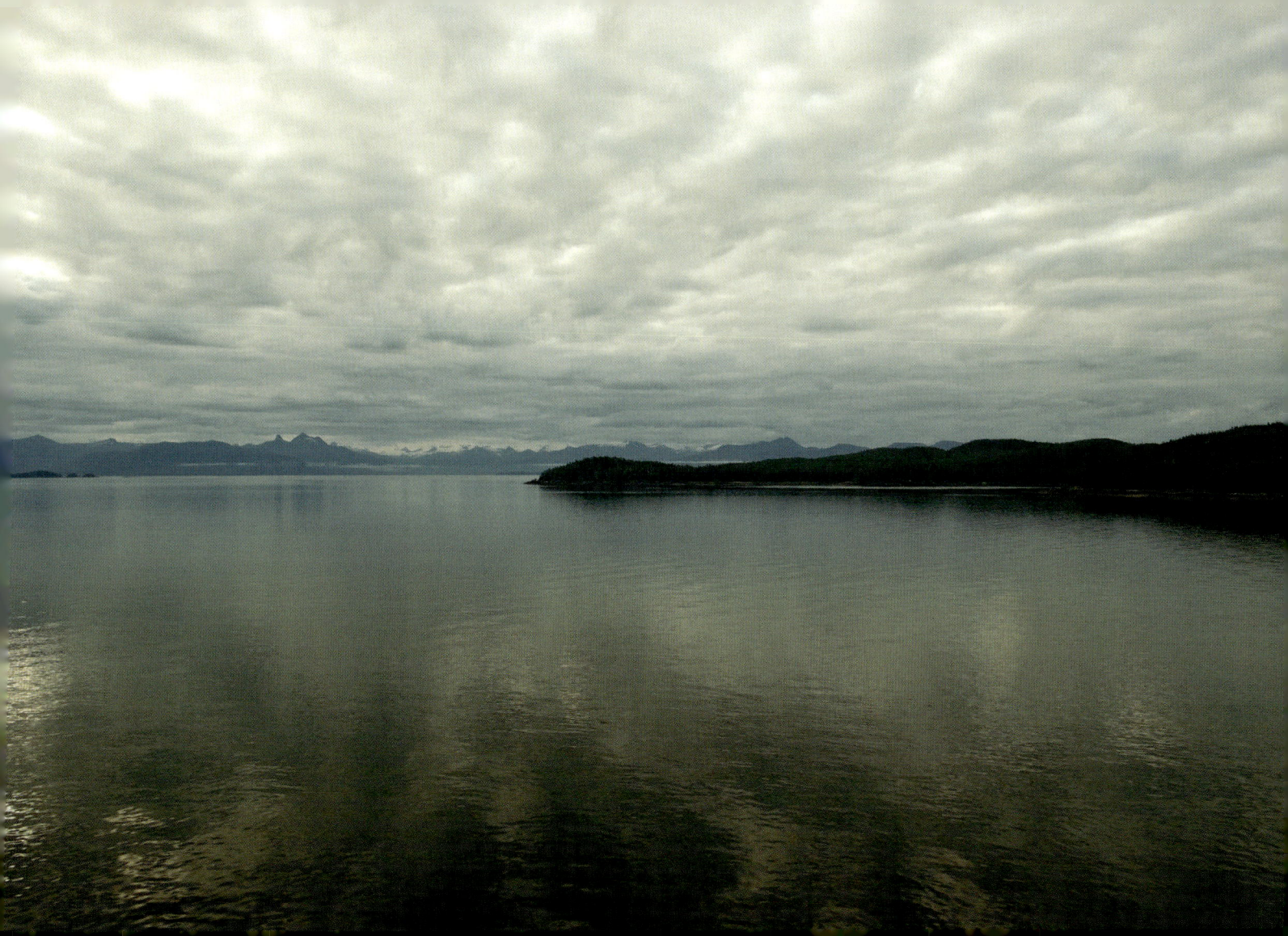

A concern without action is a wish or hope.

An action without a concern is a tradition or belief.

**Impact** occurs only when a *concern* is paired with a *specific corresponding action*.

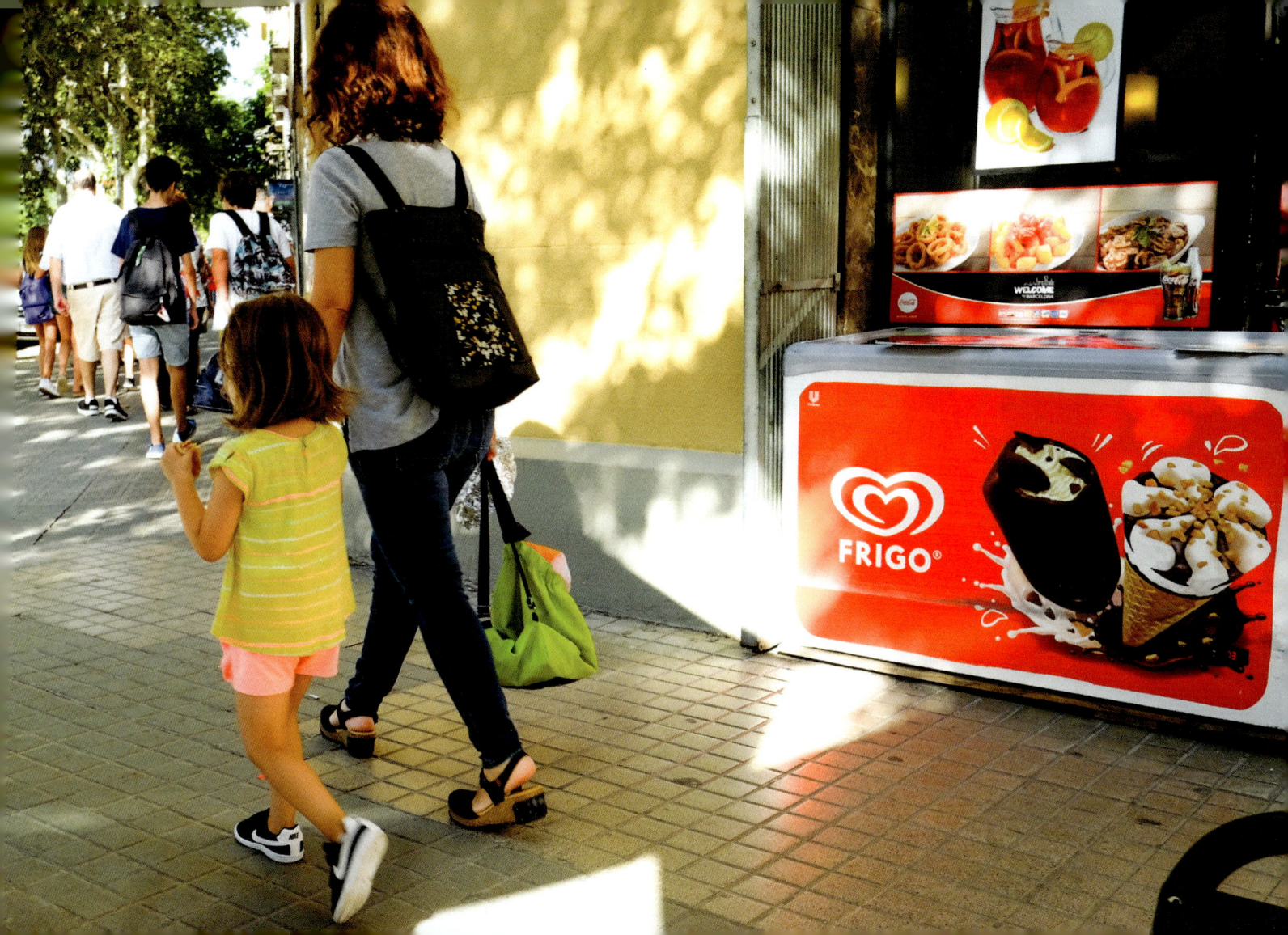

The Center for Humane Living inspires all individuals to live peaceful and compassionate lives. It provides an open hand to humanity.

## The Center for Humane Living

Inspires physical and emotional wellness, empowers relationships, leadership and lifelong learning – all enabled through an innovative approach to traditional martial arts training.

CenterforHumaneLiving.org

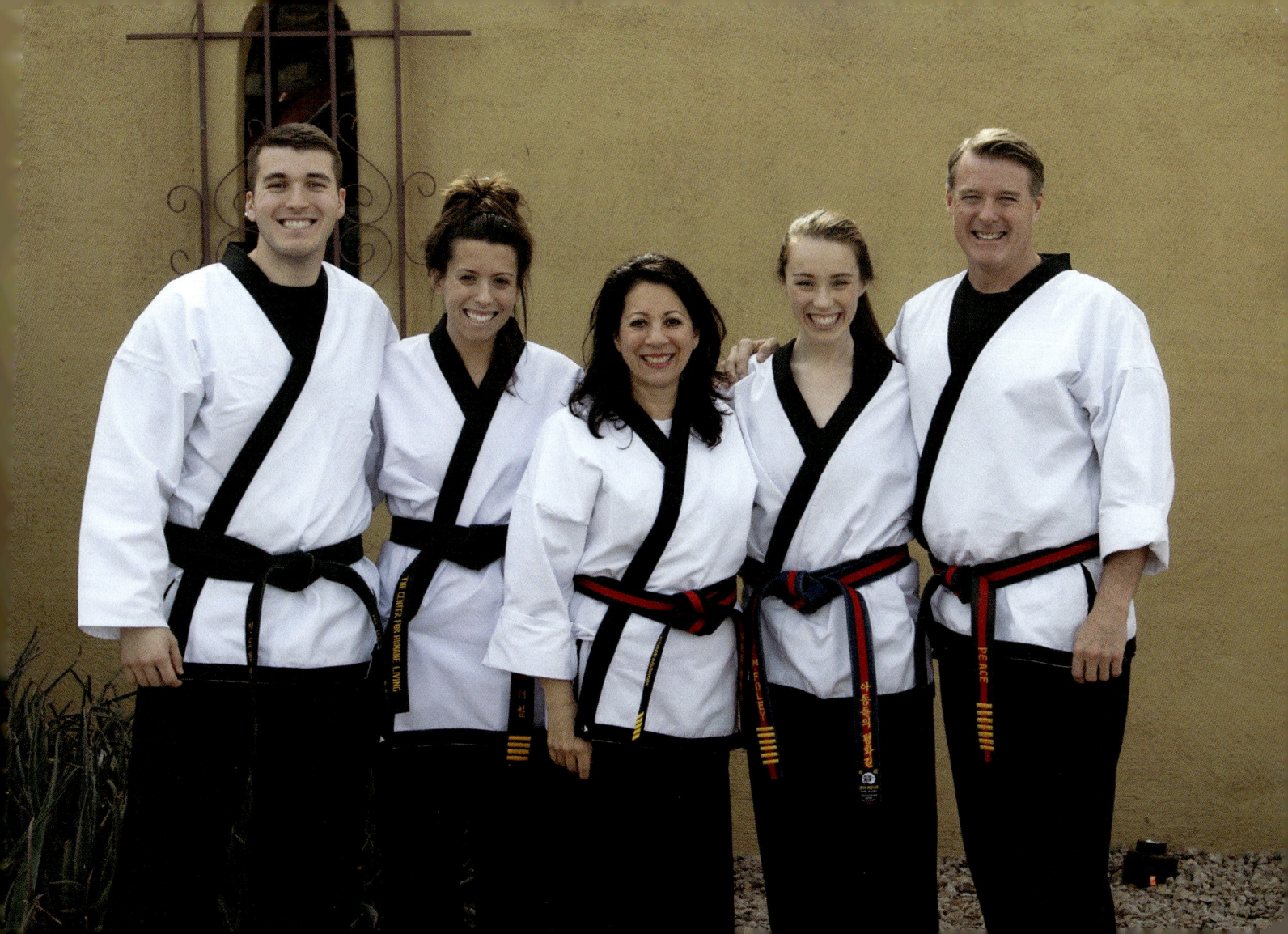

# INHALE

Reflections from a Beginner
on the Path to Mastery

*Want more reflections and writing from Dr. Foley?*

**HumaneLivingPhotography.com** is your online shop for all photo prints in this book. You can also read new works and meditations.

# About Dr. Foley

Dr. Foley received his medical degree in 1984 from The Chicago Medical School. He completed his residency in obstetrics and gynecology and his fellowship in maternal fetal medicine at The Ohio Sate University Hospital in 1988 and 1990.

Dr. Foley has published numerous scientific articles and is a reviewer for several medical journals. He is a national and international lecturer as well as an award-winning teacher and author. Dr. Foley is Past President of the Society for Maternal Fetal Medicine-National (2008) and the recipient of the Society for Maternal Fetal Medicine Lifetime Achievement Award (2013).

Dr Foley is a founding instructor and faculty member for the Dan O'Keeffe, M.D. SMFM Academy for Leadership and Development which is in its sixth year of operation training hundreds of medical leaders and professionals. He is a sought after motivational speaker and mentor.

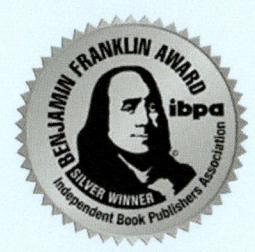

Dr. Foley is a seventh-degree black belt and the co-founder of The Center for Humane Living, a 501c3 organization whose mission is "to inspire all people to live peaceful and compassionate lives." He has been teaching martial arts and conflict management out of his center for the past 27 years and has written a "Benjamin Franklin" award-winning book, The Art of Humane Living – Martial Arts as a Path to Peace, published in 2004. He also authored Ancient Wisdom for Life Fulfillment which was published in 2010 to national acclaim.

He is married to Dr Lisa Dado who is a pediatric anesthesiologist, a fifth-degree black belt and co-founder for The Center for Humane Living. They have three children, Bonnie (fifth-degree black belt), Molly (fifth-degree black belt) and Michael (fourth-degree black belt).

***Thank you*** for bettering yourself with The Center for Humane Living.